Chezzetcook:
an
Acadian Stronghold

Ronald Labelle

Chezzetcook: an Acadian stronghold
© 2024 Ronald Labelle

All rights reserved. No part of this book may be reproduced or transmitted in any form or by any means, electronic or mechanical, including photocopying, or by any information storage or retrieval system, without permission in writing from the publisher.

The author expressly prohibits any entity from using this publication for purposes of training artificial intelligence (AI) technologies to generate text, including without limitation technologies that are capable of generating works in the same style or genre as this publication. The author reserves all rights to license uses of this work for generative AI training and development of machine learning language models.

Cover design: Rebekah Wetmore
Cover image; James Bellefontaine carrying marsh hay on his gundalow.
Editor: Andrew Wetmore

ISBN: 978-1-998149-55-1
First edition July 2024

Moose House Publications
2475 Perotte Road
Annapolis County, NS
B0S 1A0
moosehousepress.com
info@moosehousepress.com

Moose House Publications recognizes the support of the Province of Nova Scotia. We are pleased to work in partnership with the Department of Communities, Culture and Heritage to develop and promote our cultural resources for all Nova Scotians.

We live and work in Mi'kma'ki, the ancestral and unceded territory of the Mi'kmaw people. This territory is covered by the "Treaties of Peace and Friendship" which Mi'kmaw and Wolastoqiyik (Maliseet) people first signed with the British Crown in 1725. The treaties did not deal with surrender of lands and resources but in fact recognized Mi'kmaq and Wolastoqiyik (Maliseet) title and established the rules for what was to be an ongoing relationship between nations. We are all Treaty people.

Also by Ronald Labelle

Acadian Songs from Pubnico and Grand-Étang
The Acadians of Chezzetcook
La vie acadienne à Chezzetcook
La fleur du rosier – chansons folkloriques d'Acadie / Acadian Folksongs (with Helen Creighton)
Au Village-du-Bois – Mémoires d'une communauté acadienne
Tanneurs et tanneries du Bas-Saint-Laurent (1900-1930)
Contes d'Acadie par Thomas LeBlanc (critical edition)

Figure 1: Gundalow belonging to Wallace Bellefontaine before its transfer to the Nova Scotia Museum in 1980.

Introduction

My involvement in the renewal of Acadian culture in Chezzetcook began in 1982, when, as Folklore Archivist at the Université de Moncton's Centre d'études acadiennes, I obtained a modest grant from the Social Sciences and Humanities Research Council of Canada, enabling me to undertake a fieldwork project in minority Acadian communities in Nova Scotia.

The initial plan was for the study to concentrate on Eastern Nova Scotia, looking particularly at Isle Madame in Richmond County and Pomquet in Antigonish County, because these areas had rarely attracted the attention of earlier researchers.

During the planning stage, the late Professor Cyril Byrne of St. Mary's University persuaded me that it would be important to include Chezzetcook in the study. He introduced me to Father Frédéric Melanson and also to the first of my many contacts in the community.

I quickly became fascinated with Chezzetcook and decided to carry out all the interviews there myself, while sending my two research assistants to do most of the fieldwork at Isle Madame and Pomquet.

What attracted my interest in Chezzetcook was the fact that it stands out as a unique case: an important Acadian establishment in the 18th and 19th centuries, it seemed to have lost its connection to other members of the diaspora of modern-day Acadia.

When I began to meet with elderly residents in Chezzetcook, I was impressed by their wealth of historical knowledge and their retention of the French language as it had been handed down from their ancestors. What followed was a very rewarding fieldwork experience, as many residents of West Chezzetcook and Grand-Désert were able to tell me a great deal about life in the past, using the rich French idiom they had inherited.

When describing the French spoken in Chezzetcook, I avoid the word "dialect", as many Nova Scotians still make the mistake of believing that Acadians spoke a broken French, an inferior variety of the language that Francophones from elsewhere in the world would have difficulty understanding. Nothing could be further from the truth, as will become obvious in the chapters that deal with travellers from France who wrote of their visits to Chezzetcook.

When I began to interview residents of Chezzetcook, many people in the nearby Halifax area believed that few remnants of Acadian culture existed there. I discovered, on the contrary, that my informants possessed a strong command of the French language, spoken with a charming accent reminiscent of that of the Acadians in Southwestern Nova Scotia.

Upon completion of my initial research project, I continued to explore the folklore and oral history of Chezzetcook, returning to the community in subsequent years. Having to juggle research interests with archival responsibilities and graduate studies, I was forced to put aside my project of writing a book about the Acadians of Chezzetcook, but I eventually wrote up a study of the community that was submitted as a graduate research paper in the History Department at the Université de Moncton.

This study was expanded in 1991 and published as a special issue of the Acadian historical journal entitled *Société historique acadienne – les Cahiers*[1].

Given that few people in the Chezzetcook area possessed French reading skills, I decided to translate the work, adding a new chapter entitled "Acadian Voices", presenting the words of three of the elderly residents who had told their stories. The translated work was finally published by Pottersfield Press in 1995.[2]

That book has been out of print for many years, and each time local residents asked me if it would be reedited, I replied that I was waiting for the opportunity to publish a more complete study of the community and its people. That time has finally arrived.

New documentary sources have come to light since the 1990s, thanks to the many residents who have carried out research into the history of their community, and also to the availability of newly-digitized archival collections. The present study takes advantage of these new sources, thus enabling us to have a clearer view of the long and colourful Acadian history of Chezzetcook.

The past three decades have seen many changes in Chezzetcook, and now, more than ever, people there can benefit from a study that looks at their history, their way of life and their folklore. It is my hope that interest in Chezzetcook will go beyond the local sphere, because the Acadian people are now recognized as an important Francophone minority group in North America, and because Chezzetcook, with its fascinating 300-year history, provides us with an excellent example of Acadian resilience and survival.

Nearly all of the older residents I interviewed during the 1980s have passed away, and now more than ever it is important for their stories to be written down and shared so they will not be forgotten. I am very

---

1   Ronald Labelle, "La vie acadienne à Chezzetcook".
2   *The Acadians of Chezzetcook.*

grateful to all the people of West Chezzetcook and Grand-Désert who welcomed me into their homes, and to the researchers who generously shared the results of their work. This book is dedicated to them.

Sadly, the individuals who were the first to recognize the importance of documenting Acadian life in Chezzetccok are no longer with us: Lena Ferguson, who tirelessly explored a vast array of topics, producing numerous articles for the *Dartmouth Free Press;* Mgr Frédéric Melanson, who spent countless hours researching the genealogy of local families; and finally Professor Cyril Byrne, who made me aware of the fact that any study of Acadians in Eastern Nova Scotia would be incomplete without a section devoted to Chezzetcook.

This book deals essentially with the Acadian population of West Chezzetcook and Grand-Désert, although I make some references to the residents of the neighbouring village of Seaforth, who were largely of German descent. On the eastern side of Chezzetcook Inlet, a significant minority of residents were of French descent, but there the language was lost long ago, as Acadians were immersed in a majority English-speaking community.

I did not include East Chezzetcook in the study, because few traces of Acadian culture remained there when I began to carry out my research in the 1980s.

The history of Chezzetcook can be divided into four distinct phases: The period between the early 18th to the early 19th century was the time when Acadians began to build a community in Chezzetcook, and, as was the case elsewhere in the Maritimes, there were two distinct beginnings because the settlers had to start anew following the years of banishment between the mid-1750s and the mid-1760s. The first two chapters of the book trace the history of the community during its first phase, from its beginnings through to the end of the 18th century.

Chapter 3 deals with the second phase in the history of Chezzetcook, showing how the 19th century saw the development of an enterprising community with a varied economy that included fishing, agriculture, trade and brick-making. Chapter 4 presents the impressions of visitors who wrote of their encounters with the local Acadian population, while chapters 5 and 6 describe the way of life and traditions that existed during that century, before the rapid period of modernization that would come later.

The next two chapters present the way of life and culture of the people of Chezzetcook during the third phase in their history, which covers the early to mid-20th century. Chapter 7 is devoted to the recently-recovered field recordings by French folklorist Geneviève Massignon, who visited Grand-Désert in 1947 and 1961, while chapter 8 presents memories and stories by elder members of Chezzetcook, as local researcher Lena Ferguson and I recorded them during the 1970s and '80s.

The final chapter covers the most recent period, which saw both a decline and a renewal of Acadian culture in Chezzetcook. During the 20th century, as the local population became closely integrated into the growing English-speaking society in the Halifax area, French language and traditions went through an inevitable decline in Chezzetcook. This chapter chronicles the decline, but ends on a positive note, unlike the conclusion contained in my 1995 book.

The early 21st century has been a time of reawakening and renewal of Acadian identity for the people of Chezzetcook. A new phase in the community's history is just beginning, as present and future generations carve out a new place for Chezzetcook in Acadian and Maritime society.

This book tells the story up until now, and it is up to the present and future generations of Chezzetcookers to continue the story.

Ronald Labelle
April, 2024

This book is dedicated to the more than two dozen residents of West Chezzetcook and Grand-Désert, many of whom have now passed away, who welcomed me into their homes and patiently answered my questions about life in the past. The book would not have been possible without their interest and cooperation.

Figure 2: Karen Anne (Robichaud) Conrod and Sharon (Robichaud) Kirker presenting genealogical information at the Acadian 400th anniversary celebration in Chezzetcook, August 2004.

Chezzetcook: an Acadian stronghold

Introduction..5
1: Before the Acadian Expulsion...17
2: New beginnings in the Post-Expulsion era (1763-1790)..................31
3: Community growth in the 19th century..53
4: Impressions of 19th-century travelers...73
5: Building a livelihood..91
6: Folkways and traditions..128
7: Folktales and ballads—the Massignon collection.........................157
8: Voices of Acadian elders...180
9: 20th-century decline…and renewal...206
   Bibliography...223
   Acknowledgements..229
   About the author...231

Images

Figure 1: Gundalow belonging to Wallace Bellefontaine before its transfer to the Nova Scotia Museum in 1980..........4
Figure 2: Karen Anne (Robichaud) Conrod and Sharon (Robichaud) Kirker presenting genealogical information at the Acadian 400th anniversary celebration in Chezzetcook, August 2004..........10
Figure 3: West Chezzetcook, 1935. Photo by Wallace MacAskill (Nova Scotia Archives)..........14
Figure 4: One of the fine examples of traditional Acadian architecture found in Chezzetcook..........16
Figure 5: Letter from pioneer priest Jean Mandé Sigogne to Jean Baptiste Roma in June, 1804..........30
Figure 6: Tall, wooden cross said to have been erected by Mi'maq residents at Grand-Désert in the 1740s..........46
Figure 7: The 19th century church at West Chezzetcook; published by T.P. Connolly, Halifax (Nova Scotia Museum)..........54
Figure 8: Antoine Faucher, Chezzetcook's first schoolteacher..........67
Figure 9: Map showing the lands occupied by settlers around Chezzetcook Inlet in 1864 (published by A.F. Church, 1865)..........71
Figure 10: One of the 1858 portraits Cozzens describes..........75
Figure 11: The former prison at Dartmouth Cove, in 1929..........88
Figure 12: Ambrotype image of an Acadian woman from Chezzetcook captured by Frederic Cozzens in 1858..........90
Figure 13: William Lapierre at his home in 1982..........95
Figure 14: Edwin Lapierre and his fishing cabin at Threefathom Harbour in 1982..........96
Figure 15: right: the schooner "Flora MJ", captain Martin Julien, circa 1900 at Souris, PEI..........101
Figure 16: Éloi Bellefontaine working at a local sawmill in 1933....114
Figure 17: Using an ox to power the clay mixer at a Chezzetcook brickyard..........116
Figure 18: Using a portable sawmill to chop firewood..........118

Figure 19: Windmill photographed by Allen Fraser in 1930 (Nova Scotia Archives)..120
Figure 20: The bus that travelled between Chezzetcook and Halifax, passing by St. Anselm's Church, circa 1940.......................................126
Figure 21: Eugene Bellefontaine gathering clams in 1977.................127
Figure 22: Edouard Julien and Alban Bellefontaine hauling logs from a woodlot...132
Figure 23: The interior of Saint Anselm's Church after its completion around 1930. The altar at the centre was later removed during the modernization craze in the 1960s...136
Figure 24: John Lapierre and his ox with a load of hay.....................143
Figure 25: Lavinia LeBlanc, Head of Chezzetcook, 1982..................146
Figure 26: Liliane Bellefontaine, Musquodoboit Harbour, 1983.......148
Figure 27: "Dames de Sainte Anne" Membership diploma awarded to a resident of Grand-Désert in June 1922..156
Figure 28: Geneviève Massignon, at the time of her Acadian folklore research project..179
Figure 29: Douglas Lapierre holding a homemade buoy...................205
Figure 30: The pupils and staff of École des Beaux-Marais, 2018....219
Figure 31: Tricolour satchel of soil from the grounds of the Archdiocese of Paris offered to the people of Chezzetcook by the Archbishop in 1935..222
Figure 32: An Acadian flag now proudly displayed in the marsh on Chezzetcook Inlet..228

Ronald Labelle

Figure 3: West Chezzetcook, 1935. Photo by Wallace MacAskill (Nova Scotia Archives).

Chezzetcook:
an Acadian Stronghold

Ronald Labelle

Figure 4: One of the fine examples of traditional Acadian architecture found in Chezzetcook.

1: Before the Acadian Expulsion

The name Chezzetcook refers to an area about 30 kilometres east of Halifax. At the heart of the region is Chezzetcook Inlet, which reaches 10 kilometres inland from the Atlantic coast. Five communities surround the Inlet: Grand-Désert, West Chezzetcook, Head of Chezzetcook, East Chezzetcook and Lower East Chezzetcook.

This book deals mainly with the communities of Grand-Désert and West Chezzetcook, two neighbouring villages where the Acadian identity is strongest. While 18th century Acadian settlers established themselves in localities such as East Chezzetcook, Porters Lake and present-day Lawrencetown, only in West Chezzetcook, and especially in Grand-Désert, was their presence dominant enough to lead to the creation of French language communities. In other localities on the Eastern Shore, the Acadian identity was lost as the original settlers either left the area or were gradually absorbed into the English-speaking majority.

In the past, the word Chezzetcook was often spelled Chezzencook by English-speaking writers, and it is sometimes still pronounced that way. In French, it was usually spelled Chegekkouk or Chegekouke.

Father Pacifique de Valigny, a French missionary who lived and worked among the Mi'kmaq in the early 20th century, and who was an authority of the Mi'kmaq language, spelled the name "Sesitgog". According to him, the name is a shortened form of an expression meaning 'many streams caused by the ebb and flow', an apt description for the waters of the Chezzetcook Inlet.

For many centuries before the arrival of the Acadians, the Mi'kmaq people frequented the Eastern Shore, and many of the names they gave to various localities have remained, though in modified forms.

Father Pacifique quotes a late 17th century French missionary, Emmanuel Jumeau, who wrote, "Depuis Théodore jusqu'à Chibouctou on trouve Mouchkadobouet, Chegekkouk, Makanchisch et un village français

17

occupé par les Boutins, à une demi-lieue de Makanchinsch."[3]

This brief quote is interesting, as it refers to place names along a section of the coast that begins at "Théodore", the original French name for Jedore, and ends at "Chibouctou", the French rendering of "Gtjipogtog", the original name for Halifax. According to Father Pacifique, Gtjipogtog means "Great Harbour".

Mouchkadobouet is one of the 17th and 18th century French spellings for *Mosgitopogoeg* (Muskodoboit), meaning "Sparkling water".

The name "Makanchinsch", the French spelling for the Mi'kmaq *Amagantjitj*, is of particular interest, as several people in Chezzetcook told me that Threefathom Harbour used to be called "Maganchiche" by Acadian fishers.

According to Father Pacifique, the term *Amagantjitj* refers to the caressing of the waters or of the wind.[4] In her unpublished "History of Porter's Lake", Lena Ferguson opts for a different explanation, translating the term as "Little breezy place".[5]

Regarding early settlement in the area, French records from 1671 mention 13 people living at "Mouskadabouet", but no names are given. The next relevant information comes from Father Pacifique, who quotes Fr. Emmanuel Jumeau's reference to a French village situated a half league[6] from Makanchinsch, where the Boutin family resided.

Jumeau carried out most of his missionary work in New France, but he travelled around Acadia in 1685. His mention of the Boutin family would be the earliest reference regarding French settlers in the Chezzetcook area. Genealogist Mgr Frédéric Melanson identified the family as being that of Antoine Boutin[7].

The next reference to early settlers comes from le Sieur DeCostre, who complained to French officials in 1698 that an English ketch had gone to the place where a man named Petitpas resided in "Mouscadabouet"[8]. According to Mgr Melanson, Claude Petitpas Jr., born in 1663, was the eldest son of Claude Petitpas, Notary Royal in the French colony of Acadia. He is listed as living in his father's household in Port-Royal in

---

3 Pacifique, "Le Pays des Micmacs", pp. 274-5.
4 Ibid., p. 275.

5 Ferguson, "History of Porter's Lake", p.3.
6 A league is a measure of distance that corresponds to about five kilometres or three miles.
7 Melanson, "Acadian Settlement at Chezzetcook".
8 Murdoch, p. 243.

the 1686 census of Acadia and would have moved to Mouscadabouet sometime after that. At the time of the 1686 census, two of Petitpas's siblings were already living not far away at Mirligoueche (Lunenberg).

It is difficult to pinpoint the exact location of 18th century settlements situated east of Halifax, because French documents referring to "Mouscadabouet" may refer to any community in the area. In British references from the mid-18th century, "Mouscadabouet" generally corresponds to present-day Lawrencetown.

Another place name that can cause confusion is "Makanchinsch", which generally referred to Threefathom Harbour, but that was sometimes used for other localities around Porters Lake.

It is significant that Claude Petitpas, one of the first French settlers in the area, had formed an alliance with the First Nations population. This may have influenced his decision to settle in an area that was an important gathering place for the Mi'kmaq. The alliance Petitpas formed with a Mi'kmaq woman provides an example of how 17th century French settlers developed close bonds with members of the First Nations.

In 1708, the French carried out a census of the Mi'kmaq peoples residing in present-day Peninsular Nova Scotia and enumerated the French settlers living on the Atlantic coast. In this census, Claude Petitpas, his wife Marie Thérèse and seven children are included not with the French settlers, but among the "Indians" of Mouscadabouet.

Another Métis family included in the list of "Indians" is that of Maurice Mieusse (Mius), his wife Marguerite and two children. Maurice Mius was a son of Philippe Mius D'Entremont and his Mi'kmaq wife, Marie. Maurice's grandfather, also named Philippe Mius D'Entremont, arrived in Acadia as a lieutenant-major and was awarded the Barony of Pobomcoup (Pubnico) in 1653. This is one example of how early on, some of the leading families in the French colony of Acadia formed alliances with the Mi'kmaq.

Apart from the Boutin, Petitpas and Mius families, no other French or French/Mi'kmaq families are named in records referring to the Eastern Shore, but there are numerous indications that several more were living in the area. In 1746, abbé Le Loutre, who acted both as a missionary and as a French agent among the Mi'kmaq of Nova Scotia, wrote a "Description de l'Acadie", in which he mentioned having travelled a distance of 30 leagues from "Chigabenakadi" (Shubenacady) to "Chegekkouk", where ten French families were living.

The text was updated two years later, and the revised description of Acadia stated that there were several French settlements on the Eastern

Ronald Labelle

Shore, the first one being "Chegekkouk", where there were fifteen French families for whom the missionary had built a church. It was situated three leagues from Chibouctouk (Halifax): *"Il y a plusieurs habitations françoises le long de la côte de l'Est; la première est Chegekkouk, le missionnaire y a fait bâtir une église, il y a quinze familles françoises, c'est à trois lieus de Chibouktouk."*[9]

The most detailed French report describing the settlements near the Atlantic coast is also dated 1748, the year before the founding of Halifax. An anonymous author covered the entire Atlantic coast from Canso to the South Shore, and described the settlements he found along the way.

The report stated that the seacoast between Canseau (Canso) and "Mouschkodabouet" was inhabited only by Mi'kmaq hunters. "Mouschkodabouet" itself had been occupied by the French in the past but no longer was so.

The author then arrived at "Chegekkouk" where seven or eight French families lived. Next, he came to the Petitpas dwelling, beyond which was a river, followed by the uninhabited fishing station at "Makannchisch" (Threefathom Harbour). The Boutin family home was situated one half-league higher up a river.

The report then described the yet uninhabited harbour at "Chibouctou" (Halifax), and continued on to "Mirligueche" (Lunenberg) where there were 12 to 15 French families and "La Haive" (La Hève), where four or five more were found.[10]

One final document, a letter written by the abbé de l'Isle Dieu in 1750, stated that ten French families lived at "Cheggekouke."[11]

The existing written reports provide varying population numbers, which makes it difficult to trace the evolution of the Acadian population in the Chezzetcook area. The French we unable to carry out any formal census after 1713, as the territory was under British control. However, we can be fairly certain that a small Acadian, or mixed Acadian-Mi'kmaq, community existed in the Chezzetcook area from the last quarter of the 17th century until the middle of the 18th, and that it included a chapel where visiting missionaries could perform the rites of the Catholic Church.

The limited data available suggests that there were only a few families

---

9   *Documents inédits sur le Canada et l'Amérique*, pp. 43-47.
10 Library and Archives Canada, Archives de la Nouvelle-France, COL, C11D, 10/6p., «Mémoire sur l'Acadie», 1748.
11 Nova Scotia Archives, RG-1, Vol. 4, folio No. 57, "Lettre de l'abbé de l'Isle Dieu, vicaire général du Canada, 7 février 1750.

in the area at the beginning of the 18th century, but that their number grew somewhat during the following decades, possibly due to an influx of Acadian settlers from the Pigiguit (Windsor) area.[12]

And yet, in 1752, when British surveyor Charles Morris produced "A Written Description of the Coast of Nova Scotia from Halifax Harbour to Chezzetcook", all he found were the ruins of a French establishment, the only building left standing being the chapel.[13]

The mysterious disappearance of the Acadian community begs the question: What could have happened between 1748 and 1752 that would cause all the settlers to abandon Chezzetcook and surrounding areas? And this leads to a second question: Where did they all go?

While it is necessary to examine the historical context in detail in order to answer the first question, the answer to the second one is fairly obvious, thanks to an exhaustive census of Île Royale carried out by French officials in 1752. It lists all the French inhabitants of communities situated on Cape Breton Island, along with their places of origin.

While the inhabitants of some fishing communities were listed as coming directly from France or from the French colony of Plaisance (Placentia) in Newfoundland, the vast majority of those living in Port-Toulouse (St. Peter's), at Baie-des-Espagnols (Sydney) and at Mordienne (Port Morien) were listed as being from "Acadie", meaning present-day Peninsular Nova Scotia. Acadians began to move to the Port-Toulouse area shortly after the founding to the colony of Île Royale in 1713.

The family of Claude Petitpas Jr. provides an interesting case study. We know he was living at "Mouskadabouet" at the turn of the 18th century and that his descendants were among the founders of the second Acadian community of Chezzetccook. Claude Petitpas moved to Île Royale sometime between 1713 and 1721, along with his second wife, Françoise, and he is listed as a merchant living in Port-Toulouse in both the 1724 and 1726 census of Île Royale.[14]

The French sought to hire both Claude Petitpas his son Barthélémy as interpreters, as they were fluent in the Mi'kmaq language, but, being neutral Acadians, the Petitpas were not considered trustworthy, as they were known to have dealings with the British stationed at Canso.

---

12 See Ronnie-Gilles Le Blanc, "Pigiguit: l'impact du grand Dérangement sur une communauté de l'ancienne Acadie", in *Du Grand Dérangement à la Déportation – Nouvelles perspectives historiques.*
13 Winthrop Bell, *The Foreign Protestants and the Settlement of Nova* Scotia, p.402.
14 Denis Jean, "Le rôle des Métis dans l'histoire de la colonie de l'Acadie", p. 65.

Ronald Labelle

In 1728, there were complaints that Claude Petitpas was encouraging the Mi'kmaq to have peaceful relations with New England fishers at Canso.[15] The French policy at the time was to use Native warriors as proxy fighters to harass the English in every way possible.

Claude Petitpas and his son Barthélémy were then removed from the colony and sent to France. They returned to the colony however, and were finally hired as interpreters. Claude died in 1731, and his son passed away in 1747, after which the role of interpreter was taken over by Louis Benjamin Petitpas, one of Claude's sons from his second marriage.[16]

Louis Benjamin assisted Father Maillard in his missionary work among the Mi'kmaq, and that brought him to the Chezzetcook area, where he later settled, along with his brothers Joseph and Jean-Baptiste, whose families established permanent roots in the area.

While Port-Toulouse (St. Peter's) was founded around 1713, when the French first began to establish the colony of Île Royale, the communities of Baie-des-Espagnols (Sydney) and Mordienne (Port Morien) were only settled in 1749-50, at a time when approximately 300 settlers arrived from the mainland. This migration coincided with the time when Chezzetcook was being abandoned.

French correspondence regarding the Acadians' request for farmlands at Baie-des-Espagnols mentions that the new settlers had been living near Halifax.[17] The 1752 census includes a large number of members of the Boutin, Mius, Guédry and Lejeune families, all of whom had previously been living either at Chezzetcook or at other localities in the Halifax area such as Mouscadabouet and Mirligoueche (Lunenberg).

It is impossible to list the names of all the migrants who left Chezzetcook for Île Royale, as no census was carried out on the Eastern Shore at the time of their departure, but we can conclude that Baie-des-Espagnols was their most likely destination.

In order to understand why Acadian settlements on both sides of Halifax were suddenly abandoned, we need to look at the historical circumstances that brought about sudden changes of the area. Life in Acadia had always been precarious, as the French and British contested ownership of the land from the early 1600s onwards. Matters became even more complicated after the fall of French Acadia in 1713, when the Aca-

---

15 William C. Wicken, *Encounters with Tall Sails and Tall Tales*, p. 394.

16 Maxime Morin, *Le rôle politique...*pp. 100-101.

17 Robert H. J. Shears, *Examination of a Contested Landscape*, p. 30.

dians faced the choice of living under the British flag or leaving their rich farmlands to live in French-controlled Île Royale (Cape Breton) or on Île Saint-Jean (Prince Edward Island).

The vast majority chose to stay in the former Acadia, around the Bay of Fundy and the Minas Basin, and as their numbers grew during the first half of the century, so did the outlying communities of Mirligoueche and Chezzetcook.

French reports from 1746-48 paint a picture of the situation immediately before the sudden disruption caused by the arrival of Lieutenant Governor Cornwallis, who brought more than 2,000 British settlers, not to mention hundreds of soldiers, to the very heart of the Atlantic coast of Acadia. Ever since the late 1600s, the area had been dominated by a strong Mi'kmaq presence and by an elusive group of Acadians, the majority of whom could be described as a Métis population of part Mi'kmaq and part French descent. While Acadians of mixed French and Mi'kmaq heritage were found in all areas, they seem to have been most prevalent in communities around Halifax, where they combined activities such as hunting, coastal trading, fishing and farming. In contrast, the older, established communities like Grand-Pré and Port-Royal were inhabited by people of predominantly French background whose livelihood was entirely dominated by farming.

From 1749 onward, life in the Acadian homeland became even more precarious because the founding of Halifax—and the arrival of Governor Cornwallis—marked the beginning of the final conflict between the two colonial powers. The Acadians could no longer remain neutral without facing hostility from both the British and the French.

To make matters even worse, the long simmering conflict between the Mi'kmaq inhabitants and the British came to a head in 1749, when Cornwallis seized the sacred ground of Chibouctou in order to build a British garrison town. People living in Acadian communities on both sides of Halifax had close ties to the Mi'kmaq, and their inhabitants were directly threatened by the conflict. If the Acadians established cordial relations with the British in Halifax, they risked losing the friendship of the Mi'kmaq. On the other hand, if they remained close to the Mi'kmaq, they were bound to face hostility from the British.

It seems that relations between the Acadians and Governor Cornwallis began rather cordially. When Cornwallis arrived in June 1749, his first stop was a visit to the Acadian settlement at Mirligueche (Lunenberg). In his first despatch upon arriving at Halifax, he wrote: "There are a few French families on each side of the bay, about three leagues off. Some have been on board."

Regarding the Acadians he met at Mirligueche, he says: "They seem to be very peaceable; say they always looked upon themselves as English subjects".[18]

Cornwallis did not visit Chezzetcook at that time, but we can presume that the attitudes of the Acadians there would be similar to that in Mirligueche, as the two communities were closely related.

If the Acadians living close to Halifax thought they would be able to continue to live as neutral British subjects following the founding of Halifax, they found out very quickly that would be impossible. It didn't take long for the British to begin provoking hostility from the Mi'kmaq.

Unlike the Acadians, who respected the right of the Mi'kmaq to occupy their traditional lands, the British began to build the community of Halifax in the very middle of a sacred gathering site for the Mi'kmaq on the Atlantic coast. This led to a tense situation that was exacerbated when the British decided to build a sawmill at Dartmouth Cove, at the head of a crucial waterway used by the Mi'kmaq for fishing and travelling. A fatal encounter soon took place, with predictable casualties on both sides.

Governor Cornwallis and his council quickly decided that the Mi'kmaq should be driven out of Nova Scotia. The council issued an order to all British subjects

> to annoy, distress, take or destroy the Savage commonly called Micmac, wherever they are found, and all as such as aiding and assisting them, give further by and with the consent and advice of His Majesty's Council, do promise a reward of 10 Guineas for every Indian Micmac taken or killed, to be paid upon producing such Savage taken or his scalp.[19]

A guinea was the equivalent of 21 shillings, and 10 guineas represented a big prize, attracting bounty hunters from as far away as New England.

From that time on, the Acadians faced a double threat: If they "aided or assisted" the Mi'kmaq, they would be considered enemies of the British; and if they continued to cooperate with the colonial administration in Halifax, for example by supplying food and firewood to the town, their relations with the Native population would be strained.

---

18 Murdoch, p. 138.
19 Jon Tattrie, *Cornwallis: The Violent Birth of Halifax*, pp. 96-99.

Being determined to drive the Mi'kmaq out of Nova Scotia, Governor Cornwallis had effectively established a reign of terror. According to author Jon Tattrie, the bounty hunters who scoured the countryside, killing all the Mi'kmaq they found, didn't avoid murdering individuals of mixed race, and there was at least one case where the paymaster protested that some of the scalps being brought in were likely from Acadians.

French officials in Louisbourg were alarmed by the British decision to build a garrison town at Halifax and sought ways to hinder the development of the new colonial capitol. They welcomed moves by the Mi'kmaq to fight the encroachment on their territory, and even offered money to warriors who brought the scalps of slain British soldiers to Louisbourg.

While they could count on the cooperation of the Mi'kmaq, the French were faced with a difficult problem regarding the Acadians. They no doubt were aware that Acadians from Mirligueche and Chezzetcook were helping to build and supply the new British garrison town, and they must have been troubled by the news that Acadians were also acting as couriers, carrying messages from Governor Cornwallis to the military commander at Annapolis Royal.

The missionary abbé Le Loutre, who had access to all the communities around Halifax, was sent as an agent to relay orders from French officials to the Mi'kmaq and the Acadians.

No surviving documents present in detail the tactics used by the French to cut off any ties the Acadians may have formed with the British, but we know that the abandonment of Chezzetcook was partly the result of French pressures on the Acadians to leave, judging by the accounts of those who later petitioned to return from Île Royale to the Halifax area in 1754.

In October of that year, 28 Acadians who had moved to Baie-des-Espagnols (present-day Sydney) appeared before the Halifax council, requesting permission to return to their former lands. Council Minutes record:

> that upon the first settling of the English at Halifax, they were so terrified by the threats that M. Le Loutre had used and his declaring the great distresses they would be reduced to if they remained under the Dominion of the English, that they on that account had retired and were set down on the island of Cape Breton.[20]

---

20 Quoted in Shears, *Examination of a Contested Landscape*, p. 34.

Ronald Labelle

It is easy to see why the neutral Acadians who had established homes at Chezzetcook chose to abandon the area in 1749, as they faced a triple threat: they could be murdered by bounty hunters taking advantage of the fact that Chezzetcook and Mirligueche were largely Métis communities; they could be attacked by Mi'kmaq warriors who resented any collaboration between Acadians and the British occupiers of their land; and, finally, they were threatened with destruction by the French through the actions of abbé Le Loutre, who had the means to hire Mi'kmaq warriors as mercenaries.

One group of Acadians even petitioned Governor Cornwallis to declare martial law, as they were afraid of Mi'kmaq raids.[21]

Left with the choice of either seeking the protection of the British in Halifax or fleeing the area, the Acadians finally chose to relocate to Île Royale with assistance from the French agent, abbé Le Loutre.

Their decision seems to be the most practical one possible. By moving to French territory, the Acadians would no longer risk losing their longstanding alliance with the Mi'kmaq, whereas if they remained close to Halifax, they would be caught in an impossible bind. Going to Île Royale was their only realistic option, because the British garrison in Halifax would not have been able to extend protection to the outlying communities of Chezzetcook and Mirligoueche. In any case, it would have been unthinkable for the Acadians to join the British in a conflict with the Mi'kmaq, because the majority of them had family ties with First Nations communities.

The Acadians' move away from Chezzetcook in the fall of 1749 seems to have taken place very hastily, which suggests that it may have been triggered by a tragic event, rather than simply being the outcome of the difficult circumstances in which they found themselves. It could be that one or more members of the community were murdered by marauding bounty hunters from New England, the infamous "Gorham's Rangers".

But another intriguing possibility exists. Historical archaeologist Robert Shears, who excavated 18th century settlement sites at Chezzetcook and Lawrencetown, raised the possibility that the Acadians had been forced to relocate to Île Royale not by the British but rather by the French.[22] Shears found evidence of two burnt houses in the Lawrencetown area dating from the period of Acadian settlement. Archaeological evidence has shown that Acadian families were then living both at

---

21 Tattrie, p. 112.

22 Shears, p. 94.

present-day Lawrencetown and at Grand-Désert.

In his survey of the area carried out in 1752, Charles Morris wrote, "the French have been a long time settled in these two places," and stated that the two former Acadian communities were surely linked by a road.[23] Shears raises the possibility that abbé Le Loutre not only threatened the Acadians with reprisals if they remained in the British colony, but that he carried out his threat by arranging to have some of their houses burnt to the ground.

Such an event would seem improbable, if there were no other similar cases in Acadian history. We know, however, that at Beaubassin, where British and French forces faced each other on either side of the Tantramar Marshes (the present border area between New Brunswick and Nova Scotia), Acadians living on the British side were forced to move to French-held territory after their houses were torched. Historians generally agree that abbé Le Loutre was the instigator of the plan to burn the Acadian village of Beaubassin.[24]

The French commanders at Louisbourg wanted to ensure that they could count on all the manpower the Acadians living at Beaubassin could supply in the upcoming conflict with the British. Similarly, military strategy would have stipulated that any Acadians living close to the British stronghold at Halifax should leave the area immediately in order to join forces with the French.

Given the close ties that existed between the Acadian families living in the areas now known as Lawrencetown and Grand-Désert, if indeed abbé Le Loutre had arranged for the burning of some houses, it would not have taken long for the alarm to be raised among all the Acadians in the area. The decision to leave may have been a collective one, taken after some members of the community found themselves forced out.

With only a few burnt remains as evidence, it is impossible to state with certainty that the French or their Mi'kmaq surrogates torched the Acadian dwellings. Still, if the hypothesis were true, it would explain why historical documents indicate that strong tensions existed between the Acadians and the French colonial administrators at Louisbourg from the moment the migrants arrived at Baie-des-Espagnols, until they abandoned Île Royale to return to the Halifax area in 1754.

The Acadian families from Chezzetcook, Mouscadabouet and Mir-

---

23 Halifax, Nova Scotia Archives, "A Written description of the Coast of Nova Scotia from Halifax Harbour to Chezzetcook", NSA CO 217/133.
24 See Naomi E. S. Griffiths, *From Migrant to Acadian – A North American border people,* pp. 73-74.

ligoueche spent up to five miserable years on Île Royale, during which they endured constant criticism from French authorities at Louisbourg, who described them as lazy and insubordinate half-breeds ("demi-sauvages"). At one point, soldiers were even sent from the Fortress to Baie-des-Espagnols in order to watch over the Acadians.[25]

If indeed Acadian families from the Chezzetcook area had moved to Île Royale not by choice but because they had been forced out of their homes by the French, the lack of cooperation that existed between them and the colonial administration at Louisbourg would not be surprising. On the other hand, the Acadians who petitioned for the right to return to the Halifax area in 1754 did not actually mention the destruction of any of their homes by the French. Written accounts indicate only that they had suffered "threats" from French agent abbé Le Loutre.

Because we do not know the names of most the Acadians who had originally settled at Chezzetcook in the early 18th century, it is not possible to trace all their movements following the failed attempt to build a new community at Baie-des-Espagnols on Île Royale. We know that some of the returning Acadians took refuge with their Mi'kmaq kin in mainland Nova Scotia. Several families chose to return to their former communities in the Halifax area in 1754 and some were granted the right to settle at Lunenberg, the former Mirligoueche. Land was available there because the newly arrived foreign Protestants did not occupy all the lots laid out for them by colonial administrators.

The returning Acadians who had been living at Chezzetcook before their departure for Île Royale in 1749 would discover that the entire area around West Chezzetcook and Grand-Désert was now part of the new Lawrencetown Township, and that all the land had been divided into lots for Protestant families. This is how Lieutenant-Governor Charles Lawrence described the land included in the grant:

> Plan of a tract of land (…) lying and being to the Eastward of Dartmouth, and was formerly called and known by the name of Wampawk, Tawbooshomkec, Mayanshish and Shezetcook, and now to be called Lawrence Town.[26]

The name Wampack actually refers to Cole Harbour, or "Cold Harbour",

---

25 Gaston Du Boscq De Beaumont, *Les derniers jours de l'Acadie (1748-1758)*, p. 104.
26 Joan Dawson, *The Mapmaker's Eye*, pp. 119-120.

as it was referred to on maps of that period. Tawbooshomkec corresponds to the actual site of Lawrencetown, while Mayanshish encompassed the area around Porter's Lake and Grand-Désert.

Had the Acadians from Chezzetcook been allowed to return to their previous homesteads, their stay would still have been short-lived, because the Halifax Council, led by Lieutenant Governor William Lawrence and in accord with Governor William Shirley of Massachusetts, decided in June of 1755 to begin deporting all Acadians living in Nova Scotia. During the following months, they were dispersed among the British colonies, ranging from Massachusetts all the way down to Georgia.

The Acadian families that had relocated to Lunenberg were deported to North Carolina, and many eventually found freedom in Louisiana, where they flourished, their descendants now being known as "Cajuns".

The controversial decision to expel the entire Acadian population has been analyzed multiple times by historians and the Deportation is now widely condemned as an act of gross injustice. While the forceful removal of thousands of Acadians living around the Minas Basin and the present-day Annapolis Valley has been studied in depth, little attention has been given to the deportation of Acadians living near Halifax, perhaps because of their lower numbers.

According to genealogist Stephen White, about 50 Acadians from that area were exiled to North Carolina.[27] Although they only represented a small fraction of the total number who were deported, the facts surrounding their removal could contribute to our understanding of this tragic event in Acadian history.

If the colonial administrators in Halifax had been planning all along to deport the Acadian population, it is obvious that they would not have looked for a suitable location to re-settle the former inhabitants of Chezzetcook, Mouscadabouet and Mirligoueche who had just returned from Île Royale in 1754. They made up a group of no more than one hundred individuals in total, and Lieutenant Governor Lawrence could easily have detained them upon their arrival in Halifax or had them sent away immediately. The fact that his administration accepted the Acadians' request to be readmitted into the colony suggests that, as late as the fall of 1754, the British had no specific plans to deport the Acadian population. This adds an important element to the evidence suggesting that the Deportation that took place in the summer and fall of 1755 was a hastily improvised affair, with little prior planning.

---

27 Shears, *Examination of a Contested Landscape*, pp. 34-35.

Ronald Labelle

By the end of 1755, all the Acadians who had lived in the Chezzetcook area had been dispersed, and, with the exception of the Petitpas clan, the families who would begin to lay down new roots there in 1762 were an entirely new group of settlers. As was the case elsewhere in the Maritimes, the Deportation marked a clear break in Acadian history, and the 1760s was a time of rebirth.

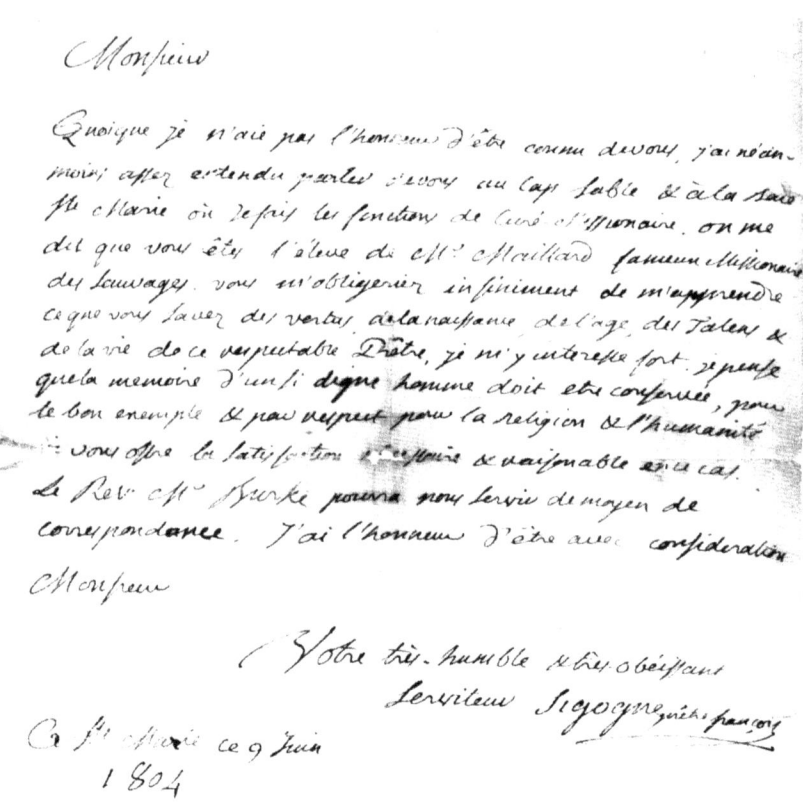

Figure 5: Letter from pioneer priest Jean Mandé Sigogne to Jean Baptiste Roma in June, 1804.

2: New beginnings in the Post-Expulsion era (1763-1790)

In 1763, the Treaty of Paris finally ended the Seven Years War, the last of the French-British conflicts that had dominated the relationship between the colonial powers in North America for a century and a half.

Once the French had lost all claim to territories in the northeastern part of the continent, the British no longer felt threatened by the existence of Acadian communities. Nevertheless, colonial officials were not prepared to grant the Acadians the same rights and privileges they gave to Protestant settlers.

While the foreign Protestants and New England Planters obtained large land grants in Nova Scotia, no provision was made for the Acadians who remained in the colony, nor for those who were hoping to return from exile. Thus, the scattered remnants of what had been the proud people of Acadia found themselves without a homeland.

For up to fifty years following the end of hostilities, Acadians wandered in exile, constantly seeking lands where they could rebuild their communities. More than one thousand ended up going to Québec, where they settled permanently in the St. Lawrence Valley and elsewhere. Close to two thousand found refuge in Louisiana, where their descendants prospered in the territory now known as "Acadiana". A smaller number of Acadians exiles remained in France, where they had been sent in 1758, while many of those who had been deported to New England three years earlier became assimilated into the local population.

It is important to point out, however, that at least two thousands Acadians died directly or indirectly from causes related to the Deportation. Several hundred drowned in shipwrecks. Others died of various diseases, while a large number of refugees either froze or starved to death while fleeing through the forest.

The group we are concerned with here is the relatively small number of Acadians who were able to re-establish communities in the Maritimes.

Ronald Labelle

Some returned from exile in France, stopping at Saint-Pierre-et-Miquelon on their way back, but most of the Acadians who built new communities in the Maritimes had never left the colony. They managed to evade capture until at least 1759, when the policy of banishment was no longer workable and was replaced by one of incarceration.

Acadians who were captured between 1759 and 1762, or who gave themselves up voluntarily, were held at places like Fort Edward in Windsor and George's Island in Halifax Harbour. When they were finally released in 1763 and 1764, they found that newly-arrived Anglo-Protestant settlers occupied most of their former lands.

Being Roman Catholic, they were disqualified from land ownership, but small groups of Acadians attempted to settle as squatters in various places, hoping to eventually obtain land tenure. In many cases, they quickly found themselves surrounded by English-speaking settlers who held legal title to the former Acadian lands, and they were forced to relocate yet again.

The second half of the 18th century saw constant moves by Acadians until they were finally able to obtain land grants that permitted them to put down permanent roots.

Three different factors explain why Chezzetcook was one of the first places where the Acadians were successful in becoming re-established. First, although Chezzetcook was included in the Lawrencetown Township grants, the eastern section of the township was not immediately occupied by Protestant settlers and remained vacant through the 1760s. Both Lunenberg and Lawrencetown had been considered as possible sites for the establishment of the foreign Protestants, but the majority of them settled in the first location, leaving part of the Lawrencetown Township vacant.

Second, French missionary abbé Maillard successfully petitioned to have several Acadian families accompany him to Chezzetcook, where he had permission to establish a base from which to minister to the Mi'kmaq population.

Finally, hundreds of Acadian prisoners were set free in 1764, following a painful period of incarceration on George's Island, and Chezzetcook was the nearest community where they could be welcomed by their compatriots.

Chezzetcook: an Acadian stronghold

The arrival of Acadian families from Île Royale, 1760

While the French missionary and agent abbé Le Loutre had caused the Acadians considerable anguish by pressuring them to abandon their original settlement at Chezzetcook, his successor, abbé Pierre Maillard, had a completely opposite influence. Abbé Maillard played a crucial role in the re-birth of Chezzetcook, and was instrumental in helping families obtain permission to settle there. After the fall of Louisbourg in 1758, Maillard had managed to convince Governor Charles Lawrence to free several families being held prisoner on Île Royale, so that they could join him in Halifax. In October 1760, Governor Lawrence wrote the following to General Whitmore, the British commanding officer at Louisbourg:

> I find myself under a necessity of Complying with a Request that Mr. Maillard has made to me, that the Families of a Louis and Joseph Petitpas may be permitted to attend him here: These two men have always had a particular attachment to Mr. Maillard·, and may be very useful as interpreters of the Indian Language and otherwise; wherefore I am to Request Your Excellency to Permit them to Come hither together with six more families Vist Abraham Lavandiere, Amand Braulds, Sigismond Braulds, Jean Baptiste Romas, Jacques Petitpas, and Jean Petitpas; whom I intend to employ, as they are recommended to me by Mr. Maillard, to be the most Skillful people in making Dikes & wares to keep off the sea from our Marsh Lands about Mines & Piziquid; and whose fidelity he assures me may be depended on.[28]

Abbé Maillard appears to have been a skilful negotiator because, in addition to obtaining permission to have his interpreters Louis and Joseph Petitpas accompany him to Chezzetcook, he was also able to secure the release of six more families held on Île Royale, and this at a time when hostilities between the British and the French had not yet officially ended. Abbé Maillard convinced the governor to accept the additional families, stating that they could supply the British with much needed expertise for the restoration of the dykes around the Minas Basin.

It may be that Maillard used that argument as a ploy, while his true intention was to provide as many Acadians as possible with lands on which to settle in Chezzetcook. That is where most of them eventually ended up, thus creating a nucleus for the budding Acadian community.

---

28 F. J. Melanson, *Genealogies of the Families of Chezzetcook, N.S.* - "Petitpas"

Ronald Labelle

Among the names mentioned in Maillard's letter are four Petitpas brothers, Louis (Benjamin), Joseph, Jacques and Jean (Baptiste), as well as their half-brother Abraham Lavandier, all of whom had been living at Port-Toulouse on Île Royale at the time of the British conquest.

There were close kinship ties between most of the initial group of settlers. The Petitpas and Lavandier families were closely related through Abraham Lavandier's father, also named Abraham Lavandier, who was the second husband of Françoise Lavergne; while the Petitpas brothers were the children of Françoise Lavergne and her first husband, Claude Petitpas.

Jean Baptiste Roma, another of abbé Maillard's assistants, was accompanied by his wife Félicité Clergé, who was the daughter of Françoise Lavergne and her third husband, Claude Clergé. Jean-Baptiste Roma was born on Île Saint-Jean (Prince Edward Island) and later moved to Port-Toulouse before joining the migration to Chezzetcook with his wife Félicité. This couple was particularly prolific, giving birth to 11 children whom they raised in Chezzetcook.

It seems that the role played by Jean Baptiste Roma as a confidant of abbé Maillard was noticed by Church officials and was talked about as far away as Church Point, in Southwest Nova Scotia. That is from where Father Jean Mandé Sigogne, the pioneer French priest in the Acadian district of Clare, addressed the following letter to Roma in 1804:

> Although I do not have the honour of being known to you, I have nevertheless heard of you at Cap Sable and at Baie Sainte-Marie, where I serve as priest and missionary. I have been told that you were a pupil of Mr. Maillard, the famous missionary to the Indians. I would be infinitely grateful if you would tell me what you know about the virtues, origins, age, abilities and life of this venerable priest. I am very interested, for I believe that the memory of such a dignified man should be preserved as an example and as a respect for religion and humanity. In offering you necessary and reasonable satisfaction regarding this, Rev. Mr. Burke is willing to act as a correspondent.[29] [translation]

While members of the Petitpas clan began to build a new settlement at Chezzetcook in the early 1760s, other relatives who had lived close to

---

29 Letter from Father Sigogne to Baptiste Roma, 9 June 1804, Acadian House Museum, Chezzetcook.

them in the Port-Toulouse area of Île Royale were looking for places to settle.

Gabriel Clergé, Félicité Clergé's brother and another half-sibling of the Petitpas brothers, had been imprisoned at the end of the siege of Louisbourg in 1758. He eventually made his way to Chezzetcook, where he married Théotiste Boudrot in 1769. Jean-Pierre Mayet, born in 1744 at Petit-de-Grat, joined the migration from Île Royale to Chezzetcook, and in 1771 he married Françoise Boudrot, a sister of Théotiste.

Another of the early settlers was Pierre Bonin, a young orphan born in 1753 at Saint-Esprit on Île Royale, who probably accompanied his uncles, the Petitpas brothers, in their move to Chezzetcook.

When the French colony of Île Royale fell to the British in 1758, hundreds of Acadians were living in the area around Port-Toulouse. Apart from those who were allowed to settle in Chezzetcook thanks to the influence of abbé Maillard, there were others who were released from imprisonment at Louisbourg by General Whitmore so that they could "remain as interpreters of the Indian language."[30]

Historical sources point to the fact that many of the pioneer settlers of Chezzetcook in the 1760s spoke both French and the Mi'kmaq language. This would enable them to maintain their ties to the Mi'kmaq population.

Finally, a few of the early settlers who came from Île Royale may have evaded capture by the British in 1758, after which they joined the move to Chezzetcook once hostilities had ended in 1763. According to genealogist Stephen White, contacts between families living in Chezzetcook and those at St. Peter's and on Île Madame continued for at least a generation, as several marriages took place in the late 18th century between residents of the two areas.[31]

Newly-released Acadian prisoners join the settlement

George's Island was one of the principal incarceration sites for Acadians captured during the years of banishment that ended in 1763. The island was used as a way station between 1755 and 1762 for the detention of Acadians who were awaiting deportation. It is likely that several of the Acadians who were held temporarily on George's Island before being sent to South Carolina had been among those who had left Chezzetcook

---

30 Melanson, *Genealogies of the Families of Chezzetcook...* - "Bonin".
31 Stephen White, personal communication, August 1987.

in 1749, only to return five years later, having tried unsuccessfully to start a new life at Baie-des-Espagnols.

The island saw its greatest number of prisoners between 1759 and 1764, when the Acadians who had put up a resistance against the British finally gave up their struggle and were rounded up and incarcerated.

French historian Edmé Rameau de Saint-Père, who first visited Nova Scotia in 1860, and who published the first book of Acadian history in 1889, described the origins of Chezzetcook in this way:

> Chezetcook, that is the name of this village, originated with a certain number of Acadian families who had been captured at various times after their banishment. They were led to Halifax, where they were held captive for a long time on an island in the middle of the south harbour and that is called île Rouge. There, they lived at times from prison rations, and at other times from the fruits of their labour, when they were permitted to work for the townspeople. Finally, 10 or 12 years after the great catastrophe, they were permitted to settle a few leagues north of Halifax at the little harbour of Chezzetcook.[32] [translation]

According to historical maps, "île Rouge" would correspond to present-day Devil's Island. However, the island in the middle of the south harbour is George's Island, which suggests Rameau de Saint-Père may have noted the wrong name.

Historians have compiled a partial list of Acadian families imprisoned at Halifax between 1759 and 1764. The list includes about 800 people and was compiled from information written down in 1763 and 1764, at the time when they were about to be released and permitted to leave either for France or the French islands in the Caribbean.

Historian Ronnie-Gilles LeBlanc noted that many Acadians who were held at George's Island were not included in the list of prisoners because they did not intend to join the migration to French territory upon their release.[33] We can assume that the prisoners whose names were not listed were looking for opportunities to become re-established in the colony. As they sought out locations where they could rebuild Acadian communities in Nova Scotia, it would not have taken them long to find out that a group

---

32 Edmé Rameau de Saint-Père, "Voyage...", p. 345.
33 Ronnie-Gilles Le Blanc, "Les Acadiens à Halifax et dans l'île George's, 1755-1764", pp. 67-71.

of their compatriots were already doing just that in Chezzetcook.

Some of the newly freed Acadians went temporarily to Chezzetcook before moving on to other localities. Amand Breau, for example, escaped from Grand-Pré in 1755, took refuge at Nepisiguit (present-day Bathurst, New Brunswick), where he was captured in 1761, and was taken to George's Island. Upon his release, he married Théotiste Bonnevie and the couple left for the French island of Miquelon. A few years later, the couple was back in the Halifax area, living at Chezzetcook.

The Breau family eventually settled at Havre-Boucher in Antigonish County, but one of their sons, Jean Breau, remained at Grand-Désert, where he was one of the first settlers on Shore Road, according to information gathered by F.-J. Melanson.[34]

François Grenon is another former prisoner who lived for a time near Chezzetcook. He escaped from the Port-Royal in 1755, only to be captured in 1761 along the Saint John River in present-day New Brunswick. Upon his release from George's Island, he left for French territory with his wife, Marie-Madeleine Breau. The couple returned to the Halifax area and went to Chezzetcook, where some of Marie-Madeleine's relatives were living. They then chose to live permanently at Arichat, on Île Madame, but some of their children stayed behind and settled at Petpeswick.[35]

Charles Bellefontaine, whose name appears on the list of prisoners held on George's Island, was a member of a large family that initially evaded capture while living along the Saint John River. Some of his siblings fled to Québec, while others were captured and eventually moved to Louisiana after their release from George's Island.

Charles and his wife, Marie Melanson, however, remained in the colony with their eight children after their release from George's Island. They lived for a time in Arichat before going to Chezzetcook. Some of their children eventually settled in Southwestern Nova Scotia, while others went to New Brunswick, but two sons, Jean-Baptiste and Alexandre, remained in Chezzetcook, where they have many descendants.

Both Bellefontaine brothers married into the Petitpas family. Jean-Baptiste married Marie Blandine Petitpas, while Alexandre Bellefontaine's wife was named Marie Henriette. The latter couple had ten children, many of whom raised families of their own in Chezzetcook.

While researching the genealogies of 15 Acadian families that settled

---

34 Melanson, *Genealogies...* - "Breau".
35 Ibid. - "Grenon".

at Chezzetcook, F. J. Melanson found evidence of at least three other families that arrived there after their release from detention.

One individual, Augustin Wolfe, followed a long and tortuous path before arriving in Chezzetcook. He was born in 1721 in the French province of Alsace that borders on Germany, and had been among the foreign settlers sent to establish Halifax. Shortly after his arrival there in 1751, Wolfe abandoned the British settlement and went to live among the Acadians of Île Saint-Jean. When the Acadians of the island were deported in 1758, he took refuge in Bellechasse, Québec.[36]

Three years later, Wolfe attempted to settle along the Saint John River, in the area around present-day Fredericton. He had probably joined a group of Acadians from the Saint John River valley, who had temporarily taken refuge in Quebec, and who were attempting to return to their former lands.[37]

Shortly after his return to Acadia, however, Wolfe was taken prisoner and brought to Halifax. Upon his release, he made his way to Chezzetcook.

Several other families who settled at Chezzetcook had been released not from George's Island, but from other centres of detention. Charles Boudrot, born at Port-Royal in 1714, was living along the Petitcodiac river in present-day New Brunswick at the time of the Deportation. Residents of that area successfully evaded capture and many fought the soldiers who had been sent to round them up. After years of resistance, they finally had to choose either to make the long trek to freedom in Québec or give up their fight.

Charles, his wife, Marie-Josephe Fougère, and their children surrendered to the British and were imprisoned at Fort Edward near Windsor. Upon their release, they made their way to Chezzetcook.

They moved to Tor Bay in Guysborough County shortly after, but at least two of their daughters stayed behind. Théotiste Boudrot became the wife of Gabriel Clergé, while Anne Boudrot married Pierre Bonin.[38]

The Boudrots' move to Tor Bay was not an isolated event, as many of the Acadians who initially settled in Chezzetcook eventually moved there. During the 1780s, large land grants were being awarded to newly-arrived United Empire Loyalists in the vicinity of Chezzetcook and many

---

36 Rapport de l'archiviste de la province de Québec, Vol. 32-33, 1951-1953, p. 7.
37 Denise Pelletier and Marie-Claire Pitre, *Les Pays-Bas*, pp. 139-142.
38 Melanson, *Genealogies...* - "Boudrot".

Chezzetcook: an Acadian stronghold

Acadians felt they had no choice but to look for land elsewhere.[39]

This explains why family names such as Bellefontaine, Bonnevie and Petitpas are found both in Chezzetcook and in the Guysborough area. Families who were unable to obtain land grants at Chezzetcook went both to the Guysborough County settlements around Tor Bay and to the Tracadie area in Antigonish County. The Girouard family, for example, after first settling at Chezzetcook, moved to Tracadie in 1783.

Jude Avery, author of a book about the history of Acadians in Guysborough County, states that the reason there was so much intermarriage between the early Acadian settlers of Tor Bay and Tracadie was that both groups had ties to Chezzetcook.[40]

One of the migrants who ended up in Tor Bay was Paul Pellerin, the husband of Marie-Louise Petitpas, a granddaughter of Claude Petitpas. Avery suggests that Claude Petitpas had frequented the Tor Bay area as far back as the late 1600s.[41] Several Acadians from the Halifax area had been active in the coastal trade from that time on, and it is likely they were familiar with the seacoast around Tor Bay.

Another family that went to Chezzetcook after being released from detention in a military fort was that of Joseph Jacques Lapierre. Born at Beaubassin, he settled with his wife, Marguerite Lebrun, along the Petitcodiac River during the 1740s, and the couple began to raise a family there.

Like Charles Boudrot and many other Acadians of the Petitcodiac district, Lapierre initially evaded capture. Lapierre and Boudrot may even have taken part in a rare, bloody battle along the Petitcodiac in which British forces sent to capture the local population were defeated, suffering over one hundred casualties.

While most of Joseph Jacques's siblings made their way to Québec after their escape from the Expulsion, his family stayed behind, taking refuge in the woods until they were forced to either surrender or starve to death. The couple were taken as prisoners and held at Fort Beauséjour in 1763, along with their eight children.

It is difficult to trace all the movements of Acadian families during those years of turmoil, but according to F.J. Melanson, the Lapierre family was in Halifax during the late 1760s, then went to live at Eastern Passage in 1770, and settled at Chezzetcook shortly after.[42]

---

39 Sally Ross, "La reconstruction d'une société", p. 62.
40 Jude Avery, *The Forgotten Acadians - a story of discovery,* pp. 28-29.
41 Idem.
42 Melanson, *Genealogies...* - "Lapierre".

The Bonnevie family provides one more example of an imprisoned family that was attracted to Chezzetcook after 1764. At the time of the Expulsion, Jacques Bonnevie and his wife, Marguerite Laure, escaped to Restigouche, at the head of Chaleur Bay, and that was where they surrendered to the British in 1761.

The couple's two eldest sons were able to flee, but were finally captured and sent to detention in Halifax, after which they lived for a time in Chezzetcook. The other five children were imprisoned at Fort Edward along with their parents, and a few of them lived temporarily in Chezzetcook before heading either to the French islands of Saint-Pierre-et-Miquelon or to other parts of Nova Scotia.

The youngest, however, Sylvain Bonnevie, married Marie Petitpas in Chezzetcook in 1769, and that is where the couple raised their children.[43]

Among the many Acadian families that took refuge in Chezzetcook after the tumultuous years of the Expulsion, there were some who only lived there for a brief time, and whose names did not get passed on to future generations. One example is included in a fascinating book of Acadian historical anecdotes entitled *Les entretiens du village*.[44]

Author Emery LeBlanc tells the story of four Le Blanc brothers, who, after being deported to Massachusetts along with their parents in 1755, made their way to the French islands of Saint-Pierre-et-Miquelon at the end of the Seven Years War in 1763.

One of the brothers, Jacques, was accompanied by his wife and young children, and the LeBlanc clan also included a sister, as well as the siblings' mother, their father having died in exile.

Four years later, the four brothers returned to Nova Scotia, arriving at Halifax. Two of them set off to find a new home and eventually settled in Memramcook, New Brunswick, while the two others remained in the Halifax area.

Emery LeBlanc tells of how Simon LeBlanc went to live in Chezzetcook, where he had heard some Acadian families were already established, while his brother Jacques settled in a nearby fishing community. The following year, Jacques drowned tragically in a boating accident near Chezzetcook, and his wife then took her children to live close to their relatives in Memramcook.

There is no further mention of Simon LeBlanc in *Les entretiens du vil-*

---

43 Melanson, *Genealogies...* - "Bonnevie".
44 Emery Le Blanc, *Les entretiens du village*, pp. 11-18.

lage, but genealogical research by Stephen White clarifies his story.[45] Simon, who was born in 1734, was single when he went to live in Chezzetcook. After his brother Jacques died and the remainder of the family left for New Brunswick, he seems to have decided to join them, because we know that he was living there at the time of his marriage in 1771. Simon LeBlanc likely only spent a year or two in Chezzetcook in the late 1760s, and that explains why no members of the LeBlanc family put down roots there.

More settlers arrive in Chezzetcook after 1780

Most of the dominant families in the Chezzetcook area can trace their ancestry to the dozen families that came either from Île Royale with abbé Pierre Maillard in 1760-61 or who arrived following the release of Acadian prisoners at the end of the Seven Years War. There are, however, a couple of families whose ancestors arrived in different circumstances.

One of these ancestors was Jean-Pierre Murphy, or "Morphi", born in Cape Breton in 1769, who arrived at Chezzetcook sometime after 1785. Despite his Irish name, Jean-Pierre Murphy spoke French and became integrated into the Acadian community of Chezzetcook upon his arrival. F. J. Melanson suggests that the Murphys may have been Irish allies of the French at Placentia, Newfoundland.[46] When the French colony in Newfoundland fell to the British in 1713, they likely moved to Île Royale along with the hundreds of French Newfoundlanders who were involved in the cod fishery.

One final pioneer settler arrived as a young French sailor in the 1790s. The story of Simon Julien is indeed unique and we are fortunate to have a complete account of the circumstances of his arrival, thanks to an article written by Adolphe Marsais, a French traveller who visited Chezzetcook in 1867.[47] This account is included in chapter 4, where I present the writings of 19th century visitors to Chezzetcook.

---

45 Stephen White, "La généalogie des trente-neuf familles hôtesses des « Retrouvailles 94 »", pp. 152-158.
46 Melanson, *Genealogies...* - Murphy.
47 Adolphe Marsais, "Un mois de séjour chez nos Acadiens", pp. 1-2.

Ronald Labelle

The pioneers of Chezzetcook: fact and fiction

With the passing of the generations, stories about how people's ancestors arrived in a community tend to become vague, while often retaining a kernel of truth. Many of the descendants of Simon Julien, for example, knew that their ancestor had been a French sailor, but they believed he had simply jumped ship at Halifax before making his way to Chezzetcook. One of his great-granddaughters, named Emma Julien, wrote an essay entitled "History of Grand Desert" when she was a student at the provincial Normal College in 1906-07. In her essay, she states that the Julien family was from Paris.

Strangely enough, oral history tells us that members of the Julien family were nicknamed "les Bretons", even though their ancestor was originally from Southwestern France, hundreds of kilometres from both Brittany and Paris.

While Simon Julien's descendants were confused as to his exact origins, they were right to recognize that he had come directly from France, and not from the former colony of Acadia, where most of the original settlers were born. Oral history going back several generations is not always factual, but it can inform us about how people perceive their cultural origins.

Liliane Bellefontaine, for example, told an interesting account of the origins of the Bellefontaine family:

> Our ancestors weren't in the Expulsion...but they lived in Port Royal for a while. And then they set off to travel, to come over here, those two brothers, Alexandre and Jean; and when they got to Halifax, they were among the others. They were Acadians, no doubt, but they weren't in the Expulsion, they left to come over here. When they got to Halifax, there was a war raid, that happened—what they call a raid. They were fighting them, you know. They were fighting the French because they were enemies...But these two moved on towards this area, these two Bellefontaines.[48] [translation]

Liliane Bellefontaine was right in assuming that her ancestors had not been victims of the Expulsion, but wasn't aware that the family had evaded capture not by escaping, but rather because they were living in a remote area along the Saint John River. Her account also fails to recog-

---

48 CEAAC, Ronald Labelle Collection, AF-182, accession no. 1138 (1982).

nize that the Bellefontaines did not come to Halifax on their own, but were brought there as prisoners of the British.

Most oral accounts of the arrival of the Acadians' ancestors in Chezzetcook seem to ignore the fact that nearly all had suffered imprisonment and were only able to seek out lands on which to settle after being released by their captors. In the Lapierre family, for example, there is an oft-repeated story about how the first Lapierres fled when the British began to deport the inhabitants of Grand-Pré. The account William Lapierre gave of his ancestors' arrival is typical of the stories told:

> They were there (at Grand-Pré). The English who came disturbed them. There was a little church there, and they locked the church. Then some of them got away through the marsh, and some came this way - the Lapierres; almost all of them were Lapierres."[49] [translation]

In fact, the ancestors of the Lapierres of Chezzetcook had left Grand-Pré more than 50 years before the Expulsion in order to settle in the new community of Beaubassin, near present-day Amherst. The story of the Lapierres escaping through the marsh in order to make their way to Chezzetcook is also fictional, as we now know that members of the founding family were held captive at Fort Beauséjour before their eventual arrival in the area. As is often the case in oral-history accounts dealing with events that took place more than a century ago, there is a kernel of truth in the story, while the family's descendants used their imagination to fill in the missing elements.

The first Lapierres who settled in Chezzetcook no doubt told their descendants how they had avoided being banished from the colony in 1755, and, with the passing of the generations, details about subsequent events may have become muddled, with the result that people concluded that their ancestors had escaped directly to Chezzetcook.

Brothers Jean and Joseph Lapierre, who arrived in the early 1770s, both raised several children who became established at Grand-Désert, so it is not surprising that some of their descendants believed that the two had arrived after evading capture during the Expulsion.[50] In fact, the brothers were both young children in 1755 and they followed their parents through the long years of imprisonment leading up to the time of

---

49 Ibid., accession no. 1084 (1982).
50 "Community History Board – Grand Desert", 2003.

their settlement in Chezzetcook.

As the community grew over the years, a few family names became more widespread than others. Thus, the name Lapierre became the most common one in Grand-Désert, while the Bellefontaine family predominated in West Chezzetcook. This would explain why local oral tradition has the Lapierre and Bellefontaine families arriving first.

Apart from the stories that have been handed down in oral tradition about the arrival of these families' ancestors, there is also an anonymous newspaper clipping from 1922, entitled "Chezzetcook, a Little Bit of Arcadia". It provides a detailed and much embellished account of the arrival of the Lapierres:

> The first settler is said to have been John Lapierre. When the Acadians were expelled from Grand Pré, John Lapierre escaped with a number of others and hid in the woods. Later, with his gun on his back and his dog at his heels, he walked and walked, looking always for a place to settle. His descendants tell what he told them of his early life – how he had to build walls in Grand Pré and work so hard there and then the British came and took it all away.
>
> An exile, a fugitive, alone save for his trusty dog, John Lapierre, with indomitable courage and energy, started his weary search for a resting place. He crossed the Lake (now called Porter's) and saw no place to settle. When he reached the "Harbor", he was exhausted. The Harbor, with its tide out, looked to him like a great desert and he so named it. After a few days rest, having decided to locate here, he returned to find his friends and Luke Lapierre came back to Grand Désert with him and the two became owners of the land. Later some six others—Charles, Peter, Oliver, Prosper, Isaiah and Joseph Lapierre—came from Grand Pré. John raised his own barley and corn and ground it by hand. During the stormy days of the first revolution in France, the Breaus and Mayettes came and when the second revolution arose the Julians came. Other early settlers were Morphi, Bonavie and Bellefontaine, which latter name Longfellow has immortalized in his Evangeline.[51]

The story of John Lapierre trekking through the woods with his dog in

---

51 "Chezzetcook, a little bit of Arcadia" (newspaper clipping), 1922, Acadian House Museum.

Chezzetcook: an Acadian stronghold

search of a safe haven certainly has little resemblance to historical fact. Stories like this one and the previous story of the Bellefontaines' arrival played a useful role, however, as they taught young people that their Acadian ancestors had endured many hardships before being allowed to settle peacefully in Nova Scotia.

It is interesting that in the quoted article, the name Murphy is written in its French form "Morphi". This supports the idea that Jean-Pierre Murphy was a member of a family that adopted a Francophone identity long ago, despite its Irish origins.

One interesting detail in the text quoted above is the statement that the name "Grand-Désert" came about because of the appearance of the mud flats at low tide. This is another fanciful attempt to explain a fact that was not well understood. William Lapierre, who was interviewed in 1980 for a newspaper article entitled "How Grand Desert got its name"[52], told a story that is somewhat closer to the truth. He had heard that the first settlers had to pay for their land grants in lumber, and therefore cut all the wood on their land, thus making it a "Grand Desert".

The confusion about the name comes from that fact that the word "désert", which in modern French has a meaning similar to the word "desert" in English, had an entirely different meaning in centuries past. The Acadians used the word to refer to any land clearing in the forest. In the 18th century, even a small area where trees had been cut down could be called a "désert".

While the village of Grand-Désert may simply have received its name because of forest clearances by the early settlers, the name suggests another intriguing possibility: It could be that the families who arrived beginning in the 1760s found that some of the woodland had already been cleared by earlier settlers, and so decided to call the place "Grand-Désert".

Archaeological excavations done in the Chezzetcook area by Robert Shears prove that a pre-Expulsion Acadian settlement was situated at present-day Grand-Désert. Shears determined that the settlement was on the drumlin peninsula of Grand-Désert Hill, at the intersection of Dyke and Range roads.[53] In his M.A. thesis, he quotes from the description of the area written in 1752, where surveyor Charles Morris wrote:

> The upland which is a high Hill has about Eighty Acres of English

---
52 Mary Alma Dillman, "How Grand Desert got its name".
53 Shears, pp. 99-100.

Grass, and further North about half a mile is another piece of upland cleared of about Twenty Acres, here are four Houses. These are all the Settlements within the Harbour, without, to the Westward, is another piece of upland cleared of about Twenty Acres. The Quantity of Hay produced from all of them may be Sufficient to support One & Fifty head of Neat Cattle besides Sheep We also know that the chapel built for visiting missionaries in the early 18th century was situated close to the shore there.[54]

It appears, then, that the name Grand-Désert would harken back to the 300-year-old settlement of the area by a small group of Acadians or of Métis families with mixed Acadian and Mi'kmaq origin.

Acadian-Mi'kmaq relations

Regarding the ties between the early Acadians and the Mi'kmaq, it is difficult to determine exactly how much contact took place between the two groups, but oral accounts that have circulated among both of them suggest they had a close relationship.

Liliane Bellefontaine told of how her ancestors lived among the Mi'kmaq people after having escaped from Halifax: "They went into the woods somehow, and they lived with the Mi'kmaq for a while. They were among the Mi'kmaq; they were all right."[55][translation]

Seeing that Chezzetcook was an important population centre for the Mi'kmaq at the time of the Acadians' arrival, it is not surprising that a legend evolved in order to explain why the two groups chose to live in the same area. Mi'kmaq elder Kevin Christmas told the story of how the Acadians' ancestors were captured on French ships and brought to Halifax by the British. The Mi'kmaq then offered to take charge of the

Figure 6: Tall, wooden cross said to have been erected by Mi'maq residents at Grand-Désert in the 1740s.

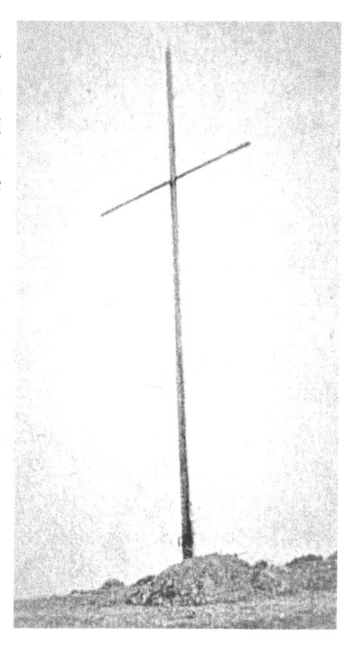

---

54 Ibid., p. 101.

Chezzetcook: an Acadian stronghold

prisoners, and so the British released the Acadians, who were taken by their hosts to Chezzetcook, where they were allowed to stay.[56]

Like many oral history accounts, this story reduces a complex set of historical circumstances to a single event, and therefore can not be taken at face value; but just as Liliane Bellefontaine's account contains a basic truth, so does this one. It teaches us that Acadian refugees in the late 18th century were welcomed and assisted by the Mi'kmaq, who contributed to their survival.

While there were historical ties between the two groups everywhere in the Maritimes, in Chezzetcook the link was particularly strong because of the presence of both Acadians and Mi'kmaq in the same community.

Historically, a large Mi'kmaq gathering took place during the summer months in the Chezzetcook area. During his first visit there in July of 1768, the missionary Charles-François Bailly baptized 47 Mi'kmaq and 16 Acadians, ranging in age from two months to seven years.[57] The fact that at least one of the Mi'kmaq children Bailly baptized had Acadian godparents is proof that there was a certain degree of contact between the two groups.

Laying down roots
During his 1768 visit to Chezzetcook, apart from baptizing children born during the previous few years, Charles-François Bailly also blessed one marriage, that of Joseph Petitpas and Marguerite Braud, both of whom had been widowed once before.

Judging from the names of parents of the Acadian children baptized, we know there were at least nine families living permanently in the Chezzetcook area. Apart from the couple already mentioned, there were Joseph Bonnevie and Marguerite Galant, François Grenon and Madeleine Braud, Pierre Landry and Anne Clergé, Antoine Lavandier and Genevieve Cenard, Jean-Baptiste Petitpas and Françoise Montaure, Louis Petitpas and Marie-Josephe Dugas, Auguste Wolfe and Catherine Allemande and finally Jean-Baptiste Roma and Félicité Clergé.

The missionary baptized three of this last couple's children in July of 1768: Prosper, Gertrude and Marguerite. The eldest of the three, Mar-

---
55 CEAAC, Ronald Labelle Collection, AF-182, accession no. 1720 (1982).
56 Kevin Christmas, personal communication, 5 May 2018, Membertou, Nova Scotia.
57 Nova Scotia Archives, *Bailly, Charles-François* (microfilm).

guerite, was four years old at the time of her baptism. This shows how rare it was for Acadians to have the services of Roman Catholic priests in the years following the Expulsion, given that parents normally sought to have their children baptized as soon as possible after birth.

The population of Chezzetcook increased quickly after the first arrivals in 1760. In 1766, Captain James Cook completed a "Navigation Chart of Chezzetcook Inlet". On the western side of the inlet, Cook included the following mention: "Eight or Nine Houses here".[58]

Five years later, it was estimated that there were 17 Acadian families in Chezzetcook, with a total of 96 persons.[59] At that time, more than one hundred other Acadians were living close by in the Halifax area, having been released from captivity there in 1763.

It seems that the colonial authorities tolerated the Acadian settlers who gravitated to the Chezzetcook area, but made no provision to supply them with land ownership. This hindered the development of Chezzetcook during the early decades of the settlement.

While Acadians in Digby County and in the Chéticamp area of Cape Breton took advantage of the large tracts of land that colonial officials in Halifax and Sydney awarded them, the inhabitants of Chezzetcook had no such luck. Many chose to leave for places in Eastern Nova Scotia where land ownership prospects were better and this explains why the population increase slowed down considerably after the initial settlement phase.

Members of the Bellefontaine and Lapierre families tell the story of how their ancestors exchanged land shortly after arriving in the area. According to this account, the Lapierres, who were fishers, moved from West Chezzetcook to Grand-Désert in order to be closer to the sea, exchanging land with the Bellefontaines, who were farmers. There is, in fact, a document dated April 29, 1788 concerning the two Lapierre brothers, Jean and Joseph, who were attempting in vain to re-obtain possession of a piece of land they had earlier sold to a Bellefontaine:

> Your memorialists have lived at the above place a great number of years, and made considerable Improvements on Lands which they had purchased of Chas. Lyons Esqu. but for Peace and Quiet, they have sold the same to Labelle Fountain, And now humbly pray, that your Excellency will be pleased to grant them an Order

---

58 David D. Scott, "Morphological Changes in an Estuary...", p. 201.
59 Bona Arsenault, *History of the Acadians*, p. 223.

Chezzetcook: an Acadian stronghold

of Survey at the above Place that they may begin again, your first Memorialist having six Children your Second three.[60]

According to Mgr Frederic Melanson,[61] the settlers sometimes received title to land situated far from their original place of habitation, which may explain the problems experienced by the Lapierre brothers.

Commenting on the difficulties the first settlers had in obtaining land, Liliane Bellefontaine refers to the long-standing problem of the oath of allegiance to the Crown, which the Acadians had refused to sign before the Expulsion, but that many agreed to sign at the time of their re-establishment, beginning in the 1760s (my questions in italics):

> You know, for a long time the French couldn't buy land around here. It was that way for quite a while. The English wouldn't give them permission to buy property, you know.
> *Did the French stay anyway?*
> The French lived here at the time the Mi'kmaqs were here, but that's as much as I can tell you. There were a lot of Mi'kmaqs here in those days.
> *It was during that time they couldn't buy land?*
> It was right at that time. But things changed after that. They agreed to sign the allegiance after that. [...] A queen sat on the throne in those days, it seems. She had promised to let them have their religion, their language and their culture. It took a long time to come.[62] [translation]

Oral history, as retold by Liliane Bellefontaine, suggests the Acadians were ready to accept the authority of the British at the time when they were becoming re-established, after the end of hostilities between France and Britain:

> They wanted to be subjects of the English, you know. They wanted to be subjects of the English if they could practise their religion and keep their language and culture. With these three things, they were happy to take the English allegiance [....] The old people talked about that. It was religion that worried them a

---

60 Nova Scotia Archives, manuscript collections: *Ungranted Petitions: La Pierre, Jean & Joseph, 1788.*
61 CEAAC, Ronald Labelle Collection, ms. 105 (1982).
62 Ibid., accession no. 1142 (1982).

> lot. They wanted to practise their religion. The English were against the Catholic religion in those days. And also, when they came here, for a long time they couldn't have a piece of land to build a Catholic church. It was quite a spell before they could get a piece of land. In Nova Scotia, the governor was Governor Lawrence [....] You know, like they say, the Acadians endured a lot so they could have peace.[63] [translation]

Among all the early settlers at Chezzetcook, a few individuals stand out because of their enterprising nature. Louis (or Louis Benjamin) Petitpas is one of them. In May of 1780, he became the spokesperson for the residents of Chezzetcook who asked for permission to cut the marsh grass that grew in abundance on the inlet:

> The Memorial of Louis Petitpas in Behalf of himself & others, humbly sheweth that a number of families have settled at chezetcouk & the environs; that they have Large families of children & are obliged to keep many Cows & find it difficult to provide hay for the wintering them; your memorialist therefore in Behalf of the above persons humbly prays a Licence may be granted to them to cut the Coarse Salt marsh Grass that grows on the east side of the said harbour to the southward of Captain allans grant along the Sea Coast and as in duty bound shall & c.[64]

The petition seems to have been received favourably, because it is appended with the following note signed by Charles Morris:

> A Licence for Louis Petitpas and others to cut salt marsh Grass from the marshes on the east side of the Harbour of Chezzetcook to the southward of land granted to Captain Allan and lying between said land and the sea Coast and extending towards Petpiswick.

Some Acadian settlers who had lived in communities around the Minas Basin and the Annapolis Valley were well aware of the potential represented by the grasses growing naturally in the tidal marsh. The question of diking these marshes would be raised many times during the follow-

---

63 Idem.
64 Nova Scotia Archives, Record RG-5, Vol. 1, series GP-3.

ing decades.

Louis Petitpas showed no hesitancy in his efforts to obtain favours from government officials. Like many of the Acadians who chose to live in the environs of Halifax during the 18th century, he combined agricultural activities with coastal navigation, carrying goods between Halifax and Boston on his schooner, the *Longsplice*. This put him in a delicate situation during the American Revolution, when he was forced to choose between remaining in British territory or moving to the rebel colonies.

His choice became apparent in May 1781, when he addressed the following petition to the Senate and House of Representatives of the Commonwealth of Massachusetts:

> The Petition of Lewis Benjamin Petitpas of Chesing Cook harbour in the Province of Nova Scotia – Merchant – Humbly shews
>
> That he was originally an inhabitant of Louisbourg formerly within the jurisdiction of the King of France but since the Conquest of that Country has lived on the English Settlements in Canada but lately in Nova Scotia where his Father's family removed; All persons of this descrzption in that Country & Commonly called French Neutrals are Considered as Enemies to the British Government & oppressed with the most intolerable taxes.
>
> Your Petitioner unwilling to submit to the Oppression & desirous of becoming a Subject of a Nation in Alliance with his own, prays that this honorable Court would grant him a permit to withdraw his property from Nova Scotia into this Commonwealth & a passport to proceed on his business with Security from Capture by American Cruisers [...][65]

Petitpas seems to have made a convincing case for himself, and his petition was immediately approved. Two days later, he sailed to St. Peter's in Cape Breton to settle his affairs, and then moved his wife and son from Chezzetcook to Boston, leaving behind daughter Marie Henriette who was already married to Alexandre Bellefontaine.

The petition by Louis Petitpas sheds light on the mentality of the Acadians in the late 18th century, the period when they were finally becoming firmly established in various parts of Nova Scotia. Although they had obtained the right to settle on British territory, it is obvious that some Acadians still considered themselves to be French citizens, hence Petit-

---

[65] Melanson, *Genealogies... - Petitpas.*

pas's desire to become "a Subject of a Nation in Alliance with his own". Few, however, went so far as to pack up and leave Nova Scotia for the new Republic to the south.

The American Revolution, while providing an opportunity for Louis Petitpas and his family to leave British territory, caused hardship to most of the Acadians who remained in Nova Scotia. According to oral history, a group of Acadians from Isle Madame took temporary refuge at Chezzetcook during the Revolution, fearing attack from the rebel colonies. In his book on Acadian history, Rameau de Saint-Père published this account he had obtained in 1860 from Boniface Fougère, an elderly resident of Saint-Pierre, Cape Breton:

> At the time of the American war, the families were forced to leave the island (Isle Madame). There were only six families left; the rest fled to Halifax and from there settled in part at Chezetcook; then, when peace returned, they came back [...] All of them seem to have taken refuge for a short time at Chezetcook. Fougère himself remained there for three years; he often saw women hauling the wood the men brought to Halifax by boat.[66] [translation]

Genealogical research by Stephen White tends to confirm this narrative. According to his findings, between 1778 and 1783, the year when the American Revolution officially ended, all of the births from Isle Madame families were recorded on mainland Nova Scotia, rather than in Cape Breton. During those years, there were also weddings where one spouse was from Isle Madame and the other from Chezzetcook.

It seems, however, that few refugees from Isle Madame settled permanently at Chezzetcook. Their home was in Cape Breton and their stay on the mainland was just one more disruption endured by a peaceful people who had been disturbed so many times since the 1750s.

After the end of the American Revolution, Acadians could finally build communities around the Maritimes without fear of attack. The main problem that remained was the difficulty they continued to have in obtaining the right to land ownership.

Until the British Parliament adopted the Roman Catholic Relief Act in 1829, Acadians and other Catholics in the British colonies would continue to be disadvantaged, as they not enjoy the same civil rights as their Anglo-Protestant neighbours.

---

66 Edmé Rameau de Saint-Père, *Une colonie féodale en Amérique*, p. 390.

3: Community growth in the 19th century

Early Church presence

Throughout the late 18th and early 19th centuries, the colonial administration in Halifax considered Chezzetcook as a Mi'kmaq mission. French Catholic missionaries were sent there because the authorities believed their influence on the Native population would be beneficial to peaceful relations in the colony. This assured that Acadians would have at least partial access to Church services.

A priest named Father Jacques carried out yearly visits to the community beginning around 1790. However, no priest was formally assigned to the community until the arrival of Father Thomas Grace, an Irishman who visited Chezzetcook regularly between 1799 and 1801. Father Grace seems to have identified himself with the French-speaking community, as he used a French version of his name in Church records, signing "Thoma de Grase".[67]

After the departure of Father Grace, nearly fifteen years would go by before Chezzetcook again received regular visits from a priest.

Until the establishment of the Diocese of Halifax in 1818, all Roman Catholic communities of Nova Scotia were attached to the Diocese of Québec. In the summer of 1803, Bishop Pierre Denaut visited the Maritime colonies, and stopped at Chezzetcook on July 6th. There, he recorded the presence of 45 Acadian families, with a total population of 224.

At that time, the Church sought to keep a distance between the Acadian and Mi'kmaq populations, and considered their communities as separate entities. In Chezzetcook, however, the Acadian and Mi'kmaq residents shared the use of a single chapel for their religious devotions.

This is how the bishop described the building: "There is but a small

---

67 Melanson, *Lectures...*, No. 5: "Chezzetcook – Culture", p. 3.

chapel, ill kept, and an uninhabitable presbytery."[68] He also noted that the building was lacking in church ornaments, sacred vessels and altar cloths.

Denaut ordered the inhabitants to build a new church and presbytery, and even laid out the specifications for their construction. The church was to be 32 feet wide and 40 feet long, along with a sacristy measuring 14 by 16 feet. The presbytery was to measure 24 feet by 26 feet.

Figure 7: The 19th century church at West Chezzetcook; published by T.P. Connolly, Halifax (Nova Scotia Museum).

This was a tall order for the small community, and one that seems to have been impossible to carry out at that time. The residents would only begin the construction eleven years later.

The original chapel mentioned by Bishop Denaut was likely a win-

---

68   Melanson, *Lectures...*, No. 4: "Chezzetcook – Christian Worship", p. 7.

dowless log building situated in Grand-Désert, not far from the site of the early 18th-century chapel that had been abandoned at the time of the Expulsion. Archaeologist Robert Shears estimated that the original chapel would have been situated near the intersection of Dyke and Range roads, and that was also the likely location of the second simple chapel.[69] In later years, a large community cross was erected on Range Road to commemorate the site.

Few religious services took place in Chezzetcook in the years following Bishop Denaut's visit. A priest named Amable Pichard briefly served the community in 1804, and Father Jacques continued his yearly visits to Chezzetcook until his health failed in 1810.

The ordinance to build a new church had not been acted upon when Father M. Mignault, who was stationed in Halifax, visited the community in the fall of 1814. Mignaud encouraged the congregation to get to work on the project, and a building site was finally chosen on high ground in West Chezzetcook, close to where the present Catholic church is.

By the summer of 1815, when construction work was well advanced, the Bishop of Québec once again visited the community. On July 18th, Bishop Plessis, who was conducting a pastoral voyage to the Catholic communities of the Maritime colonies, travelled by sloop from Halifax to Chezzetcook along with three other priests.

One of the three was Father Vincent de Paul, a Trappist monk from France who had arrived in the area entirely by accident. While returning to France in 1815 after an unsuccessful attempt at establishing a monastery in the United States, Father Vincent de Paul was delayed at Halifax for a few weeks. When a sudden change of wind caused his ship to set sail without him, he was left stranded, and spent the early summer in Halifax, waiting to find out whether he should remain there or continue on to Europe.[70]

Father Vincent de Paul just happened to be in Halifax when Bishop Plessis of Québec stopped there in 1815, and he recounted his dramatic arrival at Chezzetcook in his memoirs, of which only an English translation has survived. His writings demonstrate the difficulties of navigation in Chezzetcook Inlet:

> Monseigneur, two priests and myself were in the same boat, we had just quitted a long boat that had brought us from the town to

---
69 Shears, p. 100.
70 Luke Schrepfer, *Pioneer Monks of Nova Scotia*, pp. 22-30.

the harbour. We were about landing but had still some breakers to avoid. Two totally unexperienced [sic] young Englishmen who were rowing us led us suddenly into grave danger. The sea rose very high, and we found ourselves crossing the breakers, so that we momentarily expected to have our boat upset and ourselves sent head over heels into the midst of the waters.[71]

In his account of the pastoral visit, Bishop Plessis described the arrival of the sloop in even more dramatic fashion:

> The sloop anchored near a point. A launch was lowered to allow us to disembark. Two of the youngest sailors were sent to take the vessel to the shore. Four passengers got on [the four priests].
> All that was needed to reach the shore was to row half a dozen good strokes, but the sailors weren't very diligent. It began to rain, and we could no longer see clearly the way ahead. The boat began to drift unexpectedly, and huge waves were pushing us into the distant bay.
> A man who was rowing in a small boat nearby cried, "Get away from there or you will perish!"
> The passengers understood the danger, but to get to the shore from there it would be necessary to tackle the waves head on, which was no easy feat.
> As soon as we turned the boat, a wave lifted the launch and we could see an even larger one rolling towards us. The wave was at least 4 feet high and would certainly swamp us.
> The Divine Providence then took charge: The wave hit, and we were soaked. The terrified spectators watching from the ship could no longer even see us. The water took away Father Vincent's hat and turned the boat sideways, but we didn't overturn.
> Before the third wave could hit, we finally reached the shore. (...)
> Some Acadians came to us, and to save us a mile-long walk along the rugged shore, they took us aboard a "Warri" and brought us to the head of the harbour, two or three *arpents* from the chapel. They call "Warri" a type of small barge, with a very thick curved hull, simply trimmed with planks, with no benches, without a mast or even a rod to haul the sail. They use it to load

---

71 Vincent de Paul, *Memoir...*, pp.33-34.

the big launches with firewood that is sent from here to the capital.

It follows from this that the local inhabitants, having often to go into town, sometimes allow themselves to consume more spirits there than they should. That is about the only cause of disorder in this Christian community of 47 families.[72][translation]

The "warri" mentioned in the quote refers to a "wherry", a light, pointed rowboat used on inland waters.[73] While the gundalow was used to navigate in shallow waters in the upper part of the inlet, the wherry was the vessel of choice for the deeper waters further down.

During his two-day visit to Chezzetcook, Bishop Plessis dedicated the as-yet-unfinished church to St. Anselm of Canterbury, thus giving the future parish its name.

As work on the church was still ongoing, Bishop Plessis specified how he wanted it to be completed. He insisted that the altar should be situated at its eastern extremity, which meant that the entrance would be at the western end, facing the location of the future cemetery.[74]

His instructions were followed precisely, but the orientation was reversed when a new church replaced that one in 1894.

Bishop Plessis also asked that parishioners build a presbytery, just as the former bishop had requested in 1803, and that it have a fenced-in garden. Work began on this as soon as the church was completed, in order to accommodate Father Vincent de Paul, who was soon to return to Chezzetcook as its first resident priest.

Before leaving Chezzetcook on July 19th, the bishop, Father Vincent de Paul and Father Mignault confirmed 29 Acadians children. Oddly enough, Bishop Plessis did not mention in his journal whether any Mi'kmaq were present in either of the religious celebrations that took place during his brief visit to Chezzetcook.[75]

In his *Memoirs*, Father Vincent de Paul mentions that he returned to Chezzetcook on July 26th for the annual Mi'kmaq celebration of the feast of St. Anne. Two hundred Mi'kmaq were then gathered in the church of Chezzetcook, "which was not large enough to hold them all." This is how he described the event:

---

72 Mgr Plessis, "Voyage de 1815 en Acadie de Mgr Plessis", p. 191.
73 Centre d'études acadiennes (CEA), Ronald Labelle Collection, ms. 137 (1982).
74 Brad Sweet, *St. Anselm's an Acadian Parish. A Short History from 1750*.
75 Plessis, "Voyage de 1815 en Acadie…", pp. 190-191.

> On the eve of St. Anne's feast, they made a bonfire, and while the wood burned, they fired gunshots and danced around the fire, clapping their hands in imitation of musical instruments. This lasted for a great part of the night, however, they had previously said their evening prayers, and sung hymns and canticles.[76] [translation]

Father Vincent de Paul mentions that the Mi'kmaq who came to hear him arrived from a circuit of 15 or 20 leagues (75 to 100 kilometres). At that time, it was common for members of the Mi'kmaq community from as far away as Shubenacadie to establish a summer encampment at Chezzetcook. They chose the area partly because of its abundance of shellfish. The sites where they camped remained in evidence thanks to mounds resulting from the heaps of clamshells they left behind.

In his writings, Father Vincent de Paul always refers separately to the Acadian and Mi'kmaq populations. There is no mention of any occasion where the two groups gathered together. Church officials seem to have decided to establish a practise of keeping the Acadian and Mi'kmaq residents of Chezzetcook separate, while allowing them to use the same building for their religious devotions.

The Acadian community occupied a relatively compact area, while the Mi'kmaq were living in scattered localities, and only gathered in large numbers at Chezzetcook for special occasions, such as weddings or religious holidays.

Because he served both the Acadian and Mi'kmaq populations, Father Vincent de Paul chose to spend the winter of 1816 at Baie Sainte-Marie in southwestern Nova Scotia, where he could learn the rudiments of the Mi'kmaq language from pioneer priest abbé Sigogne.[77]

Father Vincent de Paul would remain in Chezzetcook for three years, occupying the new presbytery that was built during his tenure, and in 1817 he had a large wayside cross erected, the first of those which were to be placed at different locations in the parish. The cross was situated on a hill facing the water, not far from the church.[78] The erection of the cross inspired him to write the following:

---

76 de Paul, pp.16-19.
77 Brad Sweet, *Réfractaire and Mission Priests in Post-Deportation Acadian Education in Eastern Nova Scotia*, pp. 40-41.
78 Ephrem Boudreau, *Le petit Clairvaux – Cent ans de vie cistercienne à Tracadie en Nouvelle-Écosse, 1818-1919*, p. 28.

Chezzetcook: an Acadian stronghold

> I hope it will do a lot of good in this country, especially by being brought to the attention of the drunkards who are very numerous here. I must say, my Very Rev. Father, that drinking causes the loss of an infinite number of souls in America. However, at Chezzetcook, where we have formed a little parish, there are some truly pious people; and many young men and girls, with whom something can be done, and among whom there are many who are destined for the religious state.[79]

Despite his hopes, none of the young people to whom Father Vincent de Paul ministered were later to take religious vows. Throughout Nova Scotia, Acadians were slow to embrace religious vocations during the 19th century, despite their strong attachment to the Catholic faith. This fact is perhaps explained by the independent spirit that had always characterized the Acadian people, accustomed as they were to living outside of rigid authoritarian structures.

It was common for priests serving new Acadian parishes to take a direct interest in all aspects of local life, rather than limiting their activities to the spiritual realm, and Father Vincent de Paul was no exception. Soon after his arrival in Chezzetcook, he began cultivating several acres of land. In a letter sent to France in September 1817, he wrote: "The garden alone kept the four of us alive all summer and I m hoping that we will be kept by it during next winter." This letter suggests that three local residents were assisting him in his efforts.

He goes on to request help to expand his agricultural activities:

> I ask you to send me every kind of seeds for those vegetables for which the community makes the most use, such as cabbage, carrots, sugar beets, salads, onions, etc. Every one of them will do marvellously in the country where I live. I should like to have some hempseeds. Since flax is coming very well, I believe that hemp will come just as well here. Concerning fruit-trees, only the apple-trees are successful.[80]

In another letter written the same year, Father Vincent de Paul mentions that he was training the Mi'kmaq to take care of the land, showing them how to plant potatoes and sow turnips.[81]

---

79 Schrepfer, *Pioneer Monks*, p. 99.
80 Ibid., pp. 130-131.
81 Ibid., p. 119.

Ronald Labelle

Besides experimenting with agriculture, Father Vincent de Paul also practised medicine in the area. He had some medical knowledge learned from his father, who was a surgeon in France, and he thus obtained special permission from the Church to practise medicine and to bleed people in Chezzetcook, where no other medical help was available.[82]

Having a firm belief that Divine Providence had ordained that he be marooned in Halifax in 1815 so that he should carry out his life's work in the colony, Father Vincent de Paul felt that the best way to fulfill his religious mission would be to establish a monastery in Nova Scotia. In 1817, he concluded that Chezzetcook was not the ideal location for the project, and began to consider a move to either Cape Breton or Tracadie in Antigonish County.[83]

The following year, he left for Tracadie, where he accomplished his mission to build a monastery. After his departure for Tracadie, he would return at least once to Chezzetcook, attending festivities marking the Feast of St. Ann in 1819.

Although he only spent a few years in Chezzetcook, Father Vincent de Paul left a lasting legacy there. Father Jules Crouzier, parish priest at St. Anselm's from 1884 to 1889, recalled the story of the time when Father Vincent de Paul was caught in a violent storm at sea. He removed one of his sandals and threw it into the raging waters, after which the sea was calmed. From that time on, local fishers would fasten a strip of shoe leather to the exterior frame of their boats in order to be protected from storms.

According to the parish priest, Father Vincent de Paul was considered a saint in the locality.[84]

The practise of attaching a piece of leather to the frame of the fishing boats in memory of Father Vincent de Paul continued well into the 20th century and is still remembered by people living in Chezzetcook today. In recent years, whenever an old boat was being scuttled, people made sure they removed the leather strip that had been fastened to it in memory of Father Vincent de Paul, so that it could be kept as a precious souvenir.

Apart from the writings of Father Vincent de Paul, the only other accounts of life in Chezzetcook in the early 19th century are contained in

---

82 Blooletting was a medicinal practise used to treat several ailments from the time of Antiquity until the mid to late 19th century, when physicians finally concluded that bleeding patients was generally not an efficient form of treatment.
83 Sweet, *Réfractaire and Mission Priests...*, p. 63.
84 Boudreau, p. 30.

Chezzetcook: an Acadian stronghold

the reports on the pastoral visits of Bishop Denaut in 1803 and his successor, Bishop Plessis, in 1815. While these Québec-based bishops took a somewhat-critical view of the Acadians in general, they considered them important enough to warrant visits to their communities.

Both Bishops Denaut and Plessis travelled more than one thousand kilometres to visit the Acadian settlements in Nova Scotia in the early 19th century, but after responsibility for the settlements was transferred to the new Apostolic Vicariate in Halifax in 1817, neither Bishop Burke nor his successor, William Fraser, could be bothered to travel the 30 or so kilometres that separated them from Chezzetcook.

The Diocese of Halifax was promoted to a bishopric in 1842. Two years later, Mgr. William Walsh was named bishop, and the following year he finally carried out a pastoral visit to Chezzetcook.

The Cross, the newspaper published by the Diocese of Halifax, devoted several articles to the community between 1845 and 1849. The first one, published in August 1845, gives a detailed account of the pastoral visit of Mgr. Walsh to Chezzetcook:

> Early on Monday morning the Bishop and the Rev. Mr. Kennedy set out for the interesting French settlement of Chezzetcook. They arrived about eleven o'clock, and found the entire population drawn up to receive them. The men presented arms when the Bishop drew near. All knelt to receive his blessing, and after he had passed, a "feu de joie" was fired by the musqueteers. Nearly twenty years have elapsed since the last visitation at this secluded spot, and the expectation of the poor people knew no bounds. The church was speedily filled, and Mass was sung by the Rev. Mr. McDonnell. The opening ceremonies of the visitation were then gone through, and the Bishop addressed the congregation in French for a considerable time.[85]

It is interesting to note that the Bishop of Halifax at that time was sufficiently fluent in French to preach in that language.

Following the service in the church, the bishop led a procession to the cemetery, where five crosses had been planted. The participants followed him to the foot of the largest cross, and there he blessed the cemetery.

The following morning, Bishop Walsh celebrated a High Mass, and *The Cross* reported that "the village choir sang the Gloria, Credo and other

---

[85] *The Cross*, 23 August 1845.

parts of the Mass with considerable precision and effect". A total of 37 parishioners then received the sacrament of Confirmation, and the bishop promised to soon revisit the community in order to confirm "a great number of persons who could not then be prepared". The sacrament of Confirmation needed to be administered by the bishop himself, and the people of Chezzetcook had not received this important service during the many years when their community had been ignored by the Church.

Before leaving the community, the bishop chaired a parochial meeting, where it was resolved that a new and more spacious church should be built.

Nearly fifty years would pass before the wooden church at West Chezzetcook would be replaced by a brick one, but work to enlarge the existing building was undertaken in 1847, when the foundation was laid for an addition measuring 50 by 30 feet (15 x 9 meters).

In September 1849, the bishop presided over ceremonies inaugurating the newly-enlarged church, which included a large transept with a new chancel situated at the east end of the building. Interestingly, in an article commenting on the event, *The Cross* mentioned that, during the ceremonies, "the relic of the True Cross, which had been brought from Rome by the Bishop for the church at Chezzetcooke, was exposed for the veneration of the Faithful".[86]

The wooden church included a steeple with a belfry, and in 1897, a few years after the construction of the new church, the original bell was replaced by a massive bronze one made at a foundry in France. Not every Acadian parish had the means to obtain such an impressive bell.

The huge bell, which could be heard tolling from far out on the water, was a source of pride for the parishioners of St. Anselm's and was a testimony to their constant attachment to the Catholic faith.

19th Century hardships

The main problem faced by Acadians who tried to re-establish communities in the Maritime colonies after the British conquest was that of land tenure, and Chezzetcook was no exception. In the journal of his 1815 pastoral visit, Bishop Plessis commented on the problems experienced by the Acadians in obtaining title to lands there. A week before going to Chezzetcook, he had stopped at Tor Bay, where several Acadian

---

86 Ibid., 22 September 1849.

Chezzetcook: an Acadian stronghold

families with names such as Petitpas, Bonin, Boudreau and Richard had already settled after having abandoned Chezzetcook:

> The latter are a colony of Chezet-cook, of which further mention will be made. They left that place because American Loyalists arrived with clear titles giving them possession of 5,000 acres of land which the Acadians, being always improvident, had partially cleared without being assured of ownership.[87] [translation]

Upon arriving in Halifax, Bishop Plessis met with Lieutenant-Governor Sherbrooke, who offered to assist him in any way he could. The bishop took advantage of this offer to ask that lands that had been taken away from the Acadians of Chezzetcook be returned to them. His wish was immediately granted:

> A simple note from the prelate brought to the attention of the highly respected governor was sufficient to obtain for them a grant or entitlement to this land that they had been trying to get for four or five years without success, even though they had brought evidence before various government officials that they had spent £50 for this purpose.[88] [translation]

This quote indicates that the Acadians did not hesitate to use government channels to defend their rights, even though they were in an unfavourable position as French Catholics. Several land grant petitions from the Chezzetcook area are contained in provincial records and at the time of Bishop Plessis's visit, some of the petitioners had already been successful. At Porter's Lake in August 1814, for example, land grants were obtained by four members of the Lapierre family, Luke, Oliver, Charles and Peter, as well as by Felix Wolfe. According to Lena Ferguson, members of the Lapierre and Julien families were the original owners of the land presently occupied by the Porter's Lake Provincial Park.[89]

The earlier quote from Bishop Plessis contains a strong criticism of the Acadians, accused of being "always improvident" (*toujours imprévoyants*). The bishop's remark is typical of correspondence from Church officials in Québec, who often blamed the Acadians themselves for the prob-

---

87   Plessis, "Voyage...", p. 175.
88   Ibid., p. 187.
89   See Ferguson, "History of Saint Mary's School, Grand Desert", and "History of Porter's Lake".

lems they faced in obtaining land grants in the Maritime colonies. It illustrates a lack of comprehension on the part of officials in French Canada, who failed realize just how difficult it was for Acadians to establish their rights.

Apart from the large land grants awarded to Acadians in Cape Breton and Southwestern Nova Scotia, no provisions were made for the re-establishment of Acadians elsewhere in the Maritimes. Therefore, they had no other choice but to occupy vacant lands where they wished to settle, all the while trying to obtain the right to land ownership. If government officials in Halifax had been open to their requests, the Chezzetcook area would no doubt have become one of the principal areas of Acadian settlement in the Maritimes, as it had been one of the first to be reoccupied after the Expulsion era.

Despite all the land ownership problems faced by Acadians, the local population rose steadily throughout the first half of 19th century. Living conditions remained harsh, however, and the Nova Scotia government continued to ignore local problems until Bishop Walsh's first official visit to the community in 1845. His visit was a true revelation for Church officials in Halifax, as was reported in *The Cross*:

> We feel that too much cannot be said in favour of this interesting people. Every Catholic in the Province should be proud of them. With all the homeliness of their old French costume, so quaint and simple, they have preserved a noble simplicity and purity of morals which are seldom witnessed in these degenerate days.[90]

The newspaper then took up the cause of the community, as Chezzetcook was receiving very little support from the colonial government. Not only was its prosperity hindered by the limited land resources available to the residents, but the poor condition of the surrounding roads made it very difficult for them to take their farm produce to markets in Halifax.

The Diocese of Halifax supported their cause, as is evidenced in *The Cross*:

> We were sorry to learn that the approach to their beautiful township is in such a wretched state of repair, and that their temporal interests in this respect have been much neglected. An allocation by the Province for the construction of a proper road, especially

---

90 *The Cross*, 23 August 1845.

Chezzetcook: an Acadian stronghold

> from Lake Porter to Chezzetcook would be an act of justice as well as humanity, to a highly deserving and well-conducted people.[91]

During the following winter, economic conditions in the community reached crisis proportions, and people were forced to seek help from the government. In early March 1846, several families were granted supplies of corn meal, but they had to go all the way to Dartmouth to obtain them.

The Cross once again took interest in their plight, expressing outrage at the way they were being treated:

> Some corn meal was given out on this occasion in such proportion as the magistrates deemed equitable after an investigation of the claims of the various applicants. No blame, as we know, can be attached to these worthy functionaries, but we cannot help expressing our opinion on the unnecessary hardship to which the people of Chezzetcook have been exposed, in being compelled to walk upwards of 40 miles in such a season as the present, in order to obtain possession of a few measures of meal! What a mockery! [...] There are about 150 French families in Chezzetcook who are remarkable for their industrious and moral habits, and who seem to be entirely neglected by those who ought to take an interest in their welfare. Amongst that large population there is not one magistrate of their own religion, as we remarked last Autumn, whilst other parts of the county are well attended to, the road which leads to their interesting settlement, especially from Porter's Lake, is in a most disgraceful and neglected state. If our honest simple Acadians of Chezzetcook had been people of colour, they would, it seems, have found better.[92]

This article suggests that the Acadians suffered discrimination just like the people of African descent in 19th century Nova Scotia.

On April 4th 1846, *The Cross* quoted a letter from Reverend Alexander Macisaac, who was then resident priest at Chezzetcook, stating that the Acadians considered themselves an abandoned people:

---

91 Idem.
92 *The Cross*, 14 March, 1846.

> They seem to think themselves that if their case has not been taken into consideration, it is allowing to neglect, and that their interests are totally abandoned. Nothing is more common when they meet in groups to talk over these things, than to hear one of them exclaim with a sigh: "Ah! whatever may be the chance of others, there is none at all for a poor Frenchman." [...] The people here are in a very deplorable state. They are very few families that must not depend on their creditors for sustenance, until they raise a new crop. Exclusive of the eastern side of the harbour which is equally destitute, there are thirty families who have no kind of food, and no means of getting any, unless from a poor neighbour, who, perhaps, ere long will be as badly off himself.

The Cross concluded by suggesting that Acadians elsewhere in Nova Scotia come to the help of those in Chezzetcook, indicating that local conditions were far worse than those in areas such as Digby County:

> We would request their worthy brethren in Clare, and through the West generally, to consider the state of the people of Chezzetcook, because we think without much inconvenience to themselves, they might be able to send some seasonal relief in food. This would be an act worthy of their religion, and of the Great Country of their common origin, and we hope the hint will not be lost sight of.[93]

The lack of French-speaking priests in the Diocese of Halifax partially explains the neglect experienced by the population of Chezzetcook during most of the 19th century. The rare French-speaking priests who were assigned to the parish were very supportive and were much appreciated by the Acadian population. This was the case with Father Abel L'Hiver during the 1850s and Father Jules Crouzier in the 1880s.

Father Crouzier was originally from Southern France and was impressed by the way the local population had remained attached to their language. When he left the parish in 1889, a group of 17 parishioners published a tribute to the priest in *L'Évangéline*, the main Acadian newspaper in the Maritimes. They thanked him for having preached in favour of maintaining the French language in the community and ended their tribute by stating that they would hold the priest's advice in their hearts

---

[93] Ibid., 1846.

for a long time to come.[94]

Local schools

In 19th century Nova Scotia, schools only existed in communities that had the resources necessary for their financing and management. A school law adopted in 1811 recommended that they be opened in communities comprising of 30 families or more, but parents would have to foot half the bill. Apart from the financial hurdles involved, a school trustee system was put in place, thus creating an additional obstacle for French speaking Catholics, who did not enjoy the same rights as the Protestant population in the years before the Catholic Relief Act of 1829.

In Catholic communities, the Church tried to fill the gap by recruiting informal schoolteachers. Around 1816, a teacher named Antoine Faucher arrived in the community, along with a new parish priest from Québec named Pierre Mignault.

Faucher began to teach in a house situated near the new church. Father Mignault left after a few years, but Faucher stayed behind and was still living in Chezzetcook when French traveller Adolphe Marsais visited the community fifty years later. It is difficult to know whether Antoine Faucher continued to teach up until the opening of the first formal school in the 1840s.

Figure 8: Antoine Faucher, Chezzetcook's first schoolteacher

It became easier for Acadians to open their own schools after 1841, when the Nova Scotia government adopted a law allowing teaching to take place in English, French, German or Gaelic. In September of 1845, an article in *The Cross* indicated that children in Chezzetcook were just beginning to have access to education:

---

94 *L'Évangéline*, 22 May 1889.

Ronald Labelle

> A school has been opened, and the rising generation of both sexes will be instructed not only in their own language and other useful acquirements, but will also receive a solid religious education.

In 1867, Adolphe Marsais published an article stating that education in Chezzetcook was still in its early stages. One revealing comment contained in the Marsais article is the mention that residents were reluctant to pay for local schooling. This is one reason why it was so difficult to arrive at a well-established school system in rural Nova Scotia communities. While we are accustomed to regarding the financing of local schools as a provincial responsibility, 19th century governments were not able to cover all the costs involved.

All of the teachers mentioned in early accounts of education in Chezzetcook seem to have been French-speaking and it seems likely that when children did go to school, they had the opportunity to obtain instruction in their first language.

In an area like West Chezzetcook and Grand-Désert, where residences were scattered over a large area, the presence of a single school could not adequately serve the entire population. Pupils from Grand-Désert, for example, would have to walk several kilometres in all weather in order to attend school.

This problem limited the access they had to formal education until a petition was presented to provincial officials by "George Julien, John Julien and 86 other ratepayers of Chezzetcook School District 65".[95] The petition mentioned that among the 295 children in the district, 120 of them lived in Grand-Désert. The petition called for road work to be carried out in that locality, promising that a two-room school would be built once the work was completed.

Mr. Frank Lapierre donated the necessary land and local residents not only supplied the lumber, but also transformed it, producing all the boards and rafters and even the exterior shingles used in construction.

Thanks to Lena Ferguson's oral-history research, we know more about this school than about any other one that existed in the region during the 19th century. When Saint Mary's School opened in Grand-Désert in the fall of 1885, it included two classrooms in which each pupil was given a slate for writing. In each classroom, a central woodstove supplied the heating, thanks to a steady supply of hardwood.

---

95 Ferguson, "History of Saint Mary's School..."

Chezzetcook: an Acadian stronghold

Each room also had a wooden bucket and a dipper used for drinking water. These were not replaced by galvanized pails until around 1920. Pupils took turns fetching drinking water from a nearby well, and carried in firewood from a shed at the back. During winter months, a student was paid to light fires in the woodstoves early in the morning, so that the school would not be cold during class times.

Although Nova Scotia had initially approved the establishment of minority language schools, beginning in the 1860s, there was much political debate about the usefulness of funding public schools where teaching was carried out partly in French. At that time, there was a scarcity of trained teachers who spoke French, not only in Chezzetcook but in all Acadian regions of the province, and the government did nothing to remedy the situation.

Teachers generally obtained their training by attending the Nova Scotia Normal School. Researcher Sally Ross compiled a list of all the Acadians who studied at the Normal School in the second half of the 19th century. The list of 50 names includes only one person from Chezzetcook, Cécile Bellefontaine, who attended in 1891-92.[96]

In 1902, the provincial government finally accepted the fact that French should be part of the curriculum in Acadian schools. A commission was established to look into the problem of obtaining teachers for the ones generally referred to as "bilingual schools". Eight years later, in order to facilitate the process, the province compiled a list of 89 schools where children entering school had little knowledge of English. The list included schools from Acadian areas all over the province, but neither the school in West Chezzetcook nor the one in Grand-Désert were included, which suggests that the area was left out of the process.[97]

This is one of many examples of how, throughout their history, the residents of Chezzetcook have suffered from being the forgotten Acadians.

An evolving community

At the time of the first census of Halifax County in 1817, there were 488 people living in Chezzetcook, including 117 men, 84 women and 287 children.[98] There had been few new arrivals in the community since the

---

96 Sally Ross, *Les écoles acadiennes en Nouvelle-Écosse, 1758-2000*, pp. 42-43; 56-57.
97 Ibid., pp. 71-72.
98 Nova Scotia Archives, GG-1, Vol. 445, 35-35a. Halifax County Census, 1817.

beginning of the century, and it would seem improbable that the number of residents could have more than doubled during the 14-year span between Mgr. Denaut's population estimate of 224 in 1803 and the number in the 1817 census. However, the figures may be fairly accurate, because census statistics regarding the ages of children indicates that the birth rate was very high.

According to census reports, the population continued to increase rapidly during subsequent years, going from 488 to 1,514 between 1817 and 1851. This very significant increase may be in part due to the enlargement of census districts in the mid-19th century.

Beginning in 1851, highly-detailed census returns dealt with all aspects of local demographics. The 1851 census was the first of the detailed statistical reports that have continued to take place every ten years from that time on. It states that, among the 1,514 residents in the area, there were 973 Catholics. Given that the Acadian population was entirely Catholic, while the overwhelming number of residents in the surrounding communities were Protestants of either United Empire Loyalist or German descent, the figure of 973 would provide a fairly clear idea of the actual Acadian population in Chezzetcook in the mid-19th century.

The names enumerated in the census reports carried out in 1827, 1838 and 1851 show that the Acadian and non-Acadian areas of settlement were quite distinct. West Chezzetcook and Grand-Désert appear to have been very homogeneous areas, almost exclusively inhabited by Acadians, while outlying areas such as East Chezzetcook and Porter's Lake had a mixed population of which Protestant settlers made up the majority.

Census returns dating from the 19th century indicate that Acadians always formed the majority of the population of Chezzetcook. The 1871 census was the first to specify which members of the population were of French descent. At that time, in the territory that encompassed both East and West Chezzetcook, 901 of the 1,344 residents were of French descent. Similarly, the 1881 census reported 998 people of French descent out of 1,550.

Interestingly, the 1891 Canada census is statistically unreliable, because in that year, "French Canadian" replaced "French" on the form. While this may not have been a problem in the rest of the country, Acadians in the Maritimes generally considered the term "French Canadian" to refer only to Quebecers, and therefore hesitated to identify as such, resulting in a confusing statistical count.

Chezzetcook: an Acadian stronghold

Our reading of the manuscript census returns for 1827 onward shows that French names have always predominated in the districts that include West Chezzetcook and Grand-Désert.[99] The lists of names of family members also indicate that very few mixed marriages took place between the Acadians and people of other cultures who lived in nearby communities.

While census reports suggest that a high birth rate among Acadian families during the first half of the 19th century resulted in a rapid population increase, the growth was much slower during the second half of the century. The population more than tripled between 1827 and 1851, but remained more or less stable afterwards (an increase between 1891 and 1901 may be due to a change in census boundaries).

It appears that outmigration was the main cause for the reduction in population growth during the second half of the century. Many people from Chezzetcook left for New England at that time, joining the thousands of Maritimers who fled difficult economic conditions to look for work in industrial towns. The departures, however, did not constitute an exodus, and the

Figure 9: Map showing the lands occupied by settlers around Chezzetcook Inlet in 1864 (published by A.F. Church, 1865).

---

99 Nova Scotia Archives, Nova Scotia Census 1827, 1838, 1851, 1861; Canada Census 1871, 1881, 1891, 1901.

Ronald Labelle

continuing high birth rate made up for the loss of population, thus ensuring that the community would continue to grow.

Detailed population statistics presented in the 1901 census provide a clear picture of the demographic situation at the turn or the 20th century, thanks to census districts that distinguished between the residents of the two sides of Chezzetcook Inlet. At that time, 981 of the 1,116 residents of West Chezzetcook and Grand-Désert were of French descent. In East Chezzetcook, by contrast, only one third of the population was of French descent, 335 out of 1,006. The eastern side of the inlet was one of the early areas of Acadian settlement, members of the Petitpas family having received a large land grant there in 1809, but later settlers were primarily of English or German background, and the French language gradually fell into disuse there.

While numbers indicate that Acadians made up about 90% of the population on the western side of the inlet in 1901, the actual figure was probably even higher. At that time, the largest non-French group there was the Irish, with a total of 71 residents. A survey of manuscript census returns shows that every person with the name Murphy was entered as being "Irish", even though a large number of Murphys called themselves "Morphi" and had been completely integrated into the Acadian community for generations, speaking French as first language. The same could be said for some of the French speaking Fergusons who were counted among the 30 "Scottish" residents, as well as the Wolfes, who were among the 29 entered as being "German".

At the turn of the 20th century, West Chezzetcook was thus a solidly French-speaking community where between 90 and 95 percent of the population could be considered Acadian.

4: Impressions of 19th-century travelers

We know that Acadians from Chezzetcook sold produce at the market in Halifax from at least the 1830s, and this explains why so many visitors to the town had become aware of the existence of the Acadian community. Several 19th century travellers to Nova Scotia took trips east of Halifax in order to observe the rural lifestyle of the local inhabitants, and they generally made sure to include Chezzetcook in their excursions. Some left brief, superficial descriptions of the Acadians they encountered.

An early example would be Eugène Ney, a French diplomat who toured Nova Scotia in 1831 and wrote of his travels in a Parisian periodical dedicated to travelogues, *La Revue des Deux Mondes*.[100] This is how the diplomat described his meeting with two unidentified men from Chezzetcook:

> Upon returning from an excursion I had made to a charming lake on the Dartmouth side of the harbour, I met two peasants who were dressed just like ours. Having heard that there were still French people living in these parts, I asked them in French if they were coming from far away. "Ah! Jarniqué!", answered one of the men, "we come from more than twenty miles out in the country!" This was a village named Chenscook that is entirely French, and composed of about sixty families. There are even a great many more in Cape Breton and surroundings. They have preserved the dialect of our own peasants and they told me I was the first Frenchman from France they had ever met. [translation]

The men Eugène Ney met had probably gone to Dartmouth to trade goods. This is an example of the contacts that took place between Chezzetcook and the Halifax area throughout the century. Most visitors who

---

[100] Eugène Ney, "Voyage à la Nouvelle-Écosse", pp. 390-409.

Ronald Labelle

mentioned the Acadian population in their writings came across them either at the produce market in Halifax or on the road linking the town with Chezzetcook.

In an 1855 publication entitled *Sporting Adventures in the New World*, a British officer named Campbell Hardy wrote of his encounter with a group of young women from Chezzetcook as he was travelling near Preston:

> A little farther on, we met a party of French girls, who were trudging on to the Halifax market, with large baskets containing wild strawberries, put up in pint cases, neatly manufactured out of birch bark. We stopped and bought two cases to eat on the way, partly out of charity to the Acadian damsels, whose merry laugh and jest, uttered in their own patois, lighted up their finely chiselled features as they took our coppers. They came from Chezetcook harbour, a few miles farther on our road, where there is a large settlement of these unfortunate creatures – the remnants of the people who inhabited Nova Scotia, and parts of the other provinces, when, under the name of "l'Acadie", they belonged to France.[101]

While the author condescendingly described the laughing women of Chezzetcook as "unfortunate creatures", it is likely they were actually making fun of him, taking advantage of the fact that he couldn't understand their "merry laugh and jest", as they expressed themselves in French.

The next author to write about the residents of Chezzetcook was Frederic S. Cozzens, an American traveller who visited Nova Scotia in the early summer of 1858 and later published *Acadia or a Month with the Blue Noses*.

This book is especially valuable because of the two illustrations it contains. These are ambrotype portraits of Acadian women from Chezzetcook. The ambrotype was an early photographic process in which images were fixed on glass and later hand-tinted.

Cozzens was obviously proud of the result he obtained, as he chose to include the images in the frontispiece to his book along with the following caption: "There is nothing modem in the face or drapery of this fig-

---

[101] Lieutenant Campbell Hardy, *Sporting Adventures in the New World*, Vol. II, pp. 20-21.

Chezzetcook: an Acadian stronghold

ure. She might have stepped out of Normandy a century ago."

Figure 10: One of the 1858 portraits Cozzens describes.

Ronald Labelle

Cozzens even included a detailed account of how the portrait sitting came about:

> It may interest the reader to know that these are the first, the only likenesses of the real Evangelines of Acadia. The women of Chezzetcook appear at day-break in the city of Halifax, and as soon as the sun is up vanish like the dew. They have usually a basket of fresh eggs, a brace or two of worsted socks, a bottle of fir-balsam to sell. These comprise their simple commerce. When the market-bell rings you find them not. To catch such fleeting phantoms, and to transfer them to the frontispiece of a book published here, is like painting the burnished wings of a hummingbird. A friend, however, undertook the task. He rose before the sun, he bought eggs, worsted socks, and fir-balsam of the Acadians. By constant attentions he became acquainted with a pair of Acadian women, niece and aunt. Then he proposed the matter to them: "I want you to go with me to the daguerreotype gallery. — What for? — To have your portraits taken. — What for? — To send to a friend in New York. —What for? — To be put in a book. — What for? — Never mind 'what for,' will you go?" Aunt and niece—both together in a breath—"No." So my friend, who was a wise man, wrote to the priest of the settlement of Chezzetcook, to explain the "what for," and the consequence was—these portraits![102]

The two ambertype images produced by Frederic Cozzens in 1858 have played a huge role in the preservation of Acadian folkways, inspiring recreations of Acadian traditional dress at sites such as the *Village Historique Acadien* in Caraquet, New Brunswick.

Cozzens was greatly impressed by the Acadians he encountered in Halifax and this is how he described their trek to the market:

> In the early mornings, you sometimes see a few of these people in the streets, or at the market, selling a dozen or so of fresh eggs, or a pair or two of woollen socks, almost the only articles of their simple commerce. But you must needs be early to see them; after eight o'clock, they will have all vanished. Chezzetcook, or, as it is pronounced by the 'Alligonians, "Chizzencook," is twenty-two

---

[102] Frederic S. Cozzens, *Acadia or a Month with the Blue Noses*, pp. iv-v.

miles from Halifax, and as the Acadian peasant has neither horse nor mule, he or she must be off betimes to reach home before mid-day nuncheon. A score of miles on foot is no trifle, in all weathers, but Gabriel and Evangeline perform it cheerfully; and when the knitting-needle and the poultry shall have replenished their slender stock, off again they will start on their midnight pilgrimage, that they may reach the great city of Halifax before daybreak.[103]

His curiosity was such that he arranged an excursion to Chezzetcook, in search of the lost land of Evangeline. In his book, he describes in detail his short visit to the community. The accoun suggests that Cozzens imagined Chezzetcook in the mid-19th century to be in every way similar to a colonial Acadian village before the Expulsion, in the period depicted in Longfellow's epic poem "Evangeline":

We are re-reading Evangeline line by line. And here, at this turn of the road, we encounter two Acadian peasants. The man wears an old tarpaulin hat, home-spun worsted shirt, and tarry canvas trousers; innovation has certainly changed him, in costume at least, from the Acadian of our fancy; but the pretty brown-skinned girl beside him, with lustrous eyes, and soft black hair under her hood, with kirtle of antique form, and petticoat of holiday homespun, is true to tradition. There is nothing modern in the face or drapery of that figure. She might have stepped out of Normandy a century ago. (…) As we salute the pair, we learn they have been walking on their way since dawn from distant Chezzetcook: the man speaks English with a strong French accent; the maiden only the language of her people on the banks of the Seine.[104]

Here and there a green island or a fishing-boat rested upon the surface of the tranquil blue. For miles and miles the eye followed indented grassy slopes, that rolled away on either side of the harbor, and the most delicate pencil could scarcely portray the exquisite line of creamy sand that skirted their edges and melted off in the clear margin of the water. Occasional little cottages nestle among these green banks, not the Acadian houses of the poem, "with thatched roofs, and dormer windows projecting," but

---

103 Ibid., pp. 25-26.

comfortable, homely-looking buildings of modern shapes, shingled and un-weather-cocked. No cattle visible, no ploughs nor horses. Some of the men are at work in the open air; all in tarpaulin hats, all in tarry canvas trousers. These are boat-builders and coopers. Simple, honest, and good-tempered enough; you see how courteously they salute us as we ride by them. In front of every house there is a knot of curious little faces; Young Acadia is out this bright day, and although Young Acadia has not a clean face on, yet its hair is of the darkest and softest, and its eyes are lustrous and most delicately fringed. Yonder is one of the veterans of the place, so we will tie Pony to the fence, and rest here. (...)

The little house is divided by a partition. The larger half is the hall, the parlor, kitchen, and nursery in one. A huge fire-place, an antique spinning-wheel, a bench, and two settles, or high-backed seats, a table, a cradle and a baby very wide awake, complete the inventory. In the apartment adjoining is a bin that represents, no doubt, a French bedstead of the early ages. Everything is suggestive of boat-builders, of Robinson Crusoe work, of undisciplined hands, that have had to do with ineffectual tools. As you look at the walls, you see the house is built of timbers, squared and notched together, and caulked with moss or oakum. (...)

By this time the door-way is entirely packed with little, black, shining heads, and curious faces, all shy, timid, and yet not the less good-natured. Just back of the cradle are two of the Acadian women, "knitters i' the sun," with features that might serve for Palmer's sculptures (...) From the forehead of each you see at a glance how the dark mass of hair has been combed forward and over the face, that the little triangular Norman cap might be tied across the crown of the head. Then the hair is thrown back again over this, so as to form a large bow in front, then re-tied at the crown with colored ribbons. Then you see it has been plaited in a shining mesh, brought forward again, and braided with ribbons, so that it forms, as it were, a pretty coronet, well-placed above those brilliant eyes and harmonious features. This, with the antique kirtle and picturesque petticoat, is an Acadian portrait. Such is it now, and such it was, no doubt, when De Monts sailed from Havre de Grace, two centuries and a half ago.

---

104 Ibid., pp. 39-40.

Chezzetcook: an Acadian stronghold

> In visiting this kind and simple people, one can scarcely forget the little chapel. The young French priest was in his garden, behind the little tenement, set apart for him by the piety of his flock, and readily admitted us. A small place indeed was it, but clean and orderly, the altar decorated with toy images, that were not too large for a Christmas table. Yet I have been in the grandest tabernacles of episcopacy with lesser feelings of respect than those which were awakened in that tiny Acadian chapel. Peace be with it, and with its gentle flock. (…)[105]
>
> "It is surprising," said I to my companion, as we rolled again over the road, "that these people, these Acadians, should still preserve their language and customs, so near to your principal city, and yet with no more affiliation than if they were on an island in the South Seas!" — "The reason of that," he replied, "is because they stick to their own settlement; never see anything of the world except Halifax early in the morning; never marry out of their own set." (…)
>
> "But let me ask you," I continued, "what is the moral condition of the Acadians?" — "As for that," said he, "I believe it stands pretty fair. I do not think an Acadian would cheat, lie, or steal; I know that the women are virtuous, and if I had a thousand pounds in my pocket I could sleep with confidence in any of their houses, although all the doors were unlocked and everybody in the village knew it."[106]

Writers such as Campbell Hardy and Frederic Cozzens could only see the Acadians of Chezzetcook as picturesque peasants, being outsiders who faced a language barrier in their encounters with the population.

During the 1860s, however, three more travellers became interested in Chezzetcook. All three were well-educated Frenchmen who were able to communicate directly with the inhabitants in their native tongue.

The first and most noteworthy of these was certainly Edmé Rameau de Saint-Père. Born in 1820, he studied law in Paris and then became involved in the French colonial enterprise in Algeria. At a time when France was beginning to rebuild its overseas empire, Rameau decided it would be useful to look back at the circumstances surrounding the loss of its earlier colonies. In 1859, he published a two-volume history of

---
105 Ibid., pp. 53-56.
106 Ibid., pp. 59-60.

Ronald Labelle

France's colonies in North America and the following year, he undertook a journey through Nova Scotia and New Brunswick in order to write a detailed history of Acadia.

Not content to limit his historical research to written sources, as was customary at the time, Rameau set out to meet ordinary Acadians all over the region, questioning them about their ancestry. He later published a series of articles based on his findings, as well as a book entitled *Une colonie féodale en Amérique: l'Acadie (1604-1710)*.

Rameau had a twofold mission. On the one hand, he wanted to provide the French colonial administrators with information that could prevent them from repeating in Africa the mistakes they had made earlier in North America, but he also hoped to contribute to the survival of the French language and culture in Acadian areas of the Maritimes.

In August of 1860, Rameau visited Halifax in order to uncover some important historical information contained in the archives of the Roman Catholic Archdiocese. He also intended to visit Chezzetcook, and one can only guess at the wealth of information he would have gathered there.

Unfortunately, the delays he experienced in trying to obtain access to the Archdiocesan archives left him short of time. However, he had the opportunity to have long conversations with Father Abel L'Hiver, the French priest who had been in charge of St. Anselm's church in Chezzetcook between 1855 and 1860. This was the same priest who had greeted Frederic Cozzens during his visit to the community in 1858. Father L'Hiver introduced him to two residents of Chezzetcook, and Rameau later wrote that they were true examples of French country-dwellers, as the woman was wearing a striped skirt made of course wool, with her hair tied up and held in place by a kerchief.[107]

Rameau gathered as much information as he could from Father L'Hiver, who was very familiar with the community, having spent five years there. Here, in translation, are his notes on Chezzetcook:

> Acadian families captured in the woods during the years following their banishment and who had been brought to Halifax as prisoners originally settled the little village of Chezetcook. They remained in captivity for a long time on an island called "Île Rouge" (Georges Island), situated on the south side of the harbour. There, they survived either on prison rations or from the

---

[107] Ronnie-Gilles LeBlanc, *Le voyage de Rameau de Saint-Père en Acadie, 1860*, p. 205.

Chezzetcook: an Acadian stronghold

fruits of their labours, when they were allowed to work for the inhabitants of the town. Finally, around 1766 or 1767, twelve years or so after the great catastrophe, they were permitted to settle a few leagues north of Halifax at the harbour of Chezetcook.

In 1812, they were joined by a few French prisoners of war who were being held in Halifax. Later on, a few French sailors arrived from time to time from the Newfoundland fishery, and today, the population stands at between 1,600 and 1,800 souls. Fishing provides all these poor people with their main means of livelihood and codfish is both their staple food and their main source of trade. Like all Acadians, they have a strong attachment to the Catholic faith and to their French nationality. Being extremely isolated, they have preserved their ancestors' forms of dress and of speech and can be considered as a paleontological specimen of the Acadian people as it existed a century ago. The only other Acadians who can be compared to them are those of Chéticamp, on Cape Breton Island. They have faithfully preserved our language and their manner of dress is closer to that of French country people than that of any group of Acadians or French Canadians that I have come across, with their striped skirt, old-fashioned petticoat and women's headdress made of white muslin. This unique conservation of traditions is amazing, given that they are entirely cut off from other Acadian communities and have no communication with them.

As the shores in the Halifax area are rough and inhospitable, with scarce inhabitants, the people of Chezzetcook have few neighbours and little contact with others, apart from the short trips they make to Halifax for sales and purchases. They remain nevertheless in their little seaside hamlet, with their memories and their traditional outlooks, and they remain faithful to their beliefs, their origins and their patriotism.[108]

Rameau's observations must be interpreted in light of the fact that he only spent a few days in the Halifax area, and did not get an opportunity to closely examine the history of Chezzetcook. He may have slightly exaggerated the population figures for the community, and he seems to have been unaware of the links existing between it and the Acadian com-

---

108 Ibid., pp. 210-214.

munities in Guysborough and Antigonish counties. Nevertheless, by writing down the impressions of a priest who had lived in Chezzetcook during the 1850s, he provided us with a precious 19th century portrayal.

Coincidentally, during the few days he spent in Halifax in early August of 1860, Rameau witnessed the difficulties the Acadians of Chezzetcook were having in trying to retain the services of a French-speaking priest. Bishop Connolly had decided to send Father L'Hiver to a distant parish and to replace him with Thomas Daly, an Irish priest who spoke no French. A delegation of Acadians went to the Archdiocese to plead for the need of a French-speaking priest, but to no avail. Rameau noted that Father L'Hiver was so disheartened at seeing his work ruined and his parishioners in dismay that he chose to leave the diocese, and he finally ended up going to serve an Acadian parish in Northern New Brunswick.

Some of Rameau's observations on Chezzetcook were published in 1860 in a French magazine called *L'économiste français*,[109] and two years later, the *Revue des Deux Mondes*, the same Parisian magazine that had published Eugène Ney's account in 1831, once again presented a traveller's impressions of Chezzetcook.[110] The author this time was Édouard Polydore Vanéechout, a French mariner and writer who signed his travelogues using the pseudonym Édouard Du Hailly.

Like most 19th-century visitors, Vanéechout discovered the Acadian community thanks to a chance meeting at the Halifax market, and later made his way to Chezzetcook to see up close how the people lived. This is how he described his encounter with the locals at the market and his subsequent visit to the community:

> I was looking a little distractedly at this colourful world, when I heard someone behind me utter a few French words in a distinct accent. I turned around and saw a true Norman peasant woman (…). In front of her were eggs and a few pairs of knitted socks. When I questioned her, I learned that she lived in a village called Chezzetcook, eight leagues from Halifax, and that the population of her village was entirely French Acadian. (…). She was returning to Chezzetcook later in the day; I promised her I would to go there myself the next day.
>
> By early morning, we were in our way. The countryside we crossed had the same aspect as that found everywhere in Nova

---

109 Rameau de Saint-Père, "Un voyage en Acadie – 1860", p. 159.
110 Édouard Du Hailly, "Une station sur les côtes d'Amérique – Les Acadiens et la Nouvelle-Écosse", pp. 875-900.

Chezzetcook: an Acadian stronghold

Scotia: nothing grandiose or striking, but a succession of meadows and hillsides gracefully crowned with trees; here and there was a clear lake, where an Indian quietly glided by in a canoe, and on the shore the conical birch bark hut where a squaw, his companion, spent the day weaving baskets. Further along, the countryside was occupied by a small colony of Black fugitives from the United States. Even further, the sea reappeared on the wide horizon, and fishing boats were hauled up on the shore. There, a hundred houses were scattered in no particular order along the road: this was the village of Chezzetcook, clustered around its modest wooden church.

Entering the community, I came across a few rag-tag children playing in a hollow. How softly their childish patois resonated with the words "j'allions" and "j'étions"! Similarly, at the farm where we stopped to ask for hospitality, everything French had been carefully preserved, whether it be their dress or their speech. Now and then, an old-fashioned expression recalled how long these poor exiles had been living away from the mother country, which they always referred to as the "old country" ("le vieux pays"). One might have imagined being transported to a Norman village of two centuries ago. Here lived a Bellefontaine; the fisherman unloading his fish was a Manette, and the ploughman returning from the field was a Lapierre. Not a single unfamiliar family name.

The feeling we had can only be appreciated by someone from France. For the Englishman and for the Spaniard, who have settled all over the world, there is nothing unusual about meeting compatriots in faraway lands; but it is different for us, whose colonies, with few exceptions, have all passed into foreign hands, and it is never without emotion that we come across the remnants of the overseas empire we were unable to preserve. Our emotions were even more acute here, where for so long these remnants had been hidden away in a remote corner of Nova Scotia.

The population of Chezzetcook comprises about 1,500 souls. Originally made up of a small group of families who formed alliances, the villagers multiplied and increased their numbers without mixing with any outsiders. (…) France has long forgotten the existence of its lost children, but these people have, however, steadfastly kept the memory of their origins. (…) The history of

> this forgotten and banished people should truly be better known; no other history is so moving and enlightening as theirs. [translation]

The final traveller who wrote about Chezzetcook in mid-19th century was Adolphe Marsais, a poet and musician born in Angoulême, France in 1803 and who lived in Québec between 1854 and 1879. Marsais was a French patriot whose songs and poems praised the shared cultural heritage of France and Canada.

He travelled through Nova Scotia during the summer of 1867 and published accounts of his trip in *L'Ordre*, a Montreal newspaper founded by members of a religious organization called L'Union catholique. He was so impressed by Chezzetcook that he devoted his longest article to the Acadian community.

Here, in translation, are several excerpts from this unique article, providing an insight into local life at the time of Confederation:

> At high tide, water fills a vast basin dotted with islands covered by woods; small rowboats and sailboats glide over the flats, as if on a great lake; schooners follow the many channels, heading to Halifax with their cargo of fish, principally herring and mackerel, or else with vegetables and firewood, all of which are products sold by the farmers and fishermen of the locality. They then return with flour, lumber, provisions, textiles, etc., bought in Nova Scotia's capital city.
>
> At low tide, the basin, surrounded by rocky headlands, meadows and sand banks, dries up completely and one can even walk on its bed, which, although muddy, is quite compact. The only remaining water is then in the channels.
>
> The soil is generally rocky. (…) The countryside is filled with rounded hillocks and the greenery is a charming sight for the eyes, as this varied scenery is situated on the edge of the vast Atlantic. Topsoil is very sparse and does not support tall trees. (…) I am told that winter is not very severe and that the cold season does not last more than 4 or 5 months. In the past, there was far more snow than in recent years. Elderly residents, some of whom have reached the venerable age of 90, remember that during their youth, the snow was 4 or 5 feet thick, and that sleds were used for 3 or 4 months of the year. (…) In general, the air is healthy, which explains the fact that illness is rare in this com-

Chezzetcook: an Acadian stronghold

munity of 1,200 souls who need no doctor and no apothecary.

The excellent local parish priest, Mr. Madden, is an Irishman who speaks French very well. He was kind enough to take me to visit a fine old woman named Sophie Bonnevie, who showed me her marriage contract made out in 1792. (...) She was married 75 years ago at 19 years of age! And yet, she can still see and hear well, speaks pure French and is full of liveliness and joy. The parish priest quite rightly remarked that without the Catholic faith, his parishioners would have anglicized their names long ago and would no longer speak French.

I had an even more interesting encounter when I met with an old-timer who was born in my own home town, and who, during the past 70 years, has only twice encountered compatriots of his, seeing that he has never gone back to his native land, and no doubt will not do so in future. His story, though unremarkable, deserves to be told. His name is Simon Julien: He was 9 or 10 years old at the time of the tragic death of Louis XVI and remembers well both this event and the massacres that took place in his community at the time of the Revolution. He boarded a French ship named the *Andromaque* as a cabin boy at the age of 11 and crossed to the Gulf of Mexico, from where he sailed towards Cape Breton on a navy supply ship named the *Élizabeth*. Not far from Halifax, the ship was overtaken by a much larger British navy ship named the *Bulwark*, and he was taken to Halifax as a prisoner of war. There, he was treated kindly enough, but when he learned there were a few Acadians at Grand Desert, he escaped and went to join them. That was the name the first French settlers gave to Chezzetcook, a Mi'kmaq name, because of the open, treeless areas that existed there. He later married an Acadian woman who is still in fine health today, and he worked tirelessly, chopping wood to sell in Halifax and fishing inshore. This brave man is now 84 or 85 years old and still has all his faculties. He and his wife had a busy time of it, raising 14 children! This is not a rare thing in the area. Another inhabitant I met, Antoine Faucher, is 81 years old and combines his roles as choirmaster at the church and ladder maker. I hired him to be my driver, taking me to Halifax with his horse and wagon.

The inhabitants of Chezzetcook live on both sides of the harbour. (...) Their homes resemble those of the French Canadians on the Lower St. Lawrence but are smaller and have fewer amenities. The roofs and exterior walls are covered with shingles that are generally whitewashed. The interiors are neat and sparsely furnished. The Acadians are hard working: not only do they make red bricks at several locations, but most are able to build a house, weave fishing nets, and they can even build boats, including schooners that they build near their homes up on hills above the sea. They build them gradually, without hurrying, and when the hull is complete, they haul them to the sea using from 20 to 24 oxen that they lend to each other in a neighbourly fashion. Their main crop is hay and whatever is not necessary to feed their livestock is sold in Halifax, fetching a good price. Besides that, they sell wild berries, as well a kind of shellfish that they gather from the mud at low tide; in addition, they sell lobsters that are both large and plentiful.

The women are always producing knitted goods that they trade at the shops in town for toiletry items. Their dress is unpretentious and without any crinolines. There are no frivolous ornaments, no fancy furnishings or wagons, but at the same time, there are no beggars. The elderly people are the only ones who do not work.

The Acadians are good-natured and very polite to the strangers they meet; Sobriety is one of their main qualities. Strong drink is almost unknown in the area and there are no drinking establishments. (...) The more well-off families help those in need, and when a child is orphaned, he or she is adopted by a local family. There are among them a few English, Scottish and Irish people, all of whom are Catholics who generally speak both English and French. They all live in harmony; rarely does any disorder take place and I didn't see a single drunkard during my stay.

This Catholic community grows quickly from year to year, as there are few deaths and the maxim "go forth and multiply" seems to be in effect, but unfortunately, education there was greatly neglected until 1860. Many Acadians could neither read nor write, not having had anyone to teach them when they were young; in recent years, however, they have come to understand the value of education. Two fine and zealous teachers, a couple of French-Canadian brothers named Collerette, came from Montreal in 1860, after being hired by the Nova Scotia Superintendent of Education. They are now wisely teaching nearly 300 children who have made much progress in a short time (only 18 months).

The new school, which is spacious enough to contain 300 pupils, put on an interesting display just as I arrived, July 31st being the day for the handing out of prizes and awards. One out of every 12 children either was awarded a prize of books or received an honourable mention. (…) Money is needed to pay for school fees, and a moderate tax has been imposed for that purpose. Many fathers gladly accepted to pay the tax, although they were unaccustomed to doing so; but some residents, especially those without children, resented paying for the others, such as is often the case in Lower Canada. Whether they liked it or not, they had to pay up. Little by little, the population will become accustomed to this necessary request and will understand that the spirit needs nourishment just as much as the body. They will see that to rise up from the state of inferiority in which they have lived since the British conquest, they will need to educate the present generation.

The local church is situated on a hillock near the inlet, around the middle of the Acadian community. It is spacious and simple, but suitable; the wooden outside walls and bell tower are painted white, which creates a charming effect in the midst of the green surroundings, as green and white go so well together. Every year, three or four weddings are celebrated there. The only French priest to have resided at the rectory was Father L'Hiver, between 1856 and 1859.[111]

Marsais's article is followed by the text of a song he composed as a homage to the Acadians of Chezzetcook. Shortly after it was published in Montreal in September of 1867, the song, entitled "Un mois chez les Acadiens", was reprinted in *Le Moniteur Acadien*, the new Acadian newspaper that had just started publication in New Brunswick. It is difficult, however, to know if it was ever sung in Chezzetcook, as no mention of it was found in the community.

Although Marsais' article presents an idealized vision of the community, it provides a more detailed account than any other written by his contemporaries, and it is the most interesting one for several reasons. While many 19th-century travellers briefly stopped at Chezzetcook and wrote in passing of the quaint French-speaking peasants who lived there,

---

111 Marsais, "Un mois de séjour chez nos Acadiens", pp. 1-2.

Marsais, in contrast, spent close to a month in the community, and, being French, was able to communicate with its inhabitants in their native tongue.

The encounter the author found most fascinating was with Simon Julien, who was one of the original settlers and an ancestor of all the Juliens in the Chezzetcook area.

By sheer coincidence, Julien originally came from Adolphe Marsais's home town of Angoulême in Southwestern France, The information Marsais learned from Simon Julien himself confirms what F. J. Melanson stated about Julien's birthplace in his *Genealogies of the Families of Chezzetcook*. Melanson was also right in assuming that Simon Julien had been a prisoner in Halifax before his arrival at Chezzetcook, basing his assumption on the fact that "it is hard to conceive how else he could have landed in Nova Scotia during those many years of warfare between Britain and France".[112]

Figure 11: The former prison at Dartmouth Cove, in 1929.

---

112 Melanson, *Genealogies...* - "Julien".

The prison where Julien had been interned was likely situated at Dartmouth Cove, near Old Ferry Road, according John P. Martin, who states in his *Story of Dartmouth* that the crews of enemy ships captured offshore were usually quartered at Melville Island or at the prison that was erected in Dartmouth in 1793, and that was the scene of frequent escapes.[113]

The Marsais article also refers to Sophique Lapierre, the woman who became Simon Julien's wife in 1805. Among the other local residents mentioned, Antoine Faucher was one of the original settlers, having arrived in the area from Québec in 1814 along with abbé Pierre Mignault. Two years later, Faucher opened the first local school, near the newly-built church, and he was married to Divine Roma in 1821.

While F. J. Melanson states that Faucher was born around 1792[114], Marsais states that he was 81 years old in 1867, which would place his date of birth about six years earlier. The 94-year-old woman named Sophie Bonnevie, whom the author met in Chezzetcook, was likely one of the children of pioneer settler Sylvain Bonnevie and his wife, Marguerite.

The Marsais article is also interesting because of the brief description of the original wooden church built in Chezzetcook around 1814 and replaced by the present church 80 years later. No images of the first church are known to exist, but the article informs us that it was spacious enough and possessed a bell tower. We also learn from the article that Thomas Daly, the English-speaking priest who was in charge of the parish between 1860 and 1867, was followed by a bilingual priest named Madden.

Regarding the occupations of the settlers, Marsais generally confirms the oral traditions about shipbuilding and trade with Halifax. Interestingly, he mentions that the inhabitants made red bricks at several locations. This supports oral history accounts mentioning the existence of several small kilns during the 19th century. The author also mentions lobster as one of the products of the fishery, at a time when the market for shellfish was just beginning to develop.

If one is to believe the descriptions of 19th-century travelers, Chezzetcook was at that time a perfect example of a traditional Acadian community. So many of them were impressed by the unique character of the inhabitants that we can state with certainty that Chezzetcook in the mid-19th century had preserved many of the characteristics of Acadian life in

---

113 John P. Martin, *The Story of Dartmouth*, pp. 23 and 113.

114 Melanson, *Genealogies...*, - "Bonnevie, Boudrot, Breau, Clergé, Faucher, Grenon, Maurice, Pellerin, Richard, Robicheau, Surette".

the French colonial era. This is all the more surprising, given that the community was actually less isolated than many other Acadian villages, being in constant contact with the Nova Scotian capital.

The travellers' accounts are also proof that, one hundred years after its founding, Chezzetcook was still entirely French-speaking, even though all surrounding communities were English-speaking.

Figure 12: Ambrotype image of an Acadian woman from Chezzetcook captured by Frederic Cozzens in 1858.

5: Building a livelihood

Farming and Fishing
Like most Acadian communities during the post-Expulsion era, Chezzetcook relied primarily on farming and fishing for its livelihood. As years went by, however, local economic activities became increasingly diversified.

The 1827 Nova Scotia census, while much less detailed than those carried out in later years, still provides a fairly clear picture of the size of local farms. By comparing statistics gathered from Acadian families with those from Protestant families living in the same census area, we can see how the former were at a disadvantage. Acadian families owned, on average, three and one-half acres of cultivated land, while their Protestant neighbours of German or British descent each cultivated about ten acres of farmland.

In the early decades of the 19th century, Roman Catholics were finally obtaining land ownership rights, thanks to the Nova Scotia "Act for the Relief of Roman Catholics", adopted in 1826. Prior to the passage of this act, it was very difficult for an Acadian to obtain property, as the law stipulated that they would have to repudiate their Catholic faith in order to do so.

Acadian communities could not grow and prosper so long as there were legal obstacles put in their way. Once they became eligible to purchase property, Acadians were still disadvantaged, because the most productive land was in the hands of Protestant farmers, while the soil available to the Acadians tended to be of poor quality and less suitable for intensive agriculture.

Census returns show how agricultural practices varied among different cultural groups. While people of German descent in the surrounding area cultivated a considerable quantity of barley and oats, the three main crops in Chezzetcook were potatoes, turnips and hay.

Census figures for 1851 suggest that Chezzetcook was still recovering from the crop failures of the 1840s. The total quantity of potatoes produced in the previous year was 1,134 bushels, while figures gathered ten years later show a total crop of 6,579 bushels.

The livestock on Acadian farms consisted mostly of cows and pigs. While nearby farmers of German descent raised large herds of sheep, the number found in Chezzetcook was relatively low.

A comparison between data compiled from Acadian families and that from English-speaking Protestants in the district shows that, by the middle of the century, the former were already diversifying their economic activities, while the latter continued to rely exclusively on farming and fishing. All the non-Acadian heads of families were recorded as being either farmers or fishers, and most were entered as having both occupations. Among the 163 Acadian heads of families, 101 were identified as farmers or fishers, but 62 had other occupations. The list includes 20 brickmakers, 15 of whom combined brickmaking with farming, as well as 24 mechanics and 18 people who were involved in commerce or other trades.

Families established at the Head of Chezzetcook and at West Chezzetcook tended to concentrate mostly on farming, while the residents of Grand-Désert were actively involved in the fishery. Census returns for 1861 reflect this situation, listing 65 heads of families as being farmers, while 64 others were listed as either fishers or "farmer and fisherman". While census takers were instructed to enter the occupation of the heads of families, the fact that they often felt obliged to indicate both farming and fishing as the families' means of livelihood is proof that fishers supplemented their revenue with agricultural produce.

When the men were away on the fishing banks, their wives and older children looked after their small farms. The 1907 essay by Emma B. Julien entitled "History of Grand Desert" provides an intimate portrait of life at the time. Regarding occupations, the author states:

> The women knit, keep hens, ducks, turkeys, sheep, cows and other little animals. The men fish from April to November. (...) During the month of August, the fishermen give their work up for the time that it will take for them to make their hay. After that some of the schooners return again, not for codfish but for herring. There are 4 fishing schooners here. They leave in May and go out fishing around the Magdalen Islands. There are 4 coasting schooners. They carry bricks, lumber, gravel to Halifax. (...) Years gone by, the men never used to have a horse. Now there are more

horses than oxen and the people seem to live in a much better way.[115]

While we generally imagine our ancestors as having used horses for work and transportation, the essay by Emma Julien suggests that many 19th century families could not afford horses and went about on foot, relying on oxen to carry heavy loads.

As seen in the previous chapter, French historian Edmé Rameau de Saint-Père observed in 1860 that the cod fishery provided the population with both a food staple and a major source of income. The detailed statistics contained in the 1861 census provide a picture of a very active fishery. It reported production during the previous year of 3,197 quintals of dried codfish, 1,415 barrels of herring, 562 barrels of mackerel, 122 barrels of alewives (gaspereau) and 1,882 barrels of fish oil.

Total figures vary considerably from one census report to the next, with herring production sometimes rising to the same level as the cod fishery.

Surprisingly, lobster production was not even mentioned among census statistics for Chezzetcook until 1891. Lobster canneries were established in many communities along the Eastern Shore during the second half of the 19th century, but while the industry grew very quickly in many areas of the Maritimes, Chezzetcook lagged behind, perhaps because of the predominance of the cod fishery there.[116]

Apart from fish varieties that were exploited for commercial reasons, recreational fishing also took place, with varieties like eels and smelts being much appreciated. Eel pots were traditionally made from the branches of withe rod bushes that grew in the area.

When Geneviève Massignon visited Grand-Désert in February 1947 in the course of her survey of Acadian language and folklore, fisher Alban Lapierre described how eel traps were lowered onto the mud in the harbour. Massignon noted: *"ils font des bournes avec du raisinier pour prendre les anguilles"*.[117] "Bourne" is an old French term meaning a trap for catching eels or shellfish and "raisinier" refers to a wild grape variety English speaking Nova Scotians call withe rod.

In early spring, the fishers began to prepare for their yearly work

---

115 Emma B. Julien, "History of Grand Desert".
116 Departmetn of Marine and Fisheries, "Fisheries Statements for the year 1882", pp. 24-25.
117 Bibliothèque Nationale de France, Geneviève Massignon Fonds, B44.4, « fichier folklore acadien ».

activities. The lobster fishers made sure their traps and lines were ready by the beginning of April.

The spring fishery involved the use of nets to catch herring and mackerel that supplied bait for the fishing schooners. Mackerel was the bait of choice for lobster traps and also for the pollock fishery, whereas the boats that departed in May for the cod fishery in the Gulf of St. Lawrence would bring along a supply of herring or salt clams. According to Alban Lapierre, herring was used as bait in the spring, and was replaced by salt clams later in the fishing season.[118]

Clam digging began early in the spring. A large quantity of clams were obtained locally by digging in the mud at low tide. These were salted and packed in locally-made barrels. They were then either used by local fishers or were sold to the owners of schooners from as far away as Lunenberg.

Not all the clams were salted; throughout the summer, people from Chezzetcook brought along fresh clams when they travelled to the market in Halifax.

When the lobster season began in the spring, fishers began their annual migration to Threefathom Harbour, or "Maganchiche", the name of Mi'kmaq origin commonly used by Acadians. The fishing harbour was on an island reached by crossing a narrow channel separating it from the village of Threefathom Harbour. It wasn't linked to the mainland until a narrow causeway was built in the late 1940s.

Each fisher hauled his gear to Threefathom Harbour, along with some new lobster traps that had been made during the winter to replace the ones lost or damaged the previous year. The men all had cabins where they stayed during the week. These were built by the fishers themselves over one hundred years ago, at a time when local residents were nearly self-sufficient.

William Lapierre told of how they chopped trees in winter, then hauled the wood over the ice on Porter's Lake before having it sawed at local mills. The lumber was then ferried over to the island, where it was used to build small cabins, each equipped with a woodstove and bunks.[119]

Each Sunday during fishing season, the fishers walked about ten kilometres from Grand-Désert to Threefathom Harbour, carrying on their backs their weekly food supply, and they walked back to their homes

---

118 Ibid., tape 72-144 (1961).
119 Dillman, "How Grand Desert got its name".

Chezzetcook: an Acadian stronghold

when the week's work was done. Apart from setting traps for lobster, the fishers caught herring in nets and then salted the fish.

A schooner left for Halifax every week, carrying barrels of salt herring, which was later exported to the Caribbean unless it was kept as bait for the cod fishery. Herring was sometimes used as bait in lobster traps early in the fishing season, when mackerel was not yet available. When there was a heavy catch of herring that needed to be gutted and salted, the men sometimes needed to spend the weekend at the harbour rather than returning home. Their wives then had to pack up supplies for the coming week and walk to Threefathom Harbour, each carrying a basket of food. Although the village of Threefathom Harbour was inhabited mainly by people of German descent, most of the fishers who sailed from the harbour itself were Acadians living in Chezzetcook.Being isolated at the tip of an island,

Figure 13: William Lapierre at his home in 1982.

Being isolated at the tip of an island, Threefathom Harbour was an ideal location for smuggling during the 1920s. At the time of prohibition, schooners would go there at night to unload their cargo of rum. Bottles of illicit alcohol were sometimes stored in fishing cabins or were buried in the sand until rum runners came to pick them up. If local fishers happened to come across stashed kegs of rum that had yet to be delivered to buyers, they would then help themselves to the illicit alcohol.

The fishing cabins were also used for storing goods that washed up on shore on the rare occasions when shipwrecks happened in the area. Edwin Lapierre, for example, remembered the wreck of the *Five Onion*, a ship with a cargo of molasses. The recovered cargo provided local residents with a supply of molasses that lasted for a long time afterwards.[120] According to Lavinia LeBlanc, the molasses was shipped in large tanks

---

120 CEAAC, Ronald Labelle Collection, ms. 174 (1982).

from which it was poured into buckets once it had washed up on the shore.[121]

Figure 14: Edwin Lapierre and his fishing cabin at Threefathom Harbour in 1982.

While lost goods were sometimes recovered directly on shore, a few shipwrecks took place on the reefs off of Chétigne (or Shutin) Island, after which people rowed out to the site, hoping to recover lost cargo.

The island where the fishing harbour was situated is very low and the land there has eroded considerably over the years. During the 1940s, it became necessary to move the fishing cabins to higher ground. Ocean currents have also caused the harbour bottom to fill in, therefore reducing its depth.

Since 1949, the causeway linking the island to the mainland has been widened, making it accessible by automobile and thereby ending its isolation.

The boats used for lobster fishing were always quite small, while the

---

121 Ibid., accession no. 1296 (1982).

large schooners built in Chezzetcook were destined for the cod fishery in the Gulf of St. Lawrence. Towards the beginning of May each year, the schooners would leave for the fishing banks, where they would remain until their return in August.

Liliane Bellefontaine remembered how their departure was marked by a special mass:

> They would leave to spend the summer over there on the banks. They were gone all summer, so a mass was said before they left. They waited for that mass before leaving. I remember the mass was said for them every year, on May 1st.[122] [translation]

When the schooners set sail from Chezzetcook for the first time each year, they flew the Union Jack from each mast to mark the occasion, and it was the same when they returned in the fall. The return of the first fishing vessel in the fall was also celebrated by firing shots into the air, thus announcing to all that the fishers were back.

According to Liliane Bellefontaine:

> People were happy to see the Union Jacks flying. (...) It was just to show that their trip had been peaceful, that things had gone well. They didn't have to fly them here, to come into Chezzetcook harbour, but (...) that meant they were happy about their trip.[123] [translation]

The departure of the schooners was an important event because many of the men would not see their families again until late summer.

Some fishing schooners employed several members of the same family. Lavinia LeBlanc remembered that her first husband, Alban Julien, worked on a schooner along with his father and some of his uncles. The schooner was run by family members who hired three or four other men to do various tasks such as cleaning fish.[124]

The cod fishers faced dangers during the months they spent at sea, and their family members were never certain of seeing them return when the fishery ended in August. The first danger was that of the ice which was still drifting on the waters of the Gulf of St. Lawrence in early May. William Lapierre told of how a schooner on which he had been sail-

---

122 Ibid., accession no. 1111 (1982).
123 Ibid., accession no. 1167 (1982).
124 Ibid., accession no. 1684 (1983).

ing became caught in the ice while navigating the Strait of Canso:

> We were going through Canso. We got caught in the ice that spring. We almost went to the bottom. Oh, there was heavy ice there. There were a bunch of Germans from the west [Lunenberg County]; a bunch were on board the ship. There were 75 of them. They were tied up there; on the eastern side where the ferry crossed - a ferry took the cars across in those days. By God! we hit that ice hard. The ship was frozen there. We thought we were going to the bottom. I tell you, there was a little cove on the side there. We were shoved into that, and we had to keep a lookout all night, the ice was so thick.[125] [translation]

There was also the danger of being shipwrecked during a storm. At least two ships, the *Grand Desert* and the *Greenleaf*, were wrecked off the Magdalen Islands.

In September 1900, the *Greenleaf* had not yet returned from the Gulf of St. Lawrence and was caught in hurricane-force winds. The captain tried to anchor his ship in a sheltered bay, but the wind shifted, and she ran aground at Sandy Hook, a long sand bar that extends east from the southernmost island in the chain. Although no crew members perished, the ship was a total loss and a note of protest was signed by Captain Martin Julien, along with shipmates Angus Julien and James Lapierre, in an attempt to recover losses.[126]

The note of protest described how the schooner had left the port of Halifax on August 10th and fished in the Gulf of St. Lawrence until September 12th, when a violent storm forced the crew to take shelter in a bay. With nightfall, the wind shifted from south-south east to a northerly direction and intensified to hurricane force:

> I had no alternative left than to try and stay where I was. The wind yet increased and I parted both anchors from the bow and had to be driven ashore. The vessel struck the shore at about Two o'clock A.M. in a sandy place called "Sandy Hook" east of Amherst Island. The night was dark; we could not see the distance we were from the shore and we had to leave the vessel and run ashore amongst the breakers to save our lives. The vessel now

---
125 Ibid., accession no. 1090 (1982).
126 Eastern Shore Archives, Lena Ferguson Collection, tape 6805, Édouard Lapierre (3 March 1976).

lies badly stranded, apparently full of water, the sea always breaking over her and probabilities are that she is a total loss. All of us have lost all their clothes and personal things and even the register of the vessel I was unable to save.[127]

According to information gathered by Lena Ferguson, survivors of the wreck walked several kilometres in the howling wind before arriving at the nearest house in the village of Havre-Aubert, the island community formerly known as "Amherst". Interestingly, the French consulate in Nova Scotia is said to have paid to have a vessel sent from Pictou to take the crew members home.[128]

After sailing through the Canso Strait, ships would go to Prince Edward Island, where the men dug for clams to use as bait, if they had not already obtained a full supply in Chezzetcook. John Lapierre recalled that the use of clams as bait originated with the fishers of German descent in Nova Scotia while herring had originally been the preferred bait for those from Grand-Désert and Seaforth. William Lapierre remembered stopping at "Île Saint-Jean" (the original French name of PEI) and filling as many as 14 barrels of salt clams before heading out into the Gulf.[129]

The fact that the original French name of Prince Edward Island was still used in Chezzetcook two centuries after its English name had replaced it shows how the local population had remained close to their 18th century origins. Elsewhere in the Maritimes, Acadians long ago replaced the name "Île Saint-Jean" with the current one, Île-du-Prince-Édouard.

As William Lapierre remembered, crews also took advantage of the stop in PEI to stock up on food:

> We took some potatoes; some turnips, and then there were eggs...We took all the stuff we needed to last until August. Yeah, it was a hard living in one way. They were always soaked. They didn't have the sort of gear that people have nowadays—now they have clothes that keep the water out. Before, they just had common cotton wear that was coated with oil.[130] [translation]

With a favourable wind, the trip from Threefathom Harbour to Prince Edward Island could take less than a day. Alban Lapierre remembered once leaving the fishing harbour at 2 o'clock in the afternoon and arriv-

---
127 "Marine Note of Protest", Acadian House Museum.
128 Lena Ferguson, "The Fishing Schooners", p. 8.
129 CEAAC, Ronald Labelle Collection, accession no. 1342 (1982).

ing at PEI at 10:30 the following morning.[131]

Once they reached the fishing grounds off the Magdalen Islands, the sailors would go ashore from time to time to obtain a supply of fresh water. They would then get a chance to visit with the inhabitants of the islands, thus breaking the monotony of life aboard the ship. On these occasions, the men from Chezzetcook and Grand-Désert appreciated the opportunity to speak French with the local inhabitants, "les Madelinots".

Another way to break the monotony was to play games. There was a game called "the fox and the goose" that consisted of a wooden board with rows of holes in which pegs were placed. The goose had to remain in the same row as it moved along the board, while the fox tried to jump over it.[132] This is one example of a game played long ago that has sadly been forgotten.

William Lapierre made four trips to the fishing grounds on a schooner captained by Martin Julien. He was one of the men who would row out in small dories, jigging cod with hand lines. The 14 dories unloaded their catches three times a day. The men would row out on the open water with only a pair of oars and a jug of water on board. After a long day of fishing, no matter how tired they were, they still had to take turns doing a night watch, an hour at a time. William remembered one stormy morning when a wave hit the ship so hard that a pot of baked beans was knocked right off the stove in the galley.[133]

The sailing vessels sometimes went beyond the Magdalen Islands to fish further north in the Gulf of St. Lawrence. Alban Lapierre, who spoke to French folklorist Geneviève Massignon during both of her field trips, in 1947 and 1961, recalled that he had sailed all the way to Miscou Island in Northern New Brunswick during cod fishing season.

After learning to sail on fishing schooners, some local men signed up as crew members on ocean-going transport vessels. Étienne (or Steven) Bellefontaine, for example, left Chezzetcook to sail the world in the early years of the 20th century. He visited every continent and his ship even anchored twice in the Falkland Islands, at the southern tip of South America. He eventually returned home in 1914. When I visited him in 1982, he was in his mid-nineties and still living in the house his grand-

---

130 Ibid., accession no. 1090 (1982).
131 Bibliothèque Nationale de France, Geneviève Massignon Fonds, tape 72-144 (1961).
132 Eastern Shore Archives, Lena Ferguson Collection, tape 6805 Édouard Lapierre (3 March 1976).
133 CEAAC, Ronald Labelle Collection, accession no. 1337 (1982).

father built in West Chezzetcook.[134]

Figure 15: right: the schooner "Flora MJ", captain Martin Julien, circa 1900 at Souris, PEI.

While the workweek involved long hours of labour, Sundays were observed as holidays, the cook being the only person required to work. Édouard Lapierre, who was a cook on a vessel named *The Village Leaf*, recalled that he would be up at 4 o'clock in the morning preparing breakfast. Dinner was prepared at 9:30 and supper at 3 in the afternoon. Codfish, potatoes, salt pork, baked beans and corned beef were the food staples, but the cook also made bread, including gingerbread and raisin bread. On Sunday afternoons, the crew even had a helping of chocolate along with raisin bread.[135]

Before returning to Nova Scotia with their load of cod, the schooners would make a final stop at Prince Edward Island, this time to buy agricultural produce such as potatoes, turnips, parsnips and oats.

Once they arrived back at Threefathom Harbour, the fishers unloaded the salt cod, which was then dried on flakes before being sold in Halifax

---

134 Ibid., ms. 151 (1982).
135 Eastern Shore Archives, Lena Ferguson Collection, tape 6804, Édouard Lapierre (3 March 1976).

in early autumn. As soon as people from surrounding villages saw the schooners arriving, they would rush to the harbour to buy supplies of vegetables.

During the month of October, one final fishing activity took place in Chezzetcook Inlet and on Porter's Lake. This was the lucrative smelt fishery, which helped to provide money for the winter months. Some smelts were shipped by train to the United States, while the rest were sold either to restaurant owners in Halifax or at the market.

According to Lavinia LeBlanc, nets were spread at different places in Chezzetcook Inlet, and they remained in place until the onset of winter:

> They'd do that from October, starting October. They'd get it about a month before it started to freeze. Then the harbour would freeze and they wouldn't have a chance to get no more. But we used to go out, and they'd fish smelts, and we'd ship them to the States; put them in a barrel and freeze them, and take them to the train. (...) They were packed in ice, and they were put in barrels, you know, small barrels, not big ones. Yep, that was our Christmas money, cause that was quick money.[136]

Smelts were also caught during the winter months by ice-fishing on Porter's Lake. Some were consumed locally, but most were taken to the market in Halifax. Amable Robichaud recalled that in the early 20th century, he bought smelts locally at 2 cents a dozen and he would then sell them at the market in Halifax for four times that price.[137]

Shellfish

Shellfish production became increasingly important during the 19th century. While the mud flats at Chezzetcook were renowned for the abundant clams found there, oysters were also gathered in vast quantities.

By the mid-19th century, oysters were in high demand because they were used as bait in the offshore fishery. The 1871 census, for example, reported a production of 844 barrels of oysters the previous year, whereas the total for the entire province of Nova Scotia was 1,257 barrels.

Later on, clams began to be used as bait in the offshore fishery and

---

136 CEAAC, Ronald Labelle Collection, accession no. 1267 (1982).
137 Ibid., ms. 130 (1982).

residents gathered them to sell to ship captains from Lunenberg. In the early 20th century, a local merchant named Daniel Conrod bought hundreds of barrels of clams each year in order to sell them to the captains of fishing schooners. Clams were also taken to Halifax to be sold at the market and people sometimes went door-to-door in Chezzetcook, carrying a bucketful of clams for sale, which they measured out using a soup ladle.[138]

It is significant that lobsters were not even mentioned before the 1891 census, as the commercial lobster fishery only started in the 1880s, in response to a new demand from markets in the United States. Until that time, there was only a small-scale lobster fishery in Chezzetcook, and the catch was either consumed locally or sold at the market in Halifax.

Diking and farming the marshlands

While clams gathered on the extensive mud flats at Chezzetcook provided a much-needed source of revenue, the salt hay (or marsh grass) that grew in the marsh situated further up along Chezzetcook Inlet was also of great value as fodder for farm animals. Thanks to a petition sent to colonial administrators by Louis Petitpas and others in 1780, we know that marsh grass was used locally from the time of early settlement.

Beginning in 1834, residents began to consider diking the upper reaches of the marsh in order to expand their farmlands. They were certainly familiar with diking techniques because their Acadian ancestors had developed prosperous farms on reclaimed marshlands in the Annapolis Valley and around the Minas Basin beginning in the 17th century.

While a petition regarding the building of a dyke was sent to Halifax by members of six Acadian families with the names Lapierre, Roma, Bellefontaine, Petitpas, Faucher and Wolf, nothing seems to have resulted from the initiative. Two years later, Grand-Désert resident Paul Lapierre presented another petition, requesting permission to build a dyke to contain 100 acres of marshland on the western side of the lower part of the inlet. 17 other petitioners joined Paul Lapierre, all of whom were named either Lapierre or Wolf.

The petition mentioned that 30 acres of land were already being ex-

---

138 Eastern Shore Archives, Lena Ferguson Collection, tape J-1, Ferdinand Julien (1 March 1990).

103

ploited, while the dyke would bring a further 70 acres into use.[139] According to the petition, the dyke was to be 140 yards long, 13 feet wide and 12 feet high.

This modest plan seems to have been successful, and in 1837, a dyke drained a small lake, giving farmers access to a large quantity of salt hay. Draining the marshlands enabled farmers to harvest as much as 50 tons of hay.

An historical essay written by Emma Julien in 1907 contains an excerpt of an earlier essay the author wrote in 1902, this time in French. It explains how the dyke built during the 1930s was eventually abandoned. The excerpt appears first in the original French, to demonstrate that some pupils attending school in Grand-Désert were able to write quite proficiently in their first language:

> Le monde a fait des digues pour empêcher l'eau d'entrer et après les prés se formèrent et se couvrirent de foin. Les digues se sont cassées et l'eau est venue dedans encore une fois. Il y a encore des morceaux de bois de la digue qui avait été bâtie dans cet temps là. (People built dykes to prevent the water from coming in and then meadows appeared and were covered with hay. Then the dykes burst and the water came back in. There are still bits of wood from the dyke that was built in those days.)

In 1841, another diking petition was sent to the colonial government. It was signed by 56 heads of families with the following names: Bellefontaine, Bona, Bonnevie, Boudreau, Breau, Clergé, Crawford, Faucher, Fillis, Lapierre, Mayet, Murphy, Petitpas, Robichaud, and Roma. Eleven of the signatories were named Bellefontaine, while there were seven named Petitpas. This petition provided detailed information about the motivation behind the project:

> ...That most of your Petitioners are of French Origin, and having settled upon the Shores of Chezetcook Harbour, where the land is indifferent, Supported themselves for many years by cutting and conveying Cord wood to market, that while engaged in these occupations from their ignorance of the English language and of the forms of proceeding, much of the land around their Settlement was taken up and occupied by other Settlers, while there all

---

139 Brad Sweet, "Chezzettcook Dyke Petitions, p. 1.

places have had to be divided and subdivided to meet the necessity of increasing numbers. That immediately in front of the Settlement where your Petitioners reside, there is an extensive flat which though covered at high water, may be reclaimed and rendered available for the enlargement of the farms and general support of your Petitioners, and they humbly solicit from your honourable House a small Sum of money to aid them in the undertaking.[140]

The petitioners pledged their own labour for the task, promising 1,666 days of combined work for the construction of the dyke if the colonial government provided financing.[141]

In seeking an explanation for the failure of the government to respond favourably to the request, Brad Sweet quotes a counter petition by a man named John Gates (possibly a member of the Gaetz family of East Chezzetcook). It is likely that rights to the marshland would be contested in court, had the project been given the green light, and this could explain in part why the original petition was not approved.

Still, the local residents did not give up their fight. Many of the same 1841 petitioners added their names to a new petition in 1846, seeking assistance to reclaim 1,000 acres for "pasturage and meadow". This was at the time of the severe crop failures of 1845-47, when residents were pleading with the government for the supply of seed potatoes and other necessities.[142]

Residents of Chezzetcook were doubly handicapped, first by the fact that the majority, who spoke only French, were unable to address colonial officials in English, and second because most of them were illiterate. An "X" rather than a signature accompanies most names on the petitions. We know that a local priest wrote the petition prepared in 1846, and it is possible that the same assistance was provided in the drafting of the earlier ones.

In 1849, a new plan was proposed to dyke the Chezzetcook marshes. According to a report in The Cross, 1,800 acres of land suitable for cultivation would be reclaimed at a total cost of £2,700. The money required would be raised by selling 300 shares at a unit cost of £9. At the completion of the work, each shareholder would be granted six acres. Would-be

---
140 Nova Scotia Archives, RG-5, Series P, Vol. 52, No. 129.
141 Nova Scotia Archives, RG-5, Series P, Vol. 52, No. 107.
142 P. Lane and Associates, *Baseline Data Report and Historical Overview of the Chezzetcook Salt Marsh Prior to Highway 107 Construction*, pp. 2-8.

shareholders who did not have the money at hand could instead supply 60 days of work. The report pointed out that after the crop failures of the previous three years, many local people who could not afford to pay £9 would be unable to work for 60 days without some support from the government.[143]

The fact the project fell through suggests that the organizers were unsuccessful in raising the required sum.

In 1850, government officials finally decided to send civil engineer Charles W. Fairbanks to Chezzetcook to investigate the possibility of diking the mud flats and marshes. The engineer drafted a proposal that mapped out the area to be diked at a total cost of £7,000.[144]

It seems that no action was taken following reception of the proposal by Provincial Secretary Joseph Howe.

In 1867, a further proposal to dyke the marshes was submitted, but this time a corporation from Halifax was to direct the work, selling 5,000 shares at $10 apiece (a new Canadian currency had by then replaced the British pound).

According to Liliane Bellefontaine, Father Madden, who was resident priest at the time, convinced the inhabitants of Chezzetcook not to let outsiders take possession of their marshes, because the clams they dug on the flats, called *platains* in French, were essential to their livelihood. According to oral history accounts, the priest told them they would be "selling away their bread and butter" if they allowed the mud flats to be drained.[145]

Stories like this one show how the local priest often played the role of community leader, advising people, and serving as a spokesperson for them in various ways.

In the end, the only dyke built during the 19th century was the one situated in the narrow channel linking Chezzetcook Lake with the sea at Grand-Désert. Although this dyke was gone by the end of that century, it is remembered by the existence of "Dyke Road".

Despite the failure of attempts to fund the construction of large dykes, local farmers continued for many years to cut the salt hay that grew abundantly in the marshes at the head of Chezzetcook Inlet. The marsh was long ago divided into blocks that belonged to each family. According to Lavinia LeBlanc:

---

143 *The Cross*, November 10th 1849.
144 Nova Scotia Archives, RG-1, Series P, Vol. 259, No. 129.
145 CEAAC, Ronald Labelle Collection, accession no. 121 (1982).

Chezzetcook: an Acadian stronghold

> Everybody had a block. Some of them had two blocks. This time of year (in August), you'd see them cutting that hay and they'd be all over the marsh. They had little rigs to haul it to the boat, to dump it in the gundalow.[146]

Farmers loaded the hay onto long, flat-bottomed boats or barges known as gundalows, then floated the load down to their fields. Once the rain had rinsed away part of the salt, the hay could fed to livestock. This salt marsh hay, called *saline*, supplemented the more common type of cultivated hay called *foin doux* (sweet hay). It was so named because of its mild nature in comparison with the salt marsh hay. As local farms were not large enough to supply a great amount of cultivated hay, salt marsh hay was a welcome addition to the farm animals' diet.

The cultivated hay was the first to be harvested, and John Lapierre remembered helping his father make hay as a young boy:

> During hay season, the time when the weather was hot, the work was all done by hand. My father was handy with a scythe. He had a nice scythe. And the field was just up from our house. He would start early in the morning; at seven o'clock he started cutting hay. I went along, and I waited for him as he moved along. I enjoyed that work. I took a liking for it, and then I was always in the field with my father.[147] [translation]

The men always used oxen to haul loads of hay to the barn.

Once the cultivated hay was in, it was time to cut the salt marsh hay at the Head of Chezzetcook. To get to the hay-covered marsh, it was necessary to follow a five-kilometre-long canal known as *le grand riganeau*. The term *riganeau* comes from the French spoken centuries ago in the marshlands of the Poitou region in Western France, and is found today only in Chezzetcook. This is one of many indications of how 17th century French dialect words and expressions were preserved in Chezzetcook.

The hay cutters followed the tide up the canal in their gundalows, using two possible means of locomotion. Most of the time, the hay cutter pushed the gundalow forward by using a long pole that reached to the bottom of the canal. When the wind was favourable, a small sail was at-

---

146 Ibid., accession no. 1270 (1982).
147 Ibid., accession no. 1381 (1982).

107

tached to the mast.

The gundalow had low sides, but it was heavy-set and could hold large quantities of hay when parallel railings were attached on either side. According to Walter Myette, it could hold between two and three tonnes of hay. He recalls that each family had its own lot in the salt marshes: "I had pieces of land, lots of salt marsh that were just like owned property. It had all been leased some time before."[148] [translation]

The limits between each lot were not always clearly marked out, which sometimes caused conflicts, as Lavinia LeBlanc recounted:

> Some of them had poles, and an old piece of fence, here and there, you know. But when you see it, when it's cut it's like a lane between them, you know, a grass lane between the pieces that you can tell. I imagine it was cut years ago. Somebody would cut them with an axe or something, make a little gut, and it grew up. Cause you could easily tell what piece they owned. Sometimes they'd be arguing about it, you know.[149]

At the Head of Chezzetcook, there were no dykes to prevent the water from flooding the marsh at high tide, and it was only possible to harvest hay at low tide. The hay that grew in the highest part of the marsh was the least salted because it seldom flooded, unlike that which grew further down towards the sea. It was therefore the most valuable hay for the farmers.

Once the hay had been transported down to the village on gundalows, it was spread along the shore so that the rain would rinse out most of the salt. Then it was dried and stored in the barn, where it was mixed with cultivated hay before being fed to cattle. Farmers made sure, however, that none of the marsh hay was fed to their milk cows, because they feared the milk might take on a salty taste.

Shipbuilding

In Chezzetcook, as in many other Maritime communities, shipbuilding was a major enterprise for over one hundred years, from the beginning of the 19th century to the early decades of the 20th.

Fishing schooners were not the only vessels built in Chezzetcook.

---

148 Ibid., accession no. 1244 (1982).
149 Ibid., accession no. 1270 (1982).

Chezzetcook: an Acadian stronghold

Local Acadians were always involved in commerce, first carrying firewood to Halifax, and later bricks, sand, gravel, timber, clams and other products. They also carried goods between Prince Edward Island and Eastern Nova Scotia, and most of this trade was carried out using locally-built vessels.

Many of the schooners built in Chezzetcook in the late 19th and early 20th centuries are remembered in oral accounts. In some cases, the name of the vessel is all people remember. Among those mentioned are the *Emma M.B.*, the *Laura*, the *Minnie M.* and the *Lady Mae.*

Thanks to the extensive oral history research Lena Ferguson carried out, we know exactly when several schooners were built, and by whom:

Village Leaf: This schooner was built at Mahone Bay but owned by men from Seaforth and Grand-Désert. Anselme Lapierre was its first captain. It was large enough to carry 14 dories.

Greenleaf: Built by Martin Julien, it was owned jointly by several men from Grand-Désert and Seaforth. *The Greenleaf* is well-known because it was one of the rare ships to have been lost. It was wrecked off the Magdalen Islands in September 1900.

Sovereign: This 80-ton vessel was possibly the largest schooner built in Chezzetcook. Hauling it down to the harbour took 40 pairs of oxen, hitched up in 10 rows on either side.

Two Brothers: Built by John Bellefontaine, it had a tonnage of 30.

Widgeon: Built in 1869, owned by John Petitpas.

Condor: Built in 1873, owned by Georges Julien.

Agnes: Built by Jacob Lapierre. It was one of the smaller locally-built schooners, measuring only 40 feet in length, with a capacity of 17 tons. In 1877, it was sold by James Arnold of Jeddore for $600.[150]

Ocean Child: Built in 1879.

Seaway: Built in 1884 in Grand-Désert and owned by Gabriel Murphy.

Welcome: Built in 1884.

Princess: Built in 1889, owned by John Bellefontaine.

Maggie May: A 62-ton schooner built locally in 1891 by members of the Fillis family and later sold to John Beaver of Pleasant Harbour. It could carry 14 single-man dories.

---

150 "Bill of Sale", Acadian House Museum, West Chezzetcook, NS, Artifacts Canada accession no. 2020.28.1.

Eliza C.: Built in 1896.

Alice A.: Built in Grand-Désert in 1899.

Maggie B.: Built in 1899 by John Bellefontaine, it was later owned by Norman Chandler. It had a tonnage of 25.

Rosie M.B.: Built by four brothers of the Bonin (or Bonang) family of Grand-Désert in 1903. It was 75 feet long and had a tonnage of 75. The lumber used in the construction was obtained in the Lawrencetown area, unlike many schooners that were built using wood cut around Porter's Lake.

Shamrock: Built, or rather rebuilt, by Peter Ferguson. He bought the *Two Brothers* in 1903, rebuilt it from the keel up, and renamed it. The Bellefontaines once again became owners of the vessel around 1917 and it was one of the last to sail out of Chezzetcook

Grand-Désert: Built in 1904 at the foot of the hill on Dyke Road, it was 74 feet long and had a tonnage of 65 and was one of the last large schooners built for the cod fishery and served as a replacement for the *Greenleaf*. Martin Julien was managing owner.

Marie Stella: Built in 1906 in Grand-Désert, it belonged to Simon Lapierre. The name refers to the Acadian anthem, "Ave Marie Stella". According to Luc Bellefontaine, it was the last schooner built by the Lapierre family.

Crouzier B.: Built in 1908 by Joseph and John Bellefontaine of West Chezzetcook. It was named after Father Jules Crouzier, the well-liked priest who ministered to local parishioners during the 1880s.

The Oriole B.: Built in 1908 by Joseph and John Bellefontaine. It was 60 feet long and had a tonnage of 33.

Cecilia B.: Built by James Bellefontaine, it was one of the last schooners to sail from West Chezzetcook. In 1919, the owner sold the schooner to Craigen Young of West Petpeswick for $1,600 and the buyer agreed to pay $600 in advance. One detail contained in the written agreement of sale shows how sailing was a precarious activity: "Should the said Schooner Cecilia B of Halifax be wrecked, lost or damaged on her voyage to Halifax, the said James Bellefontaine shall refund the money."[151]

In shipbuilding, many tricks of the trade were passed on informally from one generation to the next, but the builders also used specialized technical manuals. One of these was a *Registry of Shipping with Standard Rules for Construction and Classification,* published in Nova Scotia in 1866.

Most of the materials used to build a schooner were obtained locally. When a project began, a group of men would cut all the necessary wood in the nearby forest around Porter's Lake. Logs were squared on the spot and were hauled to the village using oxen. White spruce was the most commonly used type of wood. Large tree roots were also harvested for use in making the ship's keel.

Local sawmills prepared all the necessary lumber, while blacksmiths in the area did the ironwork. Acadians have always been renowned for their woodworking skills, while blacksmithing was left to people of German or Scottish descent.

Sail-making was accomplished with materials purchased in Halifax, but local women sewed the sails, using a pattern.

Schooners were often built several kilometres from the sea, and when they were ready to be launched, it was necessary to hitch to them several teams of oxen, who slowly hauled the vessels down to Chezzetcook Inlet, sliding them over parallel logs.

According to the Nova Scotia census of 1861, during the previous year alone, 15 ships were built at Chezzetcook. Most of these were probably small fishing vessels. A ship registry published by the Department of Marine and Fisheries in 1911 lists a total of 33 schooners built in Chezzetcook or Grand-Désert, many of which belonged to Acadians. The size of these schooners varied considerably, as we can judge from the previous list.

While little is known about most of the schooners, the building of the *Oriole B.* was very well documented thanks to a letter published by the Halifax *Daily Recorder* at the time of its launching in 1908 and thanks to oral information obtained in 1978 from two of the builder's sons, Luc and Arthur Bellefontaine.[152]

The Bellefontaine family built the *Oriole B.* with help from a ship's car-

---

151 "Agreement", Acadian House Museum, West Chezzetcook, NS, Artifacts Canada accession no. 2020.11.15.
152 Lena Ferguson, "The Days of the Schooner, part 2", *Dartmouth Free Press*, 15 March 1978, 2nd section, p. 9.

Ronald Labelle

penter living in East Chezzetcook. During the winter of 1906, the men began cutting the necessary lumber on a woodlot belonging to John Bellefontaine at Porter's Lake. They started by digging out the large roots used for building the keel, knees and ribs of the schooner. The trees were felled with axe and cross-cut saw and the timbers were hand hewn with an axe. The sawmill at Porter's Lake prepared the planks.

That winter, there was very little ice on Porter's Lake, and it was impossible to use oxen to haul the wood over the lake. The men had to haul some of the wood through the forest by hand over a distance of about eight kilometres to get to West Chezzetcook. The remainder of the wood was cut the following winter when ice conditions made it possible to haul heavy loads over the lake.

Construction began in the spring of 1907 and ended with the ship's launching on March 3rd 1908. The large timbers used were bolted together, while the ribs were fastened using wooden plugs.

The *Oriole B* was one of the larger schooners, and one of the last to be built locally. Its launching was a grand occasion.

Five days later, the Halifax *Daily Recorder* published a long letter describing the event. The letter was simply signed "Acadian Fishwife", but was generally thought to be the work of writer Margaret McLaren of West Chezzetcook. The heading states "Schooner Aurel B. Launched", reflecting the confusion about the actual name of the vessel.

A story is told about how a four-year old boy named Aurèle Bellefontaine climbed a 20-foot ladder to the decks of the schooner while it was under construction. Captain John Bellefontaine cautiously climbed the ladder and brought the child down safely. According to the story, it was then decided the schooner would be named "Aurèle".

Luc Bellefontaine told a completely different story. He said his father John had asked him to suggest a name. Looking through a book about birds, he saw the name "Oriole" and suggested the schooner be named *Oriole B.*, the letter B standing for Bellefontaine. This version represents the official name given to the vessel when it was registered.

While it may seem surprising to find two completely different explanations of how the vessel was named, this is not at all unusual, because oral history accounts explaining origins often contain contradictory stories.

The article by Margaret Maclaren tells of how groups of men got together at the Bellefontaine household to help with the launching. First, the local priest blessed the schooner and christened her. Then the work began.

Chezzetcook: an Acadian stronghold

It was a long and difficult process, because the vessel had to slide along wide poles placed along the trajectory and as it advanced, it was necessary to move the poles from the back to the front.

> ... all the ropes and chains being in place, the launch was on. (...) The schooner was built in such a way that she had to be turned so as to slip more easily down the incline to the water. Now all is in readiness. The drivers of the cattle yelled, "Get up," and those who pulled the ropes roared, "Heave," and she swung round right where they wanted her. (...) Then out came Captain John with his face all wreathed in smiles, and one of those big yellow jars he held in his hand. After everyone was refreshed, the cattle were turned and the men paid out the hawsers and once more "Get up" and "Heave," and the vessel started down the hill. Captain Martin Julien was in command of everyone and everything. It was most interesting to see the long double row of oxen, fifty oxen I think, and fifty men pulling away with a will and whim which was to say the least astonishing. At last they have the schooner on the shore. (...) Afloat in the channel the schooner was later completed and fitted with two spars, a topmast and sails.[153]

It took all day to haul the schooner down to the shore, and once there, the men discovered the ice was too weak to carry it over the distance that separated it from the channel where the launching would be held. The next day, they hauled it along the shore as far as the brickyard, where the channel was deep enough to float the vessel.

Angus Roma, who was a young boy at the time of the launching, watched as thirty or more men slowly hauled the ship with oxen.[154] Luc Bellefontaine remembered that a social gathering took place when the work was over, complete with a big meal, despite the fact that the launching was taking place during Lent.[155]

The *Oriole B.* was one of the last locally-built schooners to sail the Atlantic. When steel ships began to replace wooden schooners, shipbuilding activities declined in Chezzetcook as they did elsewhere in the Maritimes.

Many small, family-run sawmills experienced difficulties caused by

---

153 Idem.
154 Eastern Shore Archives, Lena Ferguson Collection, tape 6838, Angus Roma (14 February 1977).
155 Ibid, Luc Bellefontaine (21 February 1978).

the changes in the shipbuilding industry. The 1861 Nova Scotia census gives us an idea of the importance of the lumber industry in the 19th century. It states that, in 1860 alone, 17,000 feet of pine boards were sawn in Chezzetcook, as well as 30,000 feet of spruce and hemlock.

Most sawmills were water-powered, but there was at least one powered by wind. Eloi Bellefontaine, of West Chezzetcook, owned a small sawmill that produced shingles and laths. He had built it using the mechanism from a shut-down gristmill at Porter's Lake.[156]

Figure 16: Éloi Bellefontaine working at a local sawmill in 1933.

Brickmaking

The 1861 Nova Scotia Census reflects the increasing importance of the brick industry in Chezzetcook. It lists 42 heads of families as being brickmakers. While the 1851 census reported a total of 626,000 bricks manufactured during the previous year, the figure for 1861 was even more impressive, citing a total of 936,000 bricks.

While the 1851 census was the first to mention the production of bricks at Chezzetcook, we know that the industry began earlier on. According to Joseph Purcell, there were already brickyards in a district

---

156 CEAAC, Ronald Labelle Collection, accession no. 1155 (1982).

called Grosse-Pointe at the end of the 18th century.[157] Liliane Bellefontaine stated that Lloyd Shaw, the founder of the Shaw brick company in Halifax, first learned brickmaking techniques from the men in Chezzetcook.[158]

We know for certain that the brickyards were very active before 1851 thanks to the April 4th 1846 edition of *The Cross* that included an article encouraging local brickmakers to bid for a lucrative government contract:

> ... we beg to direct their attention to an advertisement which has appeared during the last three or four weeks in the *Times* & *Acadian Recorder* in which the Government offer to receive tenders for the supply of 100,000 ch. bricks this summer. Here is an opportunity for securing employment to members, and for attracting some useful dollars to the spot.

In Chezzetcook itself, locally-made bricks were used for part of the construction of Saint Anselm parish church in 1894, thanks to Father Philias-Honoré Labrecque, a parish priest from Québec who took an active interest in the development of the community.

While the Diocese of Halifax was in favour of the construction of a simple wooden church, many parishioners hoped it could be built with local bricks. Father Labrecque intervened in their favour and the plan was adopted. The construction was a community effort, each family donating approximately 400 bricks.[159]

Unfortunately, it was not possible to build the entire structure using local bricks, because good quality clay was becoming hard to obtain locally. Bricks made in Chezzetcook were found to be too soft to be used on the exterior of the building, so their use was limited to the interior.

While St. Anselm's church is considered by many to be a testimony to the flourishing brick industry that once existed in the community, in reality, its outer walls are made from bricks manufactured in Québec.

Thousands of bricks from Chezzetcook were regularly sent to Halifax, where they were used both for building and road work. When the first tramway was built in Halifax, the base on which the tracks were laid was paved with bricks from Chezzetcook.

---

157 Joseph Purcell, *Acadian Architecture and Cultural History of Chezzetcook*, p. 13.
158 CEAAC, Ronald Labelle Collection, ms. 110 (1982).
159 Purcell, p. 13.

Figure 17: Using an ox to power the clay mixer at a Chezzetcook brickyard.

Bricks were one of the many goods that were transported to awaiting schooners using gundalows. The gundalow was also put to use to transport large quantities of sand from a breakwater beach up along the inlet to the brickyard. The sand was mixed in with clay before the bricks were molded.

According to Ulysse Murphy[160], all the brick kilns were wood fired. As a large quantity of softwood was necessary to fire up the kilns, gundalows were once again used to transport the material. A loaded gundalow could carry about three cords of wood.

Local residents spent part of the winter chopping fir trees on woodlots around the Head of Chezzetcook so that they could supply the brickyard with the necessary fuel.

The brickyard was only operative in the summer, because bricks had to be dried in the sun. The work began in early June, when clay was combined with sand in a mixer called a "pug". It was driven by an ox that walked in circles, pulling a long pole connected to the mixer in the centre.

Brick-molds, each containing either three or six bricks, were filled by hand. Women were sometimes hired to carry out the task of filling the

---

160 CEAAC, Ronald Labelle Collection, accession no. 1347 (1982).

molds. As each mold was carefully filled, the women made sure no pebbles got into the mix, which had to be entirely made up of clay and fine sand.

Boys were also hired as summer labourers to carry out various tasks, such as carrying bricks and shoveling clay.

Loading and unloading the kilns was backbreaking work. Éloi Bellefontaine remembered being hired as a helper at the brickyard when he was only 10 years old.[161]

Many residents interviewed by Lena Ferguson during the 1970 and 1980s remembered the accidental death of a young man at the brickyard, even though the accident took place in the early part of the 20th century. According to Luc Bellefontaine, a group of men were working on a steep face of clay, driving crowbars into the ground and pouring water into the cavities to break apart the deposits of clay. These deposits could be as much as 25 feet deep (8m). A young man named Roma was working down below when a huge mound of clay suddenly fell on him, crushing him to death. Some people said the victim was just a boy, one of the young helpers who worked at the brickyard during the summer.[162]

Once the bricks were shaped in the molds, they were removed and stacked in rows to be dried in the sun. This took the better part of the summer. When the weather was rainy, it was sometimes necessary to build shelters made of boards that covered the stacks of drying bricks.

By the end of the summer, it was time to fire up the kilns. Each kiln had about twenty chambers where hundreds of bricks could bake at the same time. The brickmakers were able to judge by experience how many days the bricks should be exposed to the heat. They also needed to estimate the appropriate temperature.

When the bricks were removed, the ones that had been closest to the fire in the central part of the kiln had been exposed to the highest temperature and were therefore more resistant than the rows of bricks that had been furthest from the fire. These two grades of bricks were then kept separate.

According to Angus Roma, the higher-grade bricks were also prepared differently from the others, the clay and sand being mixed together for a longer time period. The softer bricks, while unsuitable for exterior walls, could be used indoors, for instance, to build fireplaces.

---

161 Eastern Shore Archives, Lena Ferguson Collection, tape 6714, Éloi Bellefontaine (27 March 1980).
162 Ibid., tape 6756, Liliane Bellefontaine (27 April 1981).

Angus Roma remembered that young boys would lie on the ground watching the fire from the kilns, and if they fell asleep, the workers would play a trick on them, blackening their faces with soot.[163]

According to Luc Bellefontaine, as many as 13 kilns operated at different times, but some had ceased to exist before the end of the 19th century. Members of the Bellefontaine family managed most of them: Benjamin, Dennis, Andrew, Jim, Arthur, Roderick, Charles, William, Paul and Joseph

Figure 18: Using a portable sawmill to chop firewood.

Bellefontaine all ran kilns. Stephen Bellefontaine remembered that the last kilns to shut down in the early 20th century belonged to Joseph Belle-

---

163 Ibid., tape 6838, Angus Roma (14 February 1977).

fontaine, Paul Bellefontaine and Joseph Roma.[164] It is not clear how members of the Bellefontaine family obtained the specialized knowledge necessary to successfully manufacture bricks.

Luc Bellefontaine remembered that a few brickyards were owned by other families in the area, for example at East Chezzetcook, where the Redmonds and Meisners established kilns. But not all were successful at producing bricks that had the necessary strength for building purposes.

Many young men who worked at the brickyard were later able to draw on their experience to obtain work elsewhere in the brick industry. William Manette, for example, told of how he had gone to work at a brickyard at Barney's Brook, preparing brickmolds and loading and unloading the kilns. His father was a foreman at the brickyard, and several workers from Chezzetcook and Grand-Désert joined him there.[165]

Sawmills, windmills and local factories

While many young people left Chezzetcook to seek work opportunities, some were able to get by combining various occupations.

Like everywhere else in the Maritimes, the Chezzetcook area had local sawmills that provided temporary employment, and a portable sawmill was available during the early 20th century. It was hauled from one farm to the next and, at each stop, a group of men would help a family saw the logs they would need for home heating and other uses. This provided an ingenious, low-cost service to the community.

In addition, there was a windmill in the community at one time. It appeared to be in disuse in 1930, according to an archival photograph (see next page) taken that year, bearing the title: "Old type of windmill used for grinding grain at French-Acadian settlement of West Chezzetcook."[166]

Several small factories operated in the area during the late 19th and early 20th centuries. In addition, a gold mine is believed to have existed near East Chezzetcook, but it closed long ago. Companies from outside the area generally owned the local factories.

Many local women had low paying jobs in a clothing factory that operated from the 1870s until 1892. It was run in an attractive building, topped by a weathervane, that was situated beside the brook that runs from Manette's Lake to Chezzetcook Harbour. The factory seems to have

---

164 Ibid., tape 6751, Stephen Bellefontaine (3 December 1977).
165 Ibid., tape M25-A, William Manette (22 February 1992).
166 Public Archives of Nova Scotia, photograph by Allen Fraser, 1 June 1930. Accession number 8008.

been an outlet of a clothing firm in Halifax by the name of Doull and Miller. After it closed, it became a boarding house called "Brookside

Figure 19: Windmill photographed by Allen Fraser in 1930 (Nova Scotia Archives).

House" and it was finally torn down around 1920.[167]

As was the case with the brick industry, people who worked at the

---

[167] Lena Ferguson, "Chezzetcook Clothing Factory Recalled", *Dartmouth Free Press*, 2 November 1977.

clothing factory acquired specialized skills that enabled them to work in the same field once they left their home community. A man named Fred Murphy, for example, first worked at the factory and later ran a clothing store of his own.[168]

In the early 1930s, a lobster canning factory was set up with help from Acadians who had experience in the New Brunswick lobster industry. Situated on the Causeway Road at Threefathom Harbour, the factory is described in detail by Mary Jane Wolfe in chapter 8. This was at a time when small canneries were built all around the Maritimes to serve the New England market. Apart from giving the fishers an opportunity to sell their catch, they provided much needed employment for local women.

An article published in May 1939 in the Acadian newspaper *L'Évangéline* praised the existence of the canning factory, stating that 19 local fishers had united their efforts, using $6,000 they had saved at their credit union, and doing much of the construction work themselves. Their local credit union had been established with support from the parish priest, at a time when the Catholic Church encouraged participation in the co-operative movement. The article added that, aside from creating much-needed jobs, the factory had enabled the fishers to obtain a better price for their lobsters because it was run on a co-operative basis.[169]

Despite the enthusiastic tone of the article, the lobster factory soon had to close because the well it depended on could not supply enough fresh water for the boiler. The factory was then dismantled and transported to Grand-Désert, where it was rebuilt and transformed into a clam-canning factory run by an American company. According to Ferdinand Julien, clams were brought there from various places in wooden boxes named "hods". They were chucked on a table and then steamed, later to be packed and shipped to Boston.[170] As was the case with the lobster factory, much of the work was carried out by women.

The clam factory was only operational during the 1940s and 1950s, as it was forced to close when clams became less abundant.

Women who were looking for ways to earn money had one other option in the early 20th century: preparing eelgrass suitable for stuffing mattresses. An anonymous newspaper clipping from 1922 describes sev-

---

168 Eastern Shore Archives, Lena Ferguson Collection, tape 6762, Luc Bellefontaine (23 September 1976).
169 *L'Évangéline*, 18 May 1939, p. 1.
170 Eastern Shore Archives, Lena Ferguson Collection, tape J-1, Ferdinand Julien (1 March 1990).

eral traditional activities in the community, including the preparation of eelgrass for mattresses:

> For twenty years, Mrs. Romo worked at carding seaweed. She gathered it, took it into the fields, cleaned and dried it and carded it with her hands and loaded it for her husband to sell to be made into mattresses.[171]

Centenarian Margaret Lapierre informed Lena Ferguson in 1979 that Louis Romo (or Roma) carried the carded eelgrass by ox-cart to Mineville, where it was stuffed into cotton mattress cases, which were then sold in Halifax.

In the 1930s, a blight nearly wiped out all the eelgrass that grew along our shores, and that put an end to its use for mattress making. A few decades would pass before eelgrass once again became abundant.

Taking produce to Halifax

Any history of work activities in Chezzetcook must take into account the important role Halifax played in the local economy, as it provided a market for various products.

Unlike other rural communities, the residents of Chezzetcook were involved in commercial activities very early on. From the time of its founding, Halifax depended on the delivery of firewood from outlying areas like Chezzetcook. This fact is revealed in an 1834 petition to the Nova Scotia Legislative Assembly regarding the proposed dyke at the Head of Chezzetcook, where petitioners mentioned that they earned most of their revenue by selling wood to Halifax.[172] The petition stated that the inhabitants of Chezzetcook owned between 40 and 50 vessels that brought each year about 2,000 cords of firewood to Halifax, besides other wooden articles.[173]

Over the years, products such sawn timber, sand, gravel and especially bricks were added to the list of those carried to markets in Halifax. Local men also took part in the important ice trade, chopping ice on local lakes and transporting it to Halifax, where it was sold for iceboxes.

The roads leading from Chezzetcook to Halifax by way of Mineville

---

171 "Chezzetcook, a little bit of Arcadia" (newspaper clipping), 1922, Acadian House Museum, West Chezzetcook.
172 P. Lane and Associates, *Baseline Data Report...*, pp. 2-14.
173 Purcell, p. 15.

Chezzetcook: an Acadian stronghold

began to improve around 1825 and it became possible for people to walk to the market to sell a wide variety of products, including vegetables, broad beans, berries, wild rabbits, partridges, clams, smelts, chickens, eggs, butter, buttermilk, summer savoury, handmade baskets, home spun wool, hand-knit socks and mittens, woven cloth and even spring mayflowers.

As many of these products were unavailable elsewhere in Halifax, buyers depended on the weekly visits of vendors from Chezzetcook. Some even made trips from town to obtain local products like broad beans and summer savoury in Chezzetcook.[174]

Despite a gradual improvement in the roads, the trip still involved considerable difficulty, as it meant walking 30 kilometres or more, in all kinds of weather, carrying produce or bringing it by oxcart. It was even sometimes necessary for people to pull the heavy carts themselves.

Once the vendors arrived in Dartmouth, they would leave their horse or ox at a livery stable, cross the harbour on the paddlewheel ferry, and cart produce uphill to the market.

In a newspaper clipping dated 1933, Mrs. George Lapierre recounted that she had begun to make the trek to the market fifty years earlier, bringing eggs, cream, buttermilk and cheese curds. She recounted:

> We used to leave home at 8 o'clock the night before marketing days and reach Dartmouth in the early hours of the morning and then wait around for the first ferry boat to Halifax. The market was then located about the Post Office. I never had any trouble getting rid of 400 dozen fresh eggs before noon came along![175]

Wheelbarrows were sometimes used to carry buckets of clams and other produce. Some vendors would go from door-to-door in Halifax, selling clams that were dished out from a bucket using a ladle. Eventually, they began to bottle clams to sell at the market.

One enterprising man from Chezzetcook had prepared a large bucket with a partition in the middle. The top part was filled with clams, but the hidden part below carried rum to be sold in town. According to Eugene Bellefontaine, he was eventually caught by the authorities and forced to

---

174 Eastern Shore Archives, Lena Ferguson Collection, tape 6790, Annie Ferguson (28 April 1976).
175 "Recalls Old Days at Post Office Market", Acadian House Museum, West Chezzetcook, Artifacts Canada accession no. 2020.36.9

pay a stiff fine.[176]

There are many such stories from the rum-running days in Chezzetcook, such as the one about a local man who hollowed out logs of fir trees in which to hide bottles of rum, covering the extremities with wooden plugs. The vessel he used for rum running brought these hollowed-out logs to offshore suppliers and when it returned, the logs—filled with bottles—were floated to shore, where they were loaded onto carts. This enabled the rumrunner to cart his illicit stash to his clients without fear of being detected.[177]

When local ships were not engaged in the fishery, people could sometimes take advantage of the shipping that went on between Chezzetcook and Halifax, sending their products to the market on vessels carrying wood and other freight.

However, wood could not be delivered to Halifax by ship while the large sailing vessels were all far away in the Gulf of St. Lawrence. It was impossible to haul a heavy load of firewood along that distance on foot, and it was sometimes necessary to row all the way to Halifax in order to sell the wood.

As seen in the previous chapter, women would walk all night to be at the Halifax market in the morning, returning later in the day. The previously-quoted newspaper clipping describing Chezzetcook in 1922 presented an account of trips to the market by a centenarian, Mrs. Romo (or Roma). Given her age, her account harkens back to 19th century life in the community:

> Her gifts were many and varied. She acted as a barber for the village. She would go fishing with the nets herself. She would row to Halifax. She picked berries, twenty quarts at a time and carried them twenty miles to sell—knitting as she walked the way back. Mrs. Romo has only been in Halifax for a day at a time to market.[178]

In the late 19th century, Gilmore Brown, an engineer from Fredericton, New Brunswick, entertained members of his literary club with an anecdote about a meeting with a man named Bellefontaine, who had brought a load of bricks to sell in Halifax in 1886 or 1887. The members of his

---

176 Eastern Shore Archives, Lena Ferguson Collection, tape 6757, Eugene Bellefontaine (4 April 1977).
177 CEAAC, Ronald Labelle Collection, ms. 157 (1982).
178 CEAAC, Ronald Labelle Collection, ms. 157 (1982).

club were so taken by the description of the quaint Acadian from Chezzetcook that poet Bliss Carman and a few other members composed the slightly-condescending "Chezzetcook Song". The song was such a success that they even named their literary club in Fredericton "The Bellefontaine Club".[179]

Although the "Chezzetcook Song" presents a stereotypical view of the Acadians as simple, happy peasants, it is interesting because of the chorus, which lists local products that were offered for sale both at the market and elsewhere in Halifax:

> Do you want to buy the mitt, the sock, the ganzy frock,
> The juniper post, the mussel or the clam,
> The blueberry, the foxberry, the huckleberry, the cranberry,
> The smelt, the pelt, the forty-foot ladder,
> The thousand of brick or the sand?

Ladders were one wooden product that was commonly made to be sold in Halifax, while the other one, the juniper post, was used to hold up clothes lines.

Not only did people go to Halifax to sell food and goods that they produced themselves, but there were some who earned a living buying local products in order to sell them at the market. William Lapierre told of how his father-in-law would buy eggs, poultry and calves in Chezzetcook. Every weekend, he would bring meat and eggs to sell in Halifax. In summer, he also carried fresh garden produce. He would leave with his horse and cart at midnight on Friday, and would be home the following night.[180] According to his grandson, Edwin Lapierre, he made a good living as a merchant: "My grandfather, he was one of the lucky ones. He did well at the market. He always had food on the table."[181] [translation]

During the Depression years in the 1930s, many people depended on money earned in Halifax by selling clams gathered on the flats at Chezzetcook. According to William Lapierre, the wide expanse of sand in which people could dig for clams at low tide was like a gold mine for Chezzetcook.[182]

---

179 J. J. F. Winslow, "The Bellefontaine Club".
180 CEAAC, Ronald Labelle Collection, accession no. 1334 (1982).
181 Ibid., accession no. 1306 (1982).
182 Ibid., accession no. 2613 (1986).

Local residents told of many people who were able to avoid applying for relief payments during the Depression thanks to the money obtained through the sale of clams. Captains of Lunenberg schooners would pay $5 a barrel for salt clams that they used as bait during the summer fishing season. Lavinia Roma remembered that at her home, the whole family worked at shelling and salting the clams, as well as packing them in barrels. One of her brothers then took them to market.[183]

Although the trek to Halifax was exhausting, people enjoyed the social aspect of their experience at the market, where they sometimes met other Francophones. For example, there was a French Consul in Halifax who befriended the family of Napoléon Julien and who sometimes took his family on visits to the Julien home in Grand-Désert.[184]

Travelling between Chezzetcook and Halifax gradually became easier during the first half of the 20th century. A passenger train began to do the run in 1917, around the time a new indoor market opened in Halifax. Later on, a locally-run bus service was established, with a schedule devised to accommodate marketgoers. Space was provided at the back of the bus for storing baskets of produce.

Figure 20: The bus that travelled between Chezzetcook and Halifax, passing by St. Anselm's Church, circa 1940.

In hindsight, the Acadians of Chezzetcook contributed greatly to the quality of life in the provincial capital by supplying the residents of Halifax with everything from herbs to wooden ladders. This fact certainly deserves to be better recognized today.

---

183 Ibid.. Ms. 119 (1982).
184 Dillman.

Figure 21: Eugene Bellefontaine gathering clams in 1977.

Ronald Labelle

6: Folkways and traditions

Preserving Acadian material culture
It is fascinating to see how French traditions from the 18th century were maintained in Chezzetccok, given that people there rarely interacted with other Acadian groups and were in much closer contact with the English-speaking population of Halifax and surrounding areas. Chezzetcook was never an isolated community. In the fishing industry, as we have seen, the Acadians of Grand-Désert often worked with people of German descent from Seaforth and Threefathom Harbour.

Yet, despite their lack of contact with other members of the Acadian diaspora, people in West Chezzetcook and Grand-Désert were able to maintain a strong Acadian identity.

In chapter 4, we saw how several 19th century travellers described Chezzetcook as a quaint, traditional French community lying at the heart of English-speaking Nova Scotia. In the eyes of these writers, the most picturesque feature of the local Acadians was their clothing, which seemed to belong to an earlier era.

This sparked an interest in the dress worn in Chezzetcook, and the Nova Scotia Museum eventually acquired several articles of clothing dating from the mid-19th century. A 1935 report on the museum collection stated that the articles of clothing "are survivals of the original costume of the old Acadian French women of this province, as worn at the period of the French occupation, and therefore are of great interest historically."[185]

The report includes a description of a man's waistcoat or gilet that had been worn by Charles Bellefontaine (1816-1902) and is accompanied by the following note: "On everyday occasions the Chezzetcook Frenchmen wore a grey homespun coat and trousers, and a home-knitted white guernsey with indigo-blue spots in it. A soft felt hat was usually worn on the head."

---
185 Harry Piers, *Report on the Provincial Museum for 1934-35*, pp. 28-29.

Chezzetcook: an Acadian stronghold

The woman's costume included in the Nova Scotia Museum collection consists of a white net bridal cap worn only on a wedding day, a black kerchief of cotton-backed satin worn on ordinary days, a short jacket or *mantelet* of reddish-brown print cotton, and a black-and-white striped skirt of heavy homespun that had been worn by Mrs. Marguerite Bellefontaine (1824-1910) on Sundays and holidays. The report adds, "Those [skirts] worn every day and to the Halifax market were of ordinary grey homespun."

The woven skirt worn by Marguerite Bellefontaine has been used as a model for reconstructions of the Acadian traditional costume at Grand-Pré Historic Park and also at the Village Historique Acadien in Caraquet, New Brunswick. It has been part of several exhibits and one report described it in these words: "This is the only old Acadian skirt known to have survived in its original form (…) the skirt is a very rare and interesting piece."[186]

By maintaining their traditional dress through most of the 19th century, the people of Chezzetcook thus made a significant contribution to the preservation of Acadian heritage in the Maritimes.

The 1935 museum report stated: "Such types of costumes survived at Chezzetcook till about 1910." A more recent museum report, this one dated 1999, estimated that the traditional pattern of striped woven skirts lasted only until the middle of the 19th century.[187]

Both reports could bear some truth, as the traditional French costume may have begun to go out of style by the mid-19th century in most Acadian areas of the Maritimes, while remaining in use in Chezzetcook for a while longer.

Some elements of the traditional Acadian dress are certain to have remained in vogue even after the first decade of the 20th century. An anonymous article written about Chezzetcook in 1922 has this to say about clothing: "In dress, the old-fashioned handkerchief for the head and shawl for the shoulders play a prominent part, and the world's changing styles do not trouble the delightfully simple life of this Acadian village."[188]

The article provides us with a view of what the community looked like at that particular point in time, before the arrival of electricity:

---

186 Harold B. and Dorothy K. Burnham, *'Keep Me Warm One Night': Early Handweaving in Eastern Canada*, p. 64.
187 Brenda Dunn, "Certains aspects de la vie des femmes dans l'ancienne Acadie", p. 38.
188 "Chezzetcook, a little bit of Arcadia" (newspaper clipping), 1922, Acadian House Museum.

> There is no electricity and no telephones. Poles for the latter are there but they are wireless. (...) There are but few instruments of music here, but the people are good singers, many of the older ones being able to read the music of the Plain Chant and sing it. There is no hall for amusement. The houses are low. They contain a living room with a few bedrooms leading off the living room and which are just large enough to contain a bed. As a rule, the upstairs is unfinished. A small porch adjoining the house is used in summer to cook in. The stove, an old-fashioned Waterloo, with the oven half way up the stove pipe, is the only heater in the house. Not more that ten houses with a pump are to be found. All carry their water, and the houses are spotlessly clean and the floors covered with mats of their own making.[189]

From this article, it appears that few modern amenities were present in 1922, as most people still drew their water directly from outdoor wells. This was also the practice in local schools, where pupils were sent to fetch buckets of water from wells. John Lapierre, who helped to bring water to Saint Mary's school in Grand-Désert as a 12-year-old pupil in 1913, mentioned one curious fact about wells. He remembered that tiny eels could be seen at the bottom of the spring-fed well near his school and said people considered that the eels helped to keep the water pure.[190]

The article also mentioned the practice of avoiding the summer heat by using a side porch as a kitchen. This was common practice in houses throughout French Canada, where the porch was referred to as the *cuisine d'été*.

The early 20th century was a time when the community was almost self-sufficient and kept purchases to a minimum, the cast-iron kitchen stove being the only expensive product that had to be bought. Before the arrival of foundry-made stoves, all cooking had to be done using pots hung over the fire in an open hearth. The large pot used for cooking was called a *créminière*, the word Acadians used for the standard French *crémaillère*.

Cast-iron stoves not only made cooking easier, but were also more efficient for heating the house.

---

189 Idem.
190 Ferguson, *History of Saint Mary's School, Grand Desert*.

Almost all the materials needed for building were obtained locally. For example, when a new roof was put on a house, sheets of birch bark were placed beneath the wooden shingles as a protective layer. Birch bark was ideal for this purpose as it was waterproof and did not rot.[191]

Many of the solidly built houses from the 19th century are still standing, They generally include wooden beams assembled using the dovetail technique. Being skilled at woodworking, men would not only build their own houses and barns, but would make their own oars and axe handles, besides making ladders which they sold in Halifax.

One example of the Acadians' frugal nature was their practice of whitewashing houses, rather than using store bought paint. Buildings whitewashed with lime tended to gradually lose their covering and it was generally necessary to repeat the process every year. In Chezzetcook, however, an ingenious process was devised to make the lime adhere better to the wooden exterior of the houses. Lime was mixed with lard or fat before being applied to the walls, therefore becoming denser and more resistant to the elements.

Normal School student Emma Julien provided another portrait of the community in the early 20th century. In her essay "History of Grand Desert", she states that in early houses, unfinished interior walls were covered with tree bark. This practice had been dropped by the turn of the 20th century because of the availability of store-bought wallpaper.

Another detail contained in the essay has to do with footwear: "On their feet they wore wooden shoes and moccasins which they made from the skins of animals especially of cows."[192]

This interesting essay also describes communal work activities, in which twenty or more men would gather to raise a building or haul a new vessel to the shore. The author describes "chopping parties", in which firewood was prepared, and "haulings" when the wood was delivered to people who didn't own oxen or a team of horses.

Regarding women's work, she adds that "women would have knitting, carding, spinning, sewing parties" lasting all afternoon. The women would share stories as they worked together, and the session would end with a cup of tea and sometimes an evening meal.

---

191 CEAAC, Ronald Labelle Collection, accession no. 1357 (1982).
192 Julien.

Ronald Labelle

Yearly traditions: winter

In Chezzetcook, many traditional customs and habits were maintained intact and passed down from one generation to the next. It was essentially a Roman Catholic community in which seasonal activities unfolded according to a traditional sequence determined partially by the religious calendar and partially by the cycle of the seasons.

Winter was the busiest season for social activities. The men who worked outside of the area during the rest of the year were home then, and it was an ideal time for socializing.

Although many work activities stopped in winter, it was the time when firewood was obtained from woodlots at the head of Porter's Lake. There, the men chopped all the wood they would need in the coming year. As the woodlots were situated several kilometres from their homes, they hauled the logs out on sleds pulled by oxen or horses.

Figure 22: Edouard Julien and Alban Bellefontaine hauling logs from a woodlot.

When they had large quantities of wood to haul, they would organize a hauling bee, with each participant supplying one or two oxen. According

Chezzetcook: an Acadian stronghold

to Walter Myette, as many as a dozen teams of oxen could be hitched up to a load of wood.[193]

Being familiar with the local woods, many residents also had hunting camps where they set snares to trap hares during the winter. Aside from carrying the usual supplies of salt pork, bread, molasses and tea, they often brought along corn meal to make johnnycakes at their camps or cook over an open fire during lunch breaks in the woods.

Teams of horses were rarely seen in Chezzetcook because of their high cost. The task of hauling wood from the forest to the village using oxen could last more than one day.

The work all ended with a party where the host family supplied homemade beer, as Lavinia LeBlanc remembered:

> When we first went down Threefathom Harbour, that was in 1920s, we used to go to work and the neighbours used to go together, and they'd have what they called a wood cuttin' party, you know? They'd go for two or three days, and they'd cut you enough wood for the winter ... for winter, spring, for the spring, summer. And then they'd have what they called a haulin' day. They'd go with their creatures, or animals or horses or whatever they had. They'd haul it all home to you ... put it into your yard. But then you used to have to give them a party for it. And I had made a 10-gallon keg of beer. That's what they liked. It wasn't liquor that went them times. It was more that homemade brew. I had made 10 gallons of it. We had it down the basement, cellar. And we had a great big sauerkraut, pies and everything that went with it. I imagine there was about six men, with your husband that would be seven hands haulin' the wood home, you know. Well, then you'd have to ask their family too, so their family would come in the evening. Everybody would come for supper. I had it in my house.[194]

Lavinia LeBlanc remembered that hops grown in local gardens were combined with raisins, potatoes, molasses, sugar and water, all the ingredients used to make the homebrew that was shared on special occasions.

When the winter freeze-up happened on the waters of Chezzetcook

---

193 CEAAC, Ronald Labelle Collection, accession no. 1239 (1982).
194 Ibid., accession no. 1701 (1983).

Ronald Labelle

Inlet, it became possible to cross on the ice from West to East Chezzetcook. Although the Acadian population was concentrated on the western side of the inlet, there were many social contacts between communities on both sides. Liliane Bellefontaine recalls how people used to risk crossing the ice:

> Sunday afternoons, we would leave after mass to visit friends over in East Chezzetcook. It was some time into winter because the channel took time to freeze up, you know. There is a big channel over here in the middle, and we had to wait until the really cold weather had set in so the channel would freeze because we had to cross that channel. And it only lasted for a while. When the weather became warmer after that, well it was over. We couldn't go over the channel anymore. The rest of the inlet was frozen, but the channel was always dangerous, you know. Yes, that's because of the tides that come and go.[195] [translation]

During the winter, children's pastimes included sliding down hills on homemade sleds and skating on the inlet. They wore skates with blades made by local blacksmiths.

Adults would spend long winter evenings playing cards. The most popular card game was called forty-five. The players would get together informally for matches, with prizes such as wool socks, mittens, or wild hares snared in the nearby woods.

Dances organized on behalf of the local parish church were another form of entertainment during the winter. These events were called "pie socials" because women would bake pies that were auctioned off during the evening. This gave young people a chance to meet and enjoy themselves together.

At pie socials, it was common for a young man to bid on the pie baked by his girlfriend. Lavinia LeBlanc explained how a boy's rivals would sometimes get together to try to stop him from bidding successfully:

> Everybody would bring a pie, and the pie would be sold. If you were lucky enough for your boyfriend to buy it, you'd be able to sit back and eat it with him, but if he didn't buy it, you'd be half mad at him, so you wouldn't sit with him! They'd know you had a pie and they knew who was gonna buy it. They used to make it go

---

195 Ibid., accession no. 1425 (1982).

> up so high that sometimes the boys didn't have the money to buy it. (...) When they auctioned them off, if anybody knew you had a pie, then they knew you had a boyfriend or something like that. He'd have to pay high for that pie because they clubbed together so it wouldn't cost them very much to buy it. There'd be five or six boys and they'd club together and then one would bid on it. But when it came to pay, they'd all chip in. The other fellow, he'd have to pay all by himself.[196]

Over the years, parishioners held pie socials and other events in support of the church.

Pie socials would end with an evening dance featuring local fiddlers. Aimable Robichaud, whose mother's family had moved to Chezzetcook from Cape Breton, was a talented fiddler who played not only at pie socials, but also at parish picnics, weddings and fiddle contests. He said the dances included waltzes, as well as polkas, lancers and set dances, where a "caller" would give instructions for each part of the set. The fiddler accompanied each part of the dance with a different tune.[197]

The polka was one of the more popular dances. It had a form similar to that of the set, where four couples formed a square. There were five parts to the polka, and according to Aimable Robichaud, a different tune accompanied each part.

Money raised at pie socials helped to finance the finishing of the interior of Saint Anselm's church, a task that dragged on for many years after the church was built.

Christmas and New Year's were the first important feast days of the winter season. In the years when the church's interior walls were yet to be finished, Christmas decorations were placed all around them, as Sophie Lapierre recalled:

> It was all set up with wooden boards. We each did our part. We put one board after another, all tied together, and then we put big garlands on them. That was to hang in the church. I did some of that too. They made little bows that they hung up, and there were candles everywhere. The men put the boards up all the way along, then they put candles on them, and that was all lit up.[198]
> [translation]

---

196 Ibid., accession no. 1265 (1982).
197 Ibid., ms. 131 (1982).
198 Ibid., accession no. 1483-1484 (1982).

Ronald Labelle

Figure 23: The interior of Saint Anselm's Church after its completion around 1930. The altar at the centre was later removed during the modernization craze in the 1960s.

Besides being hung with candles, the boards were also decorated with fir boughs. Their fresh odour filled Saint Anselm's church at Christmas time. When it was time for the midnight mass on Christmas Eve, all the decorations had to be in place. Most members of the parish, which included all of West Chezzetcook and Grand-Désert, attended that mass.

The traditional *réveillon*, a feast that was held in all the homes after mass, even attracted Protestant families from the surrounding area. According to Sophie Lapierre, Protestants would visit their Acadian acquaintances to partake in their meal of rabbit pie, called *pâté*.

The Acadians were the only people in the area who made rabbit pie. In many families, it is still the most popular Christmas dish. The *pâté* is a large pie covered with a thick crust. To prepare it, they begin by cutting the meat from a wild rabbit into about ten pieces, after which they spread bread dough in a large pan, and spread small chunks of salt pork over the dough before adding the rest of the meat. Then they place slices of onion on top, along with some pepper and a few other spices. They spread another layer of dough over the *pâté*, and leave the dish for a few hours until the dough rises. It then cooks for about three and a half

Chezzetcook: an Acadian stronghold

hours.

Many people believe that wood stoves produced better results than modern electric ovens. Some have now altered the procedure, cooking the rabbit meat ahead of time so that the pâté doesn't take so long to bake in the oven.

The sharing of a meal was at the centre of the Christmas celebration and there was little gift giving on Christmas day, but children would sometimes receive an orange, an apple and some molasses taffy called *tamarin*. In the early part of the 20th century, Alexandre Bellefontaine began to dress up in a Santa Claus costume, vising the local school with small gifts for the children. Aurèle Bellefontaine continued the practise until the 1950s, sometimes going from house to house with peanuts and other small gifts for children.[199] In families where parents were able to afford fancy Christmas candies, children hung stockings in which to receive their gifts.[200]

New Year's Day was the one most celebrated by children. They would rise early and go through the village, stopping at each house along the way. Everywhere they stopped, they would ask to be invited in after tapping on the door with a little wooden mallet made by their fathers especially for the occasion. Aurèle Bellefontaine remembered that, as a child, he tapped on each door three times with his mallet, and upon being let in, he said "Bonjour, la bonne année!"[201] After having wished the occupants a Happy New Year, the children received taffy or molasses cookies in exchange for their greeting. As a special treat, some people bought candy canes and barley toys to hand out to their young visitors.

It was considered good luck to be visited by children early on New Year's Day. This is a custom found in many Acadian areas and also among Scots in the Maritimes and elsewhere, but the use of the wooden mallet to announce the children's arrival is a tradition exclusive to Chezzetcook, and the origin of this practice is unknown. The practise was common in the community until the middle of the 20th century. Information accompanying a mallet preserved at the Acadian House Museum in Chezzetcook states that it was used until around 1962 by a young boy in the Roma family.[202]

This is how Sophie Lapierre and Maud Bellefontaine described the

---

199 Eastern Shore Archives, Lena Ferguson Collection, tape 6753, Aurèle Bellefontaine.
200 Cathy Clarke, "103 year old woman recalls Christmases of the past", *Dartmouth Free Press*.
201 Eastern Shore Archives, Lena Ferguson Collection, tape 6753.

children's New Year's Day visit:

> (S.L.) On New Year's Day, the first day of the year, the children came to knock on the doors. And they carried a big bag. Some of them used pillowcases. They would bring that, and they'd knock on the doors and come in. You let them come in.
> (M.B.)They all had small containers, you know, to put some candies in. Oh yes, molasses taffy.
> (S.L.)Yes, and they had small mallets. We knew they were coming. We would wait for them. And some of them would bang pretty hard with those mallets. There are some who smashed the doors with them.
> (M.B.)The children were happy to go around like that. Ah, they were glad, you know, to come in and say Happy New Year.[203] [translation]

Two kinds of taffy were prepared especially for the children's visit. White taffy was made with sugar, while the dark variety called *tamarin* was made in the traditional Acadian style with molasses.[204] Once the taffy was cooked, it was pulled and stretched, and then twisted and cut into pieces that hardened once they cooled. *Tamarin* was considered to be poor people's taffy, as molasses was less expensive than refined sugar.

Lavinia LeBlanc remembered that her mother had prepared cotton bags with drawstrings for her children to gather their treats.[205]

Later in the day, the adults also celebrated the New Year with house visits, but they were greeted with offers of rum rather than candy.

Another New Year's custom was to fire a gunshot in the air at noon. Throughout Chezzetcook, shots were heard around noon, as people would fire them from their doorstep. Some people continued this custom well into the late 20th century, and it is also found among people of German descent in Nova Scotia.

The people of Chezzetcook were the only Acadians whose traditional dish on New Year's Day was sauerkraut, called *choux salés* or *choux aigres*. Acadians elsewhere in Nova Scotia prepared salted cabbage, but theirs was sliced cabbage that was preserved in a brine and then soaked

---

202 "Mallet", Acadian House Museum, Artifacts Canada accession no. 2009.001.015.
203 CEAAC, Ronald Labelle Collection, accession no. 1415 (1982).
204 Ibid., ms.156 (1982).
205 Idem.

in water for the salt to be removed before serving.

In Chezzetcook, cabbage was prepared according to the German sauerkraut recipe, which involved fermentation. Every autumn, around November, people filled a barrel with sliced cabbage and salt, adding water. This had to be done during the waxing of the moon to prevent the water from being absorbed by the cabbage. The barrel was tightly covered and a press was used to keep the liquid at the top. The barrel remained shut until New Year's Day.

It was a real treat to begin the year with a first taste of sauerkraut. According to Liliane Bellefontaine, "New Year's Day was sauerkraut day. They would all invite each other. That was the meal for the first day of the year, sauerkraut with salt pork."[206][translation]

Meals were usually accompanied with homemade bread, and some women made their own bread starter using a mixture made from water, potatoes and hops grown in local gardens.

During the long winter season, there was no need to wait for a special occasion in order to get together and socialize. Rabbit suppers were organized, and these could be followed by dances that sometimes went late into the night. According to Sophie Lapierre and Maud Bellefontaine, local priests condemned these all-night parties:

> (M.B.) During the winter, you know, during rabbit hunting time, that was the time when we used to have [rabbit suppers].
> (S.L.) They did that at night, and they finished with dances. Then after(...) you could stay until the morning.
> (M.B.) Oh yes, they'd keep it up til six o'clock in the morning, mind you. Me, I had an uncle who played the violin. He was the violin player, Uncle Fred. What a lovely player he was. He used to come home in the morning, at six o'clock in the morning. And I remember once we had gone to mass and the priest had talked from the pulpit about that, about the hour, you know. Uncle Fred, he would come home at six in the morning after having played the whole evening long.[207][translation]

William Manette remembered a dance that went on for so long that, at the end, the oil-cloth flooring had been worn right through because of all the dancing. The dancers then decided to buy new oil-cloth flooring for

---

206 Idem.
207 CEAAC, Ronald Labelle Collection, accession no. 1417 (1982).

their host's home.

A big dance was also held when a wedding took place in the community, with music supplied by local fiddlers. The wedding ceremony itself was usually held around 9 o'clock in the morning and the celebration then lasted all day.

Unlike most other Acadians, the people of Chezzetcook did not celebrate *Chandeleur* (Candlemas Day) on February 2nd. The day was only marked as a religious event including the blessing of candles at the church.

A little later in the winter, however, the yearly Mardi Gras (Shrove Tuesday) celebrations were held. Before putting away their salt pork for the 40 days of Lent, people prepared a special Mardi Gras dish called *flan au lard*. This was a type of steamed cake made from salt pork, baking soda, buttermilk, molasses and flour.[208]

A dough was prepared, in which cubes of salt pork were added. The dough would then rise in a large pan before baking. Angus Roma explained that the salt pork was fried and then the renderings were deposited in the dough, but not the grease because that would make the dish too salty.[209]

As with other winter celebrations, the meal was followed by a dance in one of the houses in the community.

No feasting took place from Ash Wednesday until the end of Lent. The adults also put away their pipes and refrained from alcohol. The pork barrel was plugged up, and remained so for the duration of Lent. People also avoided eating eggs at that time, and as an added penance, some even refrained from buttering their bread or adding milk to their tea.

Children, however, were given a break in the middle of the Lenten period. La *Mi-Carême* (Mid-Lent) was celebrated on the Thursday of the third week of Lent. In West Chezzetcook an anonymous woman called the *Mi-Carême* would walk through the village, carrying a sack or a basket filled with biscuits and small cakes. She veiled her face to avoid being recognized by the children, who waited impatiently for her at school. John Lapierre remembered how the children would be watching her walk along the shore near the school:

> They watched her from the windows. She was dressed in white, her clothes were all white. She chose a place where the children

---

208 Ferguson, "A Time of Fasting", *Dartmouth Free Press*.
209 Eastern Shore Archives, Lena Ferguson Collection, tape 6838, Angus Roma.

could see her, and they all watched her. Then, as soon as the recess came, they went to see the *Mi-Carême*. She made little molasses cakes. Ah, they were cakes about that long. And she threw them. She threw them in the yard. Then the children went to pick them up.[210] [translation]

If any of the children tried to get close enough to find out who was behind the veil, the *Mi-Carême* would raise a stick to chase them away. The children also believed she held a bag of pepper under the sheet she used as a veil, and that she would throw some in the face of any child who came too close.

Yearly traditions: spring and summer

Lenten restrictions came to a head on Good Friday, two days before Easter Sunday. Not only did people fast on that day, but they also avoided all forms of work, and made sure not to use sharp instruments that could cause bleeding. It was said that you must prevent any bleeding on Good Friday because the Lord died on that day.[211]

On Easter Sunday, in contrast, all Lenten restrictions were over and a big meal of fried eggs and salt pork took place. The ancient tradition of gathering *eau de Pâques* (Easter water) from a spring before sunrise existed in Chezzetcook at one time, but seems to have disappeared long ago, according to Liliane Bellefontaine:

> My grandmother always had her bottle. If someone had gone to get water, we would have some. It was put away for the year, the bottle of *eau de Pâques*. It was kept for sickness. I remember that. Then, that started to die out.[212] [translation]

Eau de Pâques was drunk or rubbed on the body to cure various ailments and was considered sacred, despite the fact that it was not blessed by the Church.

The children's Easter treat consisted of a gift of brightly-coloured Easter eggs. Natural dies were prepared for the eggs using lichens gathered in the forest. One type of lichen produced a pinkish colour, and

---

210 CEAAC, Ronald Labelle Collection, accession no. 1384 (1982).
211 Eastern Shore Archives, Lena Ferguson Collection, tape 6753, Aurèle Bellefontaine.
212 CEAAC, Ronald Labelle Collection, accession no. 1448 (1982).

another died the eggs green.

On Easter Sunday morning, children were told that the partridge had come by and that she had left some eggs. The children then searched through the eelgrass that banked the outside walls of the houses, and there they found the Easter eggs.[213]

The association of the partridge with Easter was one of the distinct traditions found only in Chezzetcook, as was the name "baskahou" that referred to the nest of Easter eggs gathered by the children. The term "baskahou" was likely derived from an expression in the Mi'kmaq language.

By the beginning of the spring season, all the firewood needed for the following winter had been chopped and placed in neat piles, and the men prepared to return to their farming and fishing activities or to leave for distant work sites. That was when a group of them got together to cut all the firewood that was needed for the presbytery. They held a daylong bee, and when the work was done, the parish priest invited them all to supper.

Every family in the area practised agriculture to a certain extent. Some were almost self-sufficient, while others needed to buy food supplies. This was especially true in Grand-Désert, where fishing was the dominant activity, and where arable land was scarce. Families there took advantage of the return of the schooners that carried loads of vegetables back from Prince Edward Island at the end of the fishing season.

In West Chezzetcook, some families were able to grow all the vegetables they needed, having large crops of potatoes, turnips, cabbages, beans and beets.

While the land in places was too rocky and uneven for vegetable growing, it was generally well-suited for raising cattle and poultry. Almost every family owned a few pigs, cows and chickens, as Liliane Bellefontaine remembered:

> Ah, in my young days they had plenty of food. They always had their pigs and their cows. Everybody had their cows, their pigs and their chickens, you know. And they had their hay to look after the animals. They always had two or three head of cattle; a couple of cows, a couple of steers, and they were always raising a few young animals. In a way, they were better prepared to live

---

213 Linda Hines, *Life in Old Chezzetcook*, p. 3.

than people are these days, but they had more work to do.[214] [translation]

Apart from raising animals for food, each family possessed an ox for hauling loads, as well as some sheep that produced wool. The sheep were kept on a small island named Ferguson's Island, where they grazed from May until the autumn.

Figure 24: John Lapierre and his ox with a load of hay.

All through the spring and early summer, the women were busy gardening and looking after the farm animals. They had some help from their children and from elderly men who no longer went away to work.

There were few social activities during that period, as most of the men were absent. The holidays that took place in May, June and July were above all religious celebrations.

The month of May being dedicated to the Holy Virgin, prayers were addressed to her during the entire month.

There was a children's procession, in early May, in which a statue of

---

214 CEAAC, Ronald Labelle Collection, accession no. 1452 (1982).

the Virgin Mary was crowned with flowers. Sophie Lapierre remembered that young girls were all dressed in white and carried baskets containing paper flowers prepared for the occasion, while the boys wore suits sporting white sashes.[215]

The next important religious event was the Corpus Christi procession, held in late May or June, depending on the religious calendar. It involved a large number of parishioners, including all the children who had received their first communion. Liliane Bellefontaine remembered taking part in the procession as a little girl:

> We were all dressed in white like for our first communion, and we had baskets with flowers all arranged. We had ribbons around our necks. We all walked behind like that, throwing flowers in front of the Holy Sacrament. There was what they called a *reposoir* [altar of repose]. The priest put the Holy Sacrament on that altar and gave his blessing.[216] [translation]

The next important feast day was Saint Ann's, July 26th. Elder members of the community were aware that the Mi'kmaq used to celebrate Saint Ann's Day in Chezzetcook, but by the beginning of the 20th century, they no longer had a summer encampment in the area.

To mark the feast of Saint Ann's, a novena was held in the church, where prayers were recited during nine consecutive days. Members of the local chapter of the Catholic women's organization called *Les Dames de Sainte Anne* organized a procession at the beginning and at the end of the novena. At the head of the procession, they carried a large banner obtained from the organization's home base in Quebec.

The feast day of Our Lady of Assumption, patron saint of Acadians, was considered an important holiday and was celebrated with a morning mass on August 15th, followed by a picnic organized by the local parish, and ending with an evening dance. Lobster was served at Saint Anselm's parish hall, and local fiddlers like Aimable Robichaud played from early afternoon until midnight or later.

The annual parish picnic continued throughout the 20th century. It brought in donations for the church and gave parishioners a chance to get together and dance.

By mid-August, many of the men had recently returned from the fish-

---

215 Ibid., accession no. 1475 (1982).
216 Ibid., accession no. 1170 (1982).

ery. Others had temporarily come home from various workplaces because they needed to mow their hay fields. Due to the amount of farm work that had to be done in mid-August, not everyone could take a day off to celebrate Assumption Day, according to Liliane Bellefontaine:

> August 15th, that was a holiday. Ah yes, it was a holiday, Acadia Day, you know, the Acadians' holiday. And it was a big, big celebration. It was [like a] Sunday. And it often happened that people had hay to gather, and they were afraid of losing it. So they went to ask for the priest's permission. The priest would give them permission to work in their hay fields after the church services.[217] [translation]

Yearly traditions: autumn

At the end of the summer, freshly-gathered products were used to prepare both alcoholic and non-alcoholic drinks. Malt beer was brewed around hay-making time, and beer was also made from hops. The necessary ingredients, apart from boiled hops, were raisins, potatoes, molasses or brown sugar, and yeast.

Some people preferred to make blueberry or blackberry wine, and a refreshing drink was also prepared for children, using oat flour. As John Lapierre recalled:

> My mother had some [oat flour], and she mixed water with it, then she shook it and shook it, and sometimes she put a little bit of fresh milk in it. Then she put in some sugar to sweeten it, not too sweet, but sweet enough to drink. And I tell you, I really liked that.[218] [translation]

Liliane Bellefontaine recalled how, each year, women would gather wild berries, along with a quantity of medicinal plants they used to make home remedies:

> They made a lot of their medicine themselves, you know. They picked things that they could use to heal swollen feet or swollen arms. They boiled that, then they soaked in it, and they had a lot

---

217 Ibid., accession no. 1736 (1983).
218 Ibid., accession no. 1381 (1982).

of confidence in that. I remember when we dried plantain leaves. We have a lot of it growing around the house, here.(...) They dried that in the attic, and also tansy.[219] [translation]

Plantain and tansy, both medicinal plants of European origin, were commonly used by Acadians all over the Maritimes to treat various ailments.

Apart from wild plants, many other substances were used to make home remedies. In the autumn and winter, for example, when children caught colds, they were fed a mixture of onions and molasses. If they had the flu, their parents prepared a more elaborate remedy: a poultice combining goose grease and camphor oil.

One of the tasks accomplished every fall was the gathering of eelgrass, which was locally called *boutarde*, an abbreviation of *herbe à outardes*. A large quantity of eelgrass was gathered on the sea-shore and spread around the outer walls of houses as insulation. This practise is still sometimes found, but the other main use of eel-grass, that as a substance for stuffing mattresses, disappeared following the blight in the 1930s. Up until that time, it was common for people to gather eelgrass, clean it, dry it, and finally card it by hand to make it finer. In the early 20th century, eelgrass was hauled by ox-cart to Mineville, where it was used to make mattresses that were sold in Halifax.[220]

Despite the popularity of mattresses filled with eelgrass in the early 20th century, people in Chezzetcook preferred to sleep on mattresses stuffed with straw. Straw mattresses had to be stuffed at least twice a year because they

Figure 25: Lavinia LeBlanc, Head of Chezzetcook, 1982

---

219 Ibid., accession no. 1188 (1982).
220 Ferguson, "Remember the Old Straw Mattress."

became hard and flat over time.

Feather pillows were also made locally from chicken feathers, as were feather beds, but the latter were far less common than straw mattresses.

During the winter months, it was important to have on hand an ample supply of warm blankets. Women made their own quilts by first carding wool by hand, then spreading it between layers of cotton that were stitched together. The sheep raised in the area produced enough wool not only for quilts but also to make warm clothes. Shearing, carding, spinning and weaving were all done by hand. After the sheep were sheered, the wool was washed and rinsed twice beside a stream.

Lavinia LeBlanc remembered helping several older women wash their wool when she was young. When the chore was over, she would receive a bag of wool in exchange for her services.[221]

The Acadian women of Chezzetcook were talented knitters and seamstresses, but didn't practise weaving. According to Sophie La-pierre, they sent their homespun wool to German women in neighbouring villages like Seaforth, and when the woven fabric was returned to them, they used it to make such articles as blankets, trousers and vests:

> The Germans, they lived further down. They knew how to weave. Here, they used to make things. They made stuff by the yard for the men, for their trousers. They used to wear that. Oh, yes, it was all wool, all made by hand on the loom. And they sold it by the yard to make suits. I guess it was really warm. When they put that on to go and work in the woods they didn't feel the cold. (...) That was the big German women. They did nice work, making blankets and things like that. Oh yes, it wasn't the French women.[222] [translation]

With the approach of winter, people made sure they had sufficient food supplies. Those who had not stocked up enough at the end of summer had one more opportunity to obtain agricultural products from Prince Edward Island in November. That was when schooners that normally carried merchandise such as wood, bricks and gravel made their last voyage of the year, picking up a final load of potatoes, turnips, carrots, parsnips, onions and other produce on the Island.

In mid-November, the ships sailed up Chezzetcook Inlet as far as West

---

221 CEAAC, Ronald Labelle Collection, accession no. 1689 (1983).
222 Ibid., accession nos. 1462; 1464 (1982).

Chezzetcook, where they remained until the spring. The inlet was difficult to navigate for large vessels, and could only be used when the ship's hold was empty.

Although the inhabitants of Chezzetcook often had to buy vegetables, they obtained most of the meat they needed by raising pigs, lambs, chickens and geese. In the fall, some families would butcher a steer. A herd of cattle was brought from Upper Musquodoboit and those who could afford to bought a steer to have a supply beef for the winter months. Much of the meat was pickled to be preserved in winter, but when cold weather arrived, it was possible to freeze some of the beef by boxing it and burying it in the snow.

Beef was a luxury, however, as the price of a steer was approximately 30 or 35 dollars in the early 20th century, whereas a pig could be bought for as little as five dollars.

Also in late autumn, most families butchered a pig and prepared a barrel of salt pork. Angus Roma told of how his father would bring a boxful of piglets from the market in the spring and each family would buy one, raising the pig during the summer. When it was time to butcher the pig, neighbours would gather to help in the task, and they would each receive a piece of fresh meat as a reward. This was the only time when fresh pork was available, as most of the meat was immediately salted for preservation.

The pig's blood was used for making blood pudding, the ingredients of which included milk, onions and savoury. John Lapierre remembers that his mother would first clean the tripe thoroughly, rubbing it with a small instrument shaped like a comb, and then soak it overnight before filling it with the mixture.[223]

Head cheese was also prepared by boiling the pig's head for several hours. Finally, some families made smoked ham by hanging the pig's carcass over a hardwood fire.

Geese were butchered from time to time to provide both meat and grease. Goose was a favourite dish for special oc-

Figure 26: Liliane Bellefontaine, Musquodoboit Harbour, 1983.

---

223 Ibid., accession no. 1388 (1982).

casions. According to Liliane Bellefontaine, goose meat was always served at wedding feasts.[224]

Wild game provided another source of meat, as a large number of local men went deer hunting in the fall. It was sometimes possible to keep deer meat frozen in the woodshed during winter.

The passage from autumn to winter ended the yearly cycle of traditional activities, and the change in seasons was marked with a folk custom which is still celebrated today. The eve of All Saints Day, or Hallowe'en, is traditionally the night when the souls of the dead return to earth. In Chezzetcook, young people would cover themselves with white sheets and roam near people's houses to scare the inhabitants.

Hallowe'en was called *le soir des tours*, because young people often played tricks, the most common of which was to take cabbage from farmer's fields. The custom of stealing cabbages on Hallowe'en was common among Nova Scotia Acadians and seems to take its origin from the Scots[225], who celebrated Cabbage Night on the eve of All Saints Day.

Young people would roam the community at Hallowe'en, looking for carts or sleds that they would remove from farmyards, taking them a good distance away so that the owners would have to search for them in the morning. Sophie Lapierre remembered one time when a group of young tricksters took an ox from a farmer's barn and replaced it with a young calf. The next morning, the farmer went to hitch his ox to a cart in order to fetch a load of wood, but when he entered the barn, he was stunned to find a young calf in its place.[226]

Hallowe'en was not the only time when tricks were played in Chezzetcook. The community was full of practical jokers. Some would stuff wood shavings into the hole in a lock to make it impossible to fit the key in it. There was at least one case when a practical joker stuffed field grass into a chimney so that the next person to light a fire in the stove ended up with a kitchen full of smoke.

Sophie Lapierre remembered playing a trick on a local widow who was often visited by her boyfriend. One night, she jammed the door of the widow's house, making it impossible to open it from the inside. The suiter, who preferred not to be seen leaving the house in broad daylight, finally managed to escape through a window.[227]

As the days grew short and the cold weather arrived, people would

---

224 Ibid., accession no. 1184 (1982).
225 William S. Walsh, *Curiosities of Popular Customs*, p. 510.
226 CEAAC, Ronald Labelle Collection, accession no. 1485 (1982).
227 Ibid., accession no. 1492 (1982).

watch for signs of the coming weather patterns. There were several indicators of a hard winter to come: If the wasps nests were high in the trees, if the muskrats' lairs were built on high ground or if the mountain ash had abundant fruit. All of these were seen as signs that a long, cold winter was approaching.

Folk beliefs

In Chezzetcook, as was common everywhere in the past, children were gently warned about frightening figures like the "bogeyman", who could come and take them away if they stayed out late at night. There was, however, a particular name for the bogeyman in the community. According to Claire Lapierre, children were told not to stay out too late or *kadjimouk* would come for them.

It is very likely that the name *kadjimouk* was borrowed long ago from the nearby Mi'kmaq inhabitants. The fact that local Acadians borrowed this Mi'kmaq tradition provides one interesting example of the cultural exchanges that happened in the Chezzetcook area.[228]

Many in Chezzetcook shared superstitions. This can be understood as a reaction to dangerous working conditions in the past, in which you tried to avoid doing anything that may bring bad luck.

Édouard Lapierre told of how it was considered unlucky to carry a deck of cards on board a fishing vessel. He once brought cards along when he joined the crew of his uncle's fishing boat. When his uncle found out about it, he ordered Édouard to go ashore and get rid of the cards, which he did, placing them under a rock. He remembered that the ship was having difficulty making it back to port because of a southwest wind, but as soon as they got rid of the deck of cards, the wind shifted to a more favourable northwesterly direction.[229]

As elsewhere around the Maritimes, stories were told in Chezzetcook about ghosts and buried treasure. In 1974, Wanda and Linda Manette asked their grandfather, Angus Roma, about supernatural legends. The stories he told them reflect several Acadian folk traditions. In many coastal areas, precious hoards were supposed to be protected by ghosts. In order to ward off the spirits, the treasure seekers would surround the sites with ritual objects like candles or religious medallions:

---

228 Ibid., ms. 114 (1982).
229 Eastern Shore Archives, Lena Ferguson Collection, tape 6805, Édouard Lapierre.

Chezzetcook: an Acadian stronghold

I could tell you about Red Island, where Captain Kidd was supposed to have buried a treasure. The people used to go and try to dig. There were certain things they had to have before they could dig. The first thing, they would hear a noise; they'd see something —they'd see ghosts! Somebody would appear through the bush.

Sometimes they would keep on going, keep on digging, and other times, they just cleared out. They'd get out, and then they would go again some other time; they would keep on going. They never found anything, but they were sure there was something buried on Red Island. They made holes here, there and everywhere.

One day, a fellow had gone out there for eelgrass and he had to wait for the tide before he could get his boat back out to deep water. He just lay there in the bushes, whiling the time away, and then these fellows came along. They had candles. They put candles there and they put a string around the candles, so no ghost is supposed to come.

And then after they were digging a while, this fellow heard the noise. He thought, "What the heck is goin' on?"

So he moved through the bushes, you know, and the candlelight kind of struck his face, and they see his eyes shining there, and of course, the devil would take them away! They thought that was the ghost.

But it wasn't a ghost, it was an old fellow that was just waiting for the tide. He scared them out. There were three of them. Away they went, and they didn't go back for a long time afterwards.

I have never been there to look for the treasure, but everyone that did go said they had seen a ghost or heard noise like that.

In all Acadian areas, stories are told about ghostly sights and noises, especially around sites believed to contain buried treasure. Among the tales told by Angus Roma, there is one about the time his father saw what is known as a "revenant", a deceased person who appears to someone who knew him during his life:

The old people all believed in ghosts. Me, I heard different noises. One time, right back of the hill here, about three o'clock in the morning, I was coming from the lake, and it sounded like a truck dumping rocks no more than ten feet away from me. You know

151

the sound when you dump a truckload of rocks. I went to have a look. Nothing at all! I looked everywhere around the fields by the stone wall. Nothing was touched.

My father was going to the lake the same way up there, and right in front of him was a man with a long, long whip, swishing the whip, you know, and raising the dust in front of him. And the crack of the whip you could hear. And another time, he was going to the brickyard to get his boat and the tide was high. He walked over, and as he was going down the road towards the channel, he saw somebody ahead of him and he knew right away it was a ghost, because he knew the man was dead. He heard him coughing, walking, and all of a sudden, he disappeared.

About a hunting camp, there was one up at Porter's Lake and they heard some strange noises. First of all, it was a noise like a bear coming through the woods—crashing through the woods and the alders and stuff.

My father said, "Ah, you didn't hear nothing, that's the brook."

[One of the men] said, "I didn't hear the brook. I know the brook from an animal running through the woods."

So they put the light out. The minute the light was out: Bing! Bang! in the camp. And then they'd light the light—no more!

My brother got up and tied the door. There was a nail on the door and a nail where he tied the rope to tie the door. As soon as he was in his bunk, the door was wide open. Nobody in the camp did it. They were all laying down, not sleeping a wink.

Up overhead, on the roof, and down on the stove, it was rattling the stove, they thought it was going to smash the stove to pieces. Then it would come to the bunk and scratch on the bunk where my father was.

My father had to get out, and my uncle went and took his place, and then there was no more noise. It was all over for the night.

But every night, there was something.[230]

It was generally at night that mysterious occurrences took place. One night when Sophie Lapierre was returning home late, she saw a strange light moving back and forth along the waterside. She asked her father for an explanation, and he answered that it was a 'feu follet', a fairy light that

---

230 Ibid., tape 6838, Angus Roma.

Chezzetcook: an Acadian stronghold

appears before a storm. Sure enough, a storm soon arrived.[231]
The 'feu follet' is part of folklore everywhere in French Canada, but is specifically associated with weather among Acadians. In Northern New Brunswick, it is actually called 'le feu du mauvais temps' (the bad weather light).

Local characters

Just like other rural communities in the past, Chezzetcook had its share of unusual characters. Some were fortune-tellers who were believed to possess powers of clairvoyance.

The presence of fortune telling is indicated by the 'Plan of road and principal buildings' included in the short "History of Grand-Désert" written by Emma Julien in 1907. Six buildings are shown on the plan. Along with the school and post office, there is one building identified with the title "Fortune teller".[232]

According to Claire Lapierre, a woman named Ozite Lapierre would read tea leaves, while there was also a local man who told fortunes by using a deck of playing cards.

Some individuals were feared because it was thought they practiced sorcery, while others exerted healing powers based on religious faith. Claire Lapierre told how the local midwife once went into a house believed to be haunted by sounds of chains being dragged in the cellar. The woman walked through the house, sprinkling holy water in each room, and asked the occupants if they would like her to recite prayers with them. Claire Lapierre believed someone had purposefully made noises with chains in the cellar to scare the home's occupants.

Because of the prevalence of superstitious beliefs in the past, it was not difficult to trick gullible people.

On Station Road, two houses were supposed to be haunted but, according to Claire Lapierre, these were actually used by bootleggers to hide illicit alcohol. A story was told that the owner of one of the houses had passed away without having paid for the purchase of a pair of shoes and that his spirit kept returning to try to correct the wrong.

The "revenant" legend that tells of a spirit coming back from the dead to complete unfinished business is common in folklore all over French Canada. Local bootleggers took advantage of the belief in order to scare

---
231 CEAAC, Ronald Labelle Collection, accession no. 1490 (1982).
232 Julien.

people away from their stash.

Several local characters were known to play tricks. Claire Lapierre remembered one who used to dress up in priest's garb and walk along the road wearing a Roman collar. People who didn't know him would salute him saying, 'Hello, Father' or, 'Bonjour, mon Père.'

Claire herself once played a trick on a lodger who was living in her parents' home. Seeing that the lodger had bought a new suit, she sewed the sleeves of the jacket together and he discovered the trick when he tried to put it on. She remembers that he got back at Claire and her sister by pouring water on their heads while they slept.[233]

Claire told of how a few tricksters once unfastened a man's sled from the harness that tied it to his ox. The man walked a long way with his ox before noticing that his load had been left behind.

They also played an elaborate trick on a man who was alone in his hunting cabin. They fabricated a devil's head, complete with horns made from barrel staves. They hung the devil's head in the camp, attaching a string that led outside, where they pulled on it during the night to make the head move.

The victim, who was not very religious up until that time, got such a fright that he fled, yelling that in future he would recite the rosary and go to mass every Sunday.

One man used to go through the community from early morning until evening, stopping at houses all along the way. He had an ingenious way of knowing whether or not his visit was welcome. At each house where he arrived, he would open the door and throw his hat inside. If the inhabitants had no desire to see him, they would throw the hat back out and he would leave. "He'd throw his hat in and then he'd see—if the hat didn't come out, it was safe for him to go in."[234]

As in many Acadian areas in the Maritimes, people were often given nicknames, many of which were of a satirical nature. Some were individual nicknames such as Ti-Tchinne, Tchipitte and Yock.

There was a rhyme accompanying this last name that began:

> Yock, Yock, Yock, the bamboo stalk
> Sold his wife for a pair of socks
> When the socks began to wear

---

[233] CEAAC, Ronald Labelle Collection, ms. 117 (1982).
[234] Ibid, accession no. 1121 (1982).

Chezzetcook: an Acadian stronghold

Yock, Yock, Yock began to swear[235]

Many nicknames were assigned to entire families. Aside from the Juliens being called *Les Bretons* and the Wolfes being called *Les Loups* (the wolves), there were different names for various branches of the Lapierre family in Grand-Désert. With so many people sharing the same surname, nicknames were useful in identifying individual family lines.

There were, for example, Lapierre families known as the *Baguettes*, the *Barlots*, the *Pâtés* and the *Matous*. Some Bellefontaine families also had nicknames and Liliane Bellefontaine said that her grandfather's family on her mother's side were Bellefontaines nicknamed "Bonaparte", no doubt in reference to Napoleon Bonaparte.[236]

Nicknames could be used to poke fun at people, as happened one year when a member of the *Matou* (Tomcat) branch of the Lapierre family was leading the Grand-Désert schoolchildren in the recitation of the rosary. This was during religious celebrations that took place during the month of May in honour of the Holy Virgin. While the man recited the prayers, the children began to meow like cats instead of following along. This made him so angry that he finally stopped and gave the children a scolding.

In talking about local families and local characters of the past, Claire and Elsie Lapierre didn't hide the fact that there were sometimes conflicts in the community. However, everyone who provided information for this book generally described a society in which people took time for each other. As Claire Lapierre said: "Today, you meet someone in a car, that's it—you don't have time to talk. But they had time to visit each other and have a chat. You know, it would be the same thing maybe, over and over again, but it least they had time to visit."

---

235 Ibid., ms. 117 (1982).
236 Ibid., accession no. 1139 (1982).

Figure 27: "Dames de Sainte Anne" Membership diploma awarded to a resident of Grand-Désert in June 1922.

7: Folktales and ballads—the Massignon collection

Until the 1980s, the rare folklorists who collected Acadian oral traditions in the Maritimes unfortunately neglected Chezzetcook. There was, however, one notable exception: French linguist and folklorist Geneviève Massignon visited Grand-Désert twice, the first time in early 1947 and later in 1961.

Massignon was one of the foremost French folklorists of the 20th century. Her fieldwork, carried out over a twenty-year period, took her to many parts of her native France, but her biggest contribution to research into Francophone cultures took place in Canada's Maritime provinces, where she developed a fond admiration for the Acadian people. Massignon, who lived in Paris, planned a third trip to Canada in order to continue collecting Acadian folklore, but her plans ended tragically with her sudden death in 1966 at the age of 45.

She carried out her first field research trip in difficult circumstances. With very little financial support, she sailed for Canada in the spring of 1946, somehow managing to obtain a berth on a ship carrying returning soldiers and war brides.

Arriving in Halifax, she spent the next six months travelling through eight areas of Acadian settlement in the Maritimes. In each area, she carried out lengthy interviews about oral traditions, and learned everything she could about the local Acadian dialect. Massignon then briefly visited Québec, Louisiana and New England before returning to Halifax in February of 1947, in order to board a ship bound for France.

Shortly before her ship was to set sail, she learned that an additional Acadian settlement existed not far from Halifax. Massignon therefore made a last-minute excursion to Grand-Désert, where she met Mr. Alban Lapierre at his home and took down seven French language folktales from him in shorthand.[237] Archival records left by Massignon also mention the titles of six songs collected in 1947, three from Mrs. Agnes Faucher and three from Mrs. Brigitte Lapierre.

The text of one of the songs by Mrs. Faucher, "Brave soldat revenant de guerre", was published in Geneviève Massignon's book, *Trésors de la chanson populaire française.*[238] The texts of the other songs seem to have been lost.[239]

Massignon did not get another chance to return to Canada until 1961. By then, she was working of an ambitious project to complete not one but two doctoral dissertations. The first, entitled *Les parlers français d'Acadie*, was devoted to the French language in Acadia; while the second, *Trésors de la chanson populaire française*, presented an analysis of her collection of Acadian traditional ballads.

Thanks to a Canada Council grant received in 1961, Massignon was able to spend a summer travelling through the Maritimes, equipped with a tape recorder with which she recorded hundreds of folktales and more than one thousand songs. Her brief foray to Grand-Désert in 1947 must have impressed her, because she made sure to include the community in her fieldwork plans.

On August 4th 1961, she once again visited Alban Lapierre, questioning him about fishing practices and recording a folktale from him. She also revisited Brigitte Lapierre, who gave her seven folktales and three songs. She recorded one final song from Mr. Anselme Lapierre.[240]

The precious recordings Geneviève Massignon made in 1961 were almost forgotten because, after her untimely death in 1966, the collection was simply kept in storage in France. Twenty years later, her brother finally donated the collection to the Bibliothèque Nationale, France's national library, where it was warehoused for another twenty years, until an archivist was given the task of cataloguing the collection.

Thanks to the efforts of Dr. Jean-Pierre Pichette, the Université Sainte-Anne archives were eventually able to obtain a copy of the sound recordings from Massignon's Nova Scotia fieldwork, and in 2012, I visited the Bibliothèque Nationale in Paris, where I was able to obtain copies of her

---

237 Bibliothèque Nationale de France, Geneviève Massignon Fonds, Box 46, file 1.
238 Geneviève Massignon, *Trésors de la chanson populaire française – Autour de 50 chansons recueillies en Acadie*.
239 Bibliothèque Nationale de France, Geneviève Massignon Fonds, Box 60, file 16.
240 Ibid., box 19, tapes 72-143 and 72-144.

field notes.

Geneviève Massignon's brief forays to Grand-Désert are important because she was able to meet local residents who still retained some of the traditional folktales and ballads that had been handed down since the 18th century. Her collection gives us a glimpse into the Acadian ballad and folktale tradition of the past.

Some of the songs are fragmentary, and a few of the folktales she recorded are not complete. This can be explained by the fact that by the mid-20th century, French language oral traditions were very much a thing of the past in the Chezzetcook area, following the arrival of English-language radio and television. Luckily, the two members of the community interviewed by Massignon were able to recount some stories and to sing a few examples of the old ballads they remembered.

It is important to note that, despite being a Parisian, Geneviève Massignon had absolutely no difficulty understanding everything the Lapierres told her during her visits to Grand-Désert. Listening to the recordings, it was obvious to me that they, in turn, had no difficulty understanding her. This should lay to rest the false notion some English-speaking Nova Scotians still have about Chezzetcook as a place where people spoke a broken Acadian dialect unintelligible to other Francophones.

French folksongs in Chezzetcook

Traditional ballads brought from France by the Acadians' ancestors were very much a part of local culture in Chezzetcook until the influx of new musical styles heard in dance halls and on radio beginning in the 1920s and 30s. Liliane Bellefontaine, born in 1899, recounted that even in her younger days, traditional French ballads were mostly sung by members of her parents' generation.[241] The four traditional songs Geneviève Massignon recorded from Brigitte and Anselme Lapierre are remnants of this early tradition.

Anselme Lapierre was able to sing a few verses of the ballad 'La fille au couvent', about a young girl who is sent away to a convent to keep her away from her lover. This theme is found in many French ballads.

Brigitte Lapierre sang three songs. 'Devant la porte d'un cabaret', a song she had originally performed for Massignon in 1947, is a ballad about a poor beggar who is imprisoned and who is finally set free thanks to divine intervention. The two other songs she offered are fine examples

---

241 Ronald Labelle, « Le déclin de la langue française à Chezzetcook », p. 191.

of the Acadian singing tradition and are presented here along with their melodies.

La courte paille, by Brigitte (Julien) Lapierre

'La courte paille' is an amusing song that is often included in children's collections. The most common version begins with the line 'Il était un petit navire'.

The Acadian version sung by Mrs. Lapierre, however, begins with the departure of three ships to sail around the world. They sail the seas for seven years and become lost, finally reaching land just as they have run out of food. Geneviève Massignon first collected this song from Agnes Faucher in 1947 and later recorded it from Brigitte Lapierre in 1961.

Mrs. Lapierre remembered only the middle verses of the song, but it is printed here in its entirety, thanks to additional verses found in *Chansons d'Acadie, série* 5, edited by Father Anselme Chiasson.

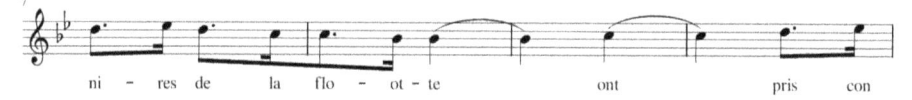

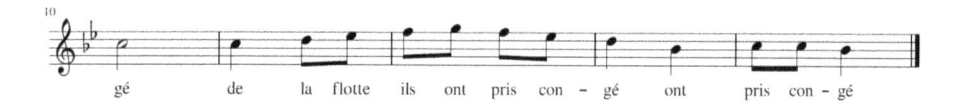

Sont trois navires de la flotte (bis)
De la flotte ils ont pris congé (bis)

C'est pour y faire le tour du monde (bis)
Sans jamais la terre aborder (bis)

Au bout de la septième année (bis)
De vivres ils avont manqué (bis)

Il faut tirer la courte paille (bis)
Quel s'ra de nous sera mangé (bis)

Oh, la plus courte arrive au maître (bis)
Oh, le grand Dieu, quel-le pitié (bis)

Il appel-le son petit mousse (bis)
« Veux-tu souffrir la mort pour moi? (bis)

Auparavant que l'on me mange (bis)
Dans la grande hune je veux monter (bis)

Mais quand il fut dans la grande hume (bis)
Se mit à rire et à chanter (bis)

« Oh, qu'as-tu donc mon petit mousse? (bis)
Qu'as-tu à tant rire et chanter? » (bis)

- Je vois la tour de Babylone (bis)
Je vois la terre de tous côtés (bis)

Je vois ma mère dans sa cuisine (bis)
Qui nous prépare à déjeuner » (bis)

Brave soldat revenant de guerre, by Brigitte (Julien) Lapierre

The second song is a beautiful ballad. It tells how a soldier returning from the wars encounters a young princess who asks for a rose he is wearing.

Many traditional French ballads tell of romantic encounters, and they usually include references to flowers or plants, each of which has its own symbolic meaning. The rose, of course, signifies that the couple are falling in love.

During Massignon's visit in 1947, both Brigitte Lapierre and Agnes Faucher performed traditional songs about a soldier returning from the wars.

The version Agnes Faucher sang is quite different from this one, as it tells the tale of a returning soldier who finds out his wife, having been wrongly informed that her husband had been killed, has remarried.[242] Brigitte Lapierre's song was finally recorded during Massignon's second field trip, in 1961. It tells of a romantic encounter between the returning soldier and the king's daughter.

♩ = 80

Bra - ve sol - dat re - ve-nant de la gue-er-re bra - ve sol - dat ve-nant de la er-re bra - ve sol - dat lon lon lon re li bra - ve sol-dat re - ve-nant de la gue-er-re

1
Brave soldat, revenant de la guerre (bis)
Brave soldat, lon lon lon le li
Brave soldat revenant de la guerre
2
Sur son chapeau, y avait une belle rose (bis)
Sur son chapeau, lon lon lon le li
Sur son chapeau, y avait une belle rose
3
La fille du roi, prit d'envie pour la rose (bis)
La fille du roi, lon lon lon le li
La fille du roi, prit d'envie pour la rose
4
Brave soldat, donnez-moi votre rose (bis)
Brave soldat, lon lon lon le li
Brave soldat, donnez-moi votre rose

Traditional French folktales in Chezzetcook

When Geneviève Massignon visited Chezzetcook in the mid-20th century, traditional French tales were beginning to be even more difficult to collect than songs. They harken back to a time when people spent their evenings gathered around a storyteller who would entertain them for hours with tales, some of which were full of magic, while others were

---

242 Massignon, Vol. 1, p. 125.

Chezzetcook: an Acadian stronghold

simply amusing stories.

Massignon was able to record two storytellers during her brief visits to Grand-Désert. One was Brigitte Lapierre, the same woman who sang her three songs, while the other was a man named Anselme Lapierre.

Each tale presented here contains a translated summary, followed by French language transcriptions of the texts as Massignon recorded them or took them down.

Five of the stories were collected both in written form in 1947 and on tape in 1961.[243] Transcriptions of the recordings are presented here along with additional elements found in the earlier written versions. The two tales collected in 1947 only are presented exactly as Massignon took them down on paper, while the three recorded in 1961 were transcribed directly from the tapes.

Massignon collected these tales more than 60 years ago and so they present a clear picture of the French language as it was spoken in Chezzetcook in the middle of the 20th century. The tales contain many archaic expressions that are no longer used in modern French. For example, the verb "nager", which now means "to swim", is used in its original meaning, signifying "rowing".

The fact that the devil appears in more than one tale indicates how religion and storytelling were interrelated. On the one hand, the fear of falling under the influence of the devil is reflected in tales where people have dangerous encounters with him; while in other tales, such as "La fille du diable", the devil is a purely fictional character who poses no threat to humans.

Une piastre le poil

told by Alban Lapierre, Grand-Désert, 1947

The theme of the crafty peasant who outsmarts his master is a familiar one in traditional folktales. In the international tale-type index, this one is identified as type number 1535, 'The Rich and the Poor Peasant'.

Interestingly, in this version, the young man's master is a priest rather than a rich man, which suggests that storytellers of the past would naturally have thought of the priest as being an authority figure.

The tale tells how a poor man brings his cattle to the market and,

---

[243] Bibliothèque Nationale de France, Geneviève Massignon Fonds, Box 46, file 1 (1947); Box 19, tapes 72-143 and 72-144.

Ronald Labelle

while returning at night, covers himself with one of the hides to keep warm. He then encounters thieves who take fright when they see him covered with an animal hide, and they abandon their stolen money. He later makes the priest believe that his new riches came from the sale of his animals' hides at a price of one dollar per hair.

The priest orders that all his cattle be butchered, expecting to make a fortune from the sale of the hides, but he quickly realizes he has been tricked.

He has the poor man stuffed into a bag and carried to the seaside to be drowned, but the crafty peasant manages to exchange places with a passing shepherd. He takes over the flock of sheep and later meets up with the priest, telling him that he was thrown to a place where he found a large quantity of sheep and other cattle.

The tale ends there, but in other versions, the foolish master asks to be put into a bag and tossed into the sea himself, so that he can obtain a large herd of cattle.

> Une fois, il y avait un homme qui avait des animaux. Il a été voir pour les tuer. Il a été vendre la peau à la ville. En s'en venant, il s'est arrêté. Il a éparé la peau dessous lui, sur l'arbre. Des voleurs ont venu là avec un sac d'argent. Ils se sont mis à compter leur argent. « Ça c'est pour moi, ça c'est pour toi. » Il a entendu ça; il a halé sa peau, la peau qu'il avait dans l'arbre. Les voleurs, ils ont eu peur; ils se sont sauvés; ils ont tout quitté l'argent là. Il a descendu de l'arbre, il a ramassé l'argent, il l'a mis dans sa voiture, il s'en est venu chez eux. Il l'a pas tout ôté. Il a mis la wagon dans la grange. Il était las.
>
> Le lendemain matin (le prêtre) a envoyé son servant voir combien il avait vendu la peau; il avait vingt-deux pièces d'animaux. Il a dit, « Servant, je les ai vendues une piastre le poil. » Il l'a amené voir l'argent qui était dans son wagon. Le servant l'a vu. Il l'a cru.
>
> Il a dit ça au prêtre, qu'il l'a vendu une piastre le poil.
>
> Le prêtre a été faire tuer ses animaux. Il a été à la ville pour vendre ses poils.
>
> Le prêtre était pas content après l'homme qui avait conté des menteries comme ça. Il voulait le faire noyer. Ils l'ont pris, ils l'ont mis dans un sac.
>
> Le prêtre était avec eux. Ils ont passé devant l'église. Le berger a passé; il y avait une bande de moutons; il était amarré dans le sac, lui. « Ah, c'est-tu bien dans le sac », qu'il a dit.

> Le berger a entendu. « Change avec moi, qu'il dit.
> - Oh non, j'irai pas, je suis trop bien. »
> Le berger lui a encore demandé, puis l'homme est sorti. Le berger s'a fourré dedans. Il a amarré le sac, puis il s'en a été avec les moutons.
> (Après) une couple de jours, le prêtre a rencontré le même homme qu'il avait fait noyer avec les trois peaux de moutons. Il dit, « Je croyais que je t'avais fait noyer. – Vous m'avez jeté où-ce qu'il y avait des moutons assez. Si vous m'aviez jeté un peu plus loin! Vous m'auriez jeté où-ce qu'il y avait des bêtes à cornes assez. »

L'ours trouvé

told by Alban Lapierre, Grand-Désert, 1947

This is an unusual story that does not have any direct parallel in other oral traditions. It tells of a boy who domesticates a bear cub that eventually grows up and goes into the wild.

Years later, the boy is a grown man with a son in school. One day, a bear enters the school, warms itself against the stove and eats the children's lunches.

When the boy's father arrives to kill the bear, he discovers it is the cub he had as a pet, now grown into a full-sized bear. As it was not rare for people to domesticate bears in the past, this story may be based on an actual event, though probably not one that happened locally.

> Un petit garçon avait été dans le bois. Il avait trouvé un petit ours. Le petit ours l'a galopé partout à l'école. Après qu'il a été gros, il s'en a été. Honoré s'est marié. Il a eu des enfants. L'ours a été dans le bois; les enfants ont été à l'école.
> Une journée, un ours a été dans l'école—les enfants avaient leur manger pendrillé—l'ours a rentré. Il a été manger. Il est rentré se chauffer les pattes sur le poêle. Les enfants s'en sont tirés à travers les châssis.
> Le petit garçon à Honoré a dit à son père qu'il y avait un ours dans l'école. Honoré y a été. Il a tiré l'ours. Quand ils sont venus à plumer l'ours, il a reconnu son ours qu'il avait trouvé dans le bois quand il était petit.

Ronald Labelle

Conte du loup et du renard
told by Alban Lapierre in 1947
and recorded from Brigitte Lapierre in 1961

The classic French folktale of Reynard the Fox actually played a role in the birth of French literature. It was the inspiration for the *Roman de Renart*, first written down in the 12th century. Medieval tales of the wily fox who tricks a dumb wolf or bear remained in the Acadian oral tradition long after they had been forgotten in France. These tales are a precious heritage that was handed down orally for centuries.

The version presented here was recorded in 1961 from Mrs. Patrick Lapierre, who learned it from her husband, Patrick. It tells of how the fox and the wolf found a keg of honey, and how the fox later ate all the honey on three consecutive days, pretending each time that he had been invited to be godfather at a christening.

When the wolf discovers he has been tricked, he wants to devour the fox, but he is tricked again when the fox promises to take him to a farm where geese are raised in a pen. When the wolf enters the pen, the noise alerts the farmer, who shoots him, and the sly fox is finally rid of him.

C'était un loup puis un renard. Ils restiont dans le bois. Ça fait que le renard était toujours plus fin que le loup. Ils cherchaient du miel; ils allaient voir pour des barils de miel. Le renard savait où ce qu'il était, le baril de miel. Ils sont partis ensemble, tous les deux, pour aller voir pour un baril de miel. Ils l'ont trouvé.

Le renard, il dit au loup, « Il faut pas y toucher; il faut pas le manger aujourd'hui. Serrons-le pour une autre fois. » Il était plus fin, le renard, puis ils s'en avont revenus.

Bien, le lendemain, il dit, « Moi, je suis demandé pour aller au baptême. Ah bien, j'irai pas. – Ah, le loup lui dit, on refuse pas le baptême. On refuse pas le baptême. »

Il voulait être fin. Il voulait s'en aller tout seul, puis manger une partie du baril de miel, puis il voulait pas en donner au loup.

Il s'en est venu et le loup lui a demandé, « Comment est-ce que vous l'avez donc appelé? – Bien commencé. »

Ah, le lendemain, il dit, « Je suis encore demandé pour aller au baptême, mais j'y irai pas. Non, j'irai pas; je sons ensemble. – Bien, le loup dit, refuses pas le baptême. Tu refuses pas le bap-

Chezzetcook: an Acadian stronghold

tême. Vas! »

Ah bien, il y a été. Il a mangé bien à moitié. Il s'en a venu et le loup lui a demandé, « Comment ce que vous l'avez donc appelé aujourd'hui? – Bien à demi. »

Bien, la troisième journée, il dit, « Je suis encore demandé pour aller au baptême, mais j'irai pas. – Ah, le loup dit, vas, refuses pas le baptême, on refuses pas le baptême. »

Il y a été. Il mange tout le baril de miel net. Il en a pas laissé pour le loup.

Il s'en est venu, puis le loup lui a demandé, « Comment est-ce que vous l'avez appelé aujourd'hui? – Bien fini. »

Tout était fini.

Bien, une journée ils sont partis et le loup dit au renard, il dit, « Il faut aller voir le baril de miel, il dit, on a pas été le voir depuis le temps qu'il est là. »

Bien, il se fiait pas d'y aller. Il disait qu'il se sentait pas vaillant aujourd'hui pour y aller. « Ah bien, allons voir. »

Ils ont parti; ils ont été. Le renard se tenait tout le temps derrière. Il traînait la patte. Le loup a été le premier. Il a trouvé plus de miel, le miel était tout mangé.

« Ah bien, je m'en vais te manger! Tu as tout mangé le miel en arrière de moi, qu'il a dit. Je m'en vais te manger. – Ah, mange-moi pas, il dit, mange-moi pas. Je t'emmènerai dans un endroit où-ce qu'il a des gooses assez. »

C'était dans un endroit où c'était une fermier qui avait beaucoup de gooses. Puis c'était le soir; il rentre dans le têt et puis le renard, lui, il était fin. Il a pas rentré, lui.

Puis le loup se battait après les gooses. Ils ont fait un grand train et puis le fermier s'en a aperçu. Il a entendu. Il est venu avec son fusil et puis l'a tué le loup.

Ça fait que le renard s'en est tiré comme il faut.

Conte du renard et l'ours
      recorded from Brigitte Lapierre, Grand-Désert, 1961.

This is another brief tale about Reynard the Fox. This time, the dumb animal he chooses as his victim is not a wolf but a bear.

Storytellers would sometimes weave together several episodes of the

Ronald Labelle

tales about a clever fox. This particular episode is one of the most common ones found in the French oral tradition, but Mrs. Lapierre added an unusual detail: After the unsuspecting bear is tricked into going ice fishing using his tail—and loses it when it freezes in the ice—the storyteller concludes that this is why all bears now have short tails.

> Il y avait un renard qui avait été voler quelque affaire. Le renard avait venu avec du poisson et puis c'était un beau poisson.
> L'ours lui dit, « Où-ce que t'as donc pris ça? – Il y en a assez dans le lac, il dit, tu peux t'en pêcher. – Avec quoi? – T'as rien qu'à t'en aller là, puis faire un trou, puis te fourrer la queue dans le lac, il dit, puis t'en pêcheras sur ta queue, avec ta queue. »
> Il a resté là jusqu'au lendemain matin. Il a resté là toute la nuit. Et puis c'était le lendemain, ça commençait le jour.
> L'ours, il voulait sortir de là, et puis sa queue était gelée, bien gelée. Il pouvait pas la haler en dehors. Il a tant fait qu'il a cassé sa queue. Il a perdu sa queue.
> Ils disent que c'est comme ça que les ours avaient la queue courte.
> Le renard était le plus fin.

Conte des trois frères *or* Le simple

told by Alban Lapierre in 1947
and recorded from Brigitte Lapierre in 1961.

This is a classic folktale about three brothers who set off together. The two eldest mock their younger sibling, treating him like a simpleton. However, when the king makes a plea for help, the younger brother comes to the rescue thanks to the magic tools he has found, and he is rewarded with the princess's hand in marriage. He finally forgives his brothers and has them released from the prison where they were locked up.

This story is best known as a Norwegian folktale because it was first published in a classic collection of tales from Norway in 1852. The tale is very rare in the French tradition, but it somehow found its way to Chezzetcook, where Alban Lapierre told it to Geneviève Massignon in 1947. Massignon recorded a second version of the tale in 1961, this time from Brigitte Lapierre.

Chezzetcook: an Acadian stronghold

In 1963, when French folklorists published the second volume of *Le conte Populaire français*, the standard reference work of French folktales, they included Alban Lapierre's tale under the title 'Les tâches du roi' (The King's Tasks).[244] In this way, a tale from the Acadian oral tradition in Chezzetcook made its way into one of the most important reference works in international folklore scholarship.

The version presented here is a transcription of the one recorded from Brigitte Lapierre in 1961, with the addition of some details taken from the version first told by Alban Lapierre in 1947. In her telling, Brigitte Lapierre uses a few English expressions like "I wonder" and "so hard".

One of the tasks accomplished for the king involves a sheet of "mascoui", a common Acadian term derived from the Mi'kmaq word for birch bark.

> Ils étiont trois frères. Le plus jeune, il voulait toujours savoir qu'est-ce qui allait et il aimait savoir beaucoup. Et puis les deux autres se moquiont de lui. Ils s'en alliont une fois dans le bois, dans le chemin, puis ils entendiont de quoi qui faisait du train. Ce petit jeune-icite, il dit à ses frères, « I wonder qu'est-ce que… Je sais pas qu'est-ce que c'est ça, ce train là. – Ah bien, ont dit ses frères, c'est rien. »
>
> Bien, il a parti, il a laissé ses frères là puis il s'en a été là. Il a trouvé une pelle plantée là, qui bêchait tout seul. Il avait une bourse avec lui, de quoi qui était grand assez pour le prendre. Il fourre la pelle dans sa bourse.
>
> Il s'inquiétait pour ses frères. Il s'en va avec eux. Eux se moquent de lui. Ils disent, « Qu'est-ce que t'as donc vu encore? – Ah, pas grand-chose, rien qu'une pelle qui était là. »
>
> Ils avont été plus loin. Là il a trouvé une hache qui coupait tout seul. Ça semblait une hache qui coupait du bois. Bien il a été voir. « Il faut que je check ça. »
>
> Bien, il prend la hache, puis il le fourre encore avec sa pelle. Il a tout emporté ça.
>
> Then, il a été plus loin. Il entendait de l'eau qui dripait. Il dit, « Il y a de l'eau qui drip. Il faut que j'aille voir qu'est-ce que c'est que ça. »

---

244 Paul Delarue et Marie-Louise Tenèze, *Le conte populaire français*…, tome 2, pp. 481-482.

Il a été voir. C'était un petit ruisseau qui coulait, puis c'était comme dans une feuille de mascoui, l'eau tombait, coulait dedans. Il bouche ça avec de la mousse. Là, l'eau coulait pas so hard. Il ramasse la feuille et l'emporte.

Ça a adonné après ça qu'il y avait un roi qui avait un gros arbre qui poussait devant son palais. Il voulait le faire couper. Ça lui faisait trop d'ombrage et ça ôtait la lumière. Puis beaucoup ont essayé de couper l'arbre. Il a dit que s'il se trouvait quelqu'un pour l'ôter, il marierait sa fille et puis il aurait la moitié de son trône. Il voulait faire couper cet arbre-là, puis faire une belle fontaine.

Il y a joliment du monde qui a été voir, mais ils se lassaient vite. Quand ils coupiont une partie de l'arbre avec leur hache, ça s'épaississait. Ils coupaient un morceau, puis deux repoussaient après que c'était coupé. Ça s'en allait pire.

Eux, ces trois hommes-icite, ils ont essayé. Les deux plus vieux ont essayé avant. Puis ceux qui aviont essayé, le roi les a enlevés tout net. Il s'est fâché. Il les punissait. Ils étiont obligés de couper l'arbre, puis boucher une fontaine. Ça fait qu'il fallait la pelle et puis la hache et puis l'eau après ça pour remplir la fontaine. Le troisième l'avait, le jeune qui avait ramassé toutes les affaires dans le bois. Il a fait tout ce que le roi voulait avoir.

Les deux autres, ils y ont été. Ils ont essayé. Ils les ont envoyés en prison. Puis le troisième y a été. Il a mis sa hache qu'il avait trouvée dans le bois, puis il a coupé l'arbre comme le roi voulait l'avoir. L'arbre a tombé.

Après ça, il a pris sa pelle et puis il a bêché la fontaine comme le roi voulait l'avoir. Et puis il a pris sa feuille de mascoui qu'il avait, il a débouché la mousse, puis la fontaine s'est emplie pleine d'eau.

Ça fait que c'est lui qui a marié la fille du roi. C'est lui qui l'a mariée, puis après ça, il a fait ôter ses deux frères hors de la prison. Le roi a accordé que ses frères soient ôtés de la prison.

Conte de l'homme qui s'était donné au le diable
recorded from Brigitte Lapierre, Grand-Désert, 1961.

This is another classic tale in the French tradition. It tells of a man who sells his soul to the devil and who bargains for more time when the devil comes to claim his prize. In 18th and 19th century France, it was one of the

Chezzetcook: an Acadian stronghold

tales that circulated in "chapbooks", low-priced booklets that peddlers sold door-to-door.

In Brigitte Lapierre's version, the man sells his wife's soul to the devil, rather than his own. On the devil's first visit, the husband gets rid of him by tricking him into transforming himself into a rat that gets thrown into the stove. On his second visit, the man plays his fiddle, causing the devil to dance without being able to stop. After that, the devil leaves and doesn't return during the woman's lifetime.

Mrs. Lapierre later mentioned that there was also a third episode, in which the husband saved his wife by making the devil sit on a chair from which he was powerless to get up.

> C'était un homme que sa femme s'avait donné au diable. Ça fait, un tel temps il est venu, puis son mari voulait pas que le diable l'emportit. Il en avait besoin. Il voulait la garder encore plus longtemps.
>
> L'homme de la femme dit au diable, « J'ai entendu dire que le diable était capable de se virer en souris puis en rat. – Ah, oui. » Il a commencé à se mettre en rat puis à courir dans la place.
>
> Et puis l'homme a pris un sac. Le rat se fourre dans le sac. Il y avait un beau gros feu. Il a rouvri le couvert du poêle; il l'a fourré dedans et le sac a brûlé.
>
> Puis le diable qui brûlait, il dit, « Quitte-moi aller, quitte-moi aller! Si tu veux me laisser aller, il dit, je laisserai ta femme un an et un jour plus loin. »
>
> Bien, il l'a laissé aller, then. Le diable s'est tiré. Sa femme était encore avec lui.
>
> Et puis au bout d'un an, une journée, il a encore venu le voir.
>
> Cet homme-icite, l'homme de la femme, il savait bien jouer du violon. Le diable est venu, puis il lui a dit, « J'ai entendu dire que le diable pouvait bien danser. – Ah oui, il dit, le diable est capable de danser. »
>
> Ça fait qu'il s'est mis à danser et puis il a fait lasser le diable.
>
> Le diable était assez las qu'il voulait plus danser. Il dit, « Laisse-moi aller, laisse-moi aller. »
>
> Il l'a laissé, then. Il s'en a été et il est plus revenu. Il a plus venu trouver l'homme après ça.

Ronald Labelle

Conte du capitaine qui a engagé le diable
recorded from Brigitte Lapierre, Grand-Désert, 1961.

This story is actually a devil legend similar to one found in many Maritime Acadian communities. It tells of the time a fishing boat captain who was short one crew member foolishly said he would even hire the devil if he showed up.

In Acadian legends, the devil never passes up an invitation, so he arrives disguised as a fisher.

One evening during the fishing trip, the captain notices that his new hire has hoofs rather than feet and realizes that he has hired the devil. When they reach the shore, he pays the devil double what he owes him, in order to be rid of him.

The devil leaves angrily, because what he really wanted to gain was the soul of the captain.

> Il y avait un homme qui aimait pas travailler fort. Il était engagé avec le diable. C'était un pêcheur. C'était un capitaine de bâtiment. Il l'a rencontré dans la rue.
>
> « Il manque un homme », il a dit à cet homme-ci. Il manquait un homme et lui avait dit qu'il s'engagerait quand même qu'il s'engagerait avec le diable. Il avait pas bien parlé.
>
> Ça fait que c'était le soir quand il a été dans la rue, il a rencontré un homme. Cet homme-icite lui a demandé s'il voulait pas aller à la pêche avec lui. Il dit oui, puis il y a été.
>
> Puis quand ils ont été un élan à la pêche, une soirée, il faisait pas beau, il faisait mauvais temps, puis ils étiont trempes, les pieds. Il s'est assis, puis il s'est chauffé les pieds. Ils se chauffiont en bas, les pieds sur le poêle.
>
> Puis le capitaine était en haut de la cabane puis il watchait faire. Puis c'était pas des pieds qu'il avait, cet homme-là, c'était des pattes de cheval. Et puis il a reconnu que c'était pas un homme qu'il avait engagé. Il avait engagé le diable.
>
> Ça fait qu'il a descendu en bas. Il dit. « Sais-tu, je m'en vais vous dégager. »
>
> Ah, il voulait pas. Il voulait pas être dégagé. Il l'a dégagé du bateau avec ça. Il a donné deux fois plus de morue à lui, du poisson qu'ils aviont pris, pour se clairer de lui. Ça fait qu'il s'en a été.
>
> Il s'est fâché, le diable, puis il a pris sa morue, puis il l'a tout tiré en l'air. Ça fait qu'il s'est délivré du diable.

Chezzetcook: an Acadian stronghold

Les petits enfants perdus dans le bois

told by Alban Lapierre in 1947,
and recorded from him in 1961

In 1947, Alban Lapierre dictated to Geneviève Massignon his version of the well-known tale popularized in Grimms' collection as 'Hansel and Gretel'. Massignon later recorded the same tale from him in 1961. The recorded tale has not been transcribed here because it is very similar to the well-known version. Unfortunately, Massignon only took down a summary of the version told by Lapierre in 1947.

Yet, this earlier version is interesting because it differs from the familiar Grimms' fairy-tale. Here, the children are not deliberately sent away by their parents, but get lost while picking berries. They sleep under a tree and arrive the next day at the house of the witch, who feeds them cake to fatten them.

At the end, after they have freed themselves from the witch, they are reunited with their parents, who were looking for them all along. The children's parents are thus seen in a positive light in the Acadian version.

> Un petit garcon et une petite fille ramassaient des grainages dans le bois; ils s'avont écartés; la nuit est venue, ils s'avont couché sous l'arbre.
>
> Ils ont marché su' une maison. C'était une sorcière; elle avait un gâteau,
>
> les enfants l'ont mangé. Elle voulait les faire engraisser. Un jour, la sorcière a ramené une brassée de bois pour faire un beau feu pour faire cuire le petit garçon.
>
> La petite fille a mis du bois dans le poêle; tous les deux ont mis la vieille dans le poêle et elle a brûlé. Les petits étaient tout seuls.
>
> Les parents les cherchaient; ils les ont retrouvés.

Conte de la fille du diable

told by Alban Lapierre in 1947 and
recorded from Brigitte Lapierre in 1961

This fairy-tale, as told by the two Grand-Désert storytellers, usually begins when a young man becomes a captive of the devil as a penalty for having lost to him in a game of chance. The versions told in Grand-Désert simply begin when a young man is hired to work for the devil and then becomes his captive. The devil gives the young man impossible tasks to accomplish in order to win his freedom and receive one of the daughters in marriage. He carries out the tasks with the help of the youngest of the devil's three daughters, and she escapes with him, using her magic powers to get away from her father.

This is one of the most complex fairy tales found in the French-speaking world, and is full of magic.

The version recorded from Brigitte Lapierre is presented here, along with a few details added from Alban Lapierre's earlier telling. The two Grand-Désert storytellers could not recall the tale in its entirety, but they did retain the central episodes, where the girl uses her supernatural powers to save the young man.

First, she magically cuts down a forest of trees, her suitor having been unsuccessful using a blunt ax. Then, she magically empties water from a lake, where the young man had only been given a leaky basket with which to do the job. Later, when the devil disguises his daughters to confound the young man, she tells him how to recognize her because of her red dress, whereas her sisters are in blue and green.

The couple finally escapes, but the young man ignores the girl's instructions about which horse to choose in the stables, and so, once again, she needs to use magic to elude the devil who is in pursuit. She changes shapes twice to fool her father, who keeps catching up to them on a faster horse.

At the end, the couple cross a bridge at the limit of the devil's domain and are finally free.

As they approach the bridge, the devil is about to overtake them, but the girl takes out a loaf of bread in which she has stuck pins. Her father feels a sharp pain as if the pins were sticking in him and he gives up the pursuit.

This unusual detail is rarely included in the classic tale and corresponds directly to a belief present in Acadian sorcery legends, in which pins stuck into an object magically cause a victim to feel pain, as if they were being thrust into their own body.

As is the case in the other tales, the telling includes a few Acadian expressions derived from English, such as "watchait" (to watch) and "driver" (to drive).

> C'est le conte sur un diable qui avait trois filles. Il y avait un homme paresseux; il voulait pas travailler fort. Il s'est engagé à couper du bois, puis il trouvait ça malaisé, couper du bois. Il ai-

mait pas travailler Ça fait que le diable a venu dans le milieu du bois et puis il a engagé John – c'est John qu'il s'appelait – pour faire son ouvrage. Puis John avait une hache qui avait pas de taillant. Il pouvait pas couper le bois avec ça. Il s'est mis à brailler. Il était pas capable de le faire. Il y a une des filles du diable qui venait le voir. Elle lui apportait à manger. Elle lui a demandé, « Qu'est-ce qui te fait donc pleurer? - Ah, bien, ton père m'a donné une hache pas de taillant puis il faut que je coupe tout ce bois-ici. » Elle dit, « Pleurez pas; assisez-vous ». Elle était capable, la fille du diable, elle était capable de tout faire couper. Le diable est venu après et tout était fini.

Il lui a donné une autre job then à faire : vider un lac avec un panier qui perdait son eau. La même fille l'a trouvé. Elle lui a demandé qu'est-ce qu'il avait à brailler. « Bien c'est ton père qui me fait vider le lac avec un panier. Je suis pas capable de le faire. – Couche toi puis dors, elle dit, délasses-toi. » Il se couche et il dort. Après, l'eau était toute séchée. Le diable a venu; c'était tout paré comme il voulait l'avoir.

Le troisième coup, il y avait un chien, puis le chien était tout curly. Il lui dit, « Il faut que tu enlèves tous les curls qu'il y a dans le poil du chien. Si tu peux faire ça, il dit, tu seras clair. » Il s'en a été, puis il a pris un bois, puis il a amarré le chien là-dessus, mais quand il ôtait le bois, les curls s'en venaient back. Bien, la fille a venu, puis elle a ôté les curls du chien.

Le diable avait trois filles. S'il avait fait ces ouvrages-là, il marierait une des filles après qu'elles passeront dans le trou de clé d'une porte. Le diable voulait pas lui donner celle qui lui portait son dîner. Elle lui avait dit, « Il y a une qui sera en vert, l'autre sera en bleu, puis l'autre sera en rouge. Ça sera moi. Tu choisiras moi. » Lui watchait pour prendre laquelle qu'il allait choisir. Ça fait qu'il a choisi le rouge. C'était elle.

Puis après ça, ils étaient pour s'en aller. Ils vouliont avoir un cheval pour les amener. Ils voulaient s'en aller et puis elle a revenu : « Tu prendras un cheval, elle disait à Jean, puis tu prendras pas les autres qui paraissont farouches puis capables. Tu prendras le cheval qui fait rien dans l'étable, le vieux cheval qui tient la tête en bas. »

Lui, il a été à la grange pour prendre le cheval. Il a pas fait comme elle avait dit de faire. Il a pris un des chevals qui paraissait capable et puis ils s'avont été. Elle lui a dit, « C'est pas ça que je t'ai dit de faire. Il va nous attraper. »

Ils ont commencé à driver. Bientôt, voilà le vieux cheval qui venait.

Elle dit, « Il vient; il va nous attraper. »

Il venait vite su' eux.

« Bien, je vais te dire qu'est-ce qu'on va faire, elle dit, je vais me virer en church et puis toi, quand tu viendras là, tu sonneras la cloche. »

Puis le church était là, puis l'homme sonnait la cloche et puis le diable a venu. Il a dit, « Vous avez pas vu un cheval puis un homme puis une femme passer? – Non, je sonnais ma cloche. » C'est tout ce qu'il a pu faire avec eux.

Il savait qu'ils étiont pas bien loin. Il est allé plus loin et puis bientôt encore, après qu'ils étaient partis, voilà le diable qui s'en venait chez eux again.

Sa femme lui demandait, « Les as-tu vus? – Non, j'ai rien vu. »

Sa femme dit, « Bien, c'était à eux que tu as parlé. »

Il part encore et le voilà encore qui vient. « À c'tte heure, elle dit, moi je vais me virer en pomme de choux et puis toi, tu vas couper les pommes de choux. »

Il a fait encore pareil; il a demandé s'il avait pas vu du monde passer. « Non. » Il a encore été back chez eux.

Sa femme lui a encore dit, « C'est à eux que tu parlais. »

À c'tte heure, il fallait qu'il drivit vite assez pour qu'ils pouviont passer la ligne, la ligne du diable. L'autre terre était bénie. Le diable pouvait pas aller plus loin. Ce coup-là, il y avait un pont. Il fallait qu'ils traversent le pont avant.

Elle avait des épingles dans un pain; ça piquait trop le diable. Il a pas pu les attraper. Ils ont pu traverser le pont.

Quand ils sont arrivés là, il a coupé la queue de son cheval et il l'a tiré au diable. Le diable a pris la queue de son cheval et il s'en a été back chez eux.

C'était tout fini. Ça fait que c'est elle qui l'a sauvé.

Chezzetcook: an Acadian stronghold

Le vieux matelot

told by Alban Lapierre in 1947,
and later recorded from Brigitte Lapierre in 1961.

This is the classic tale that folklorists refer to as 'The Grateful Dead'. In the French tradition, it is best known in its literary form under the title *Jean de Calais*.

Like the previous tale, it is usually a long one containing several episodes. Although the version presented here does not include every episode, the two storytellers remembered the essential elements of the story.

It tells of a sailor who is cast adrift and arrives on an island where he helps to settle a debt between two ghosts, one a baker and the other a shoemaker. Later, he arrives at a robber's den, where a princess is being held captive. He frees the princess and escapes with her in a rowboat, taking along the robber's gold.

They encounter a ship whose captain takes on the princess along with the gold, but, once again, the sailor is cast adrift. He is magically saved from his predicament by a talking bird sent by one of the ghosts he had earlier helped.

The hero then reaches a ship that takes him to shore. There, he is hired as a stablehand by the king.

When the ship captain arrives and pretends to have been the princess's saviour, the sailor reveals the truth and is granted her hand in marriage.

Une fois, il y avait un vieux matelot. Il est allé voir pour une job pour aller sur la mer. Un capitaine l'a engagé pour trois mois. Au bout de trois mois, il devait être payé, qu'il fut sur l'eau ou qu'il fut sur la terre.

Ses trois mois sont venus et il se trouvait sur l'eau. Le capitaine l'a payé, puis il lui a donné son meilleur canot, une bonne paire d'avirons et de quoi à manger.

Le matelot a nagé pour deux jours et une nuit avant qu'il ait vu la terre. Il a arrivé à une île. Il a couché là entre deux fosses.

Il y avait un boulanger et un cordonnier qui étaient chacun dans une fosse. Le cordonnier devait un pain au boulanger et le boulanger lui disait, « Paie-moi mon pain; paie-moi mon pain! » Alors, le vieux matelot a donné dix cents au boulanger.

Il s'en a été le lendemain matin. Il a pris son canot, ses rames et il a nagé deux jours et une nuit. Il a encore vu la terre. Il a nagé vers cette terre-là, puis c'était une île de forbans.

Il y avait des canots et une maison. Il a été à la maison, puis il a cogné à la porte. Le forban est venu à la porte. Il lui a dit, « Bonjour » et lui a demandé s'il était forban. Il a dit, « Oui, je suis un bon forban. »

Le forban a dit, « Je vais m'en aller trouver les autres forbans. Vous resterez ici, vous, puis on va vous donner les clés de trois chambres. Vous les débarrez, mais la quatrième chambre, vous la débarrez pas! » Il a débarré les trois chambres. La première, c'était l'or, l'argent, la myrrhe; la deuxième, c'était des fusils puis des sabres; la troisième, c'était des hardes, des habits de soie.

La quatrième chambre, il l'a débarrée, l'a rouvri. Il y avait une fille pendrillée par les cheveux. C'était la fille du roi. Il descendit la fille.

Il lui dit, « Change d'habits; prends les plus beaux qu'il y a dans la chambre. » Lui, il a pris un coffre d'or, puis ils ont parti.

Ils ont pris le plus beau canot qui était là. Ils ont nagé encore pour trois jours. Ils ont vu un bâtiment à voiles au loin. Il a commencé à secouer son aviron en l'air et le bâtiment est venu à lui.

Il a demandé s'ils les prendriont à bord du bâtiment. Ils ont dit que oui. Ils ont amené la fille en haut avec le coffre d'or puis ses avirons.

Après ça, ils ont coupé l'amarre du canot et ils ont envoyé le matelot en dérive tout seul avec rien du tout, pas d'avirons. Il a commencé à drifter dans l'eau.

Le vieux matelot braillait. Un petit oiseau est venu sur le bout du canot. L'oiseau, c'était le cordonnier avait été sauvé par le matelot. Il a dit, « Jette-toi à l'eau » par trois fois.

Le matelot a dit, « Si je me jette à l'eau, je me noierai. ».

La troisième fois, il a écouté l'oiseau. Il s'a jeté à l'eau et il s'est trouvé sur le pont d'un bâtiment en pleines voiles. C'était pas le même mais il allait au même quai.

Le capitaine lui dit, « Avez-vous été volé? » Il a dit oui.

« Ce bâtiment icite, il sera rendu trois jours avant l'autre. » C'était un bâtiment du roi pareil.

Ils sont arrivés trois jours avant et le matelot a été demander au roi pour de l'ouvrage. Le roi dit, « J'ai pas grand-chose à faire droite à c'tte heure, mais je vous donnerez 50 cents par jour pour nettoyer l'étable des chevals. » Il a pris ça, 50 cents par jour pour soigner les chevals du roi.

Le roi espérait son bâtiment qui venait. Comme de fait, au bout des trois jours, le bâtiment du roi a venu.

Le roi a été à bord; il a reconnu sa fille. Il a demandé au capitaine où il avait trouvé sa fille. Le capitaine savait l'histoire. Il a conté au roi qu'il l'avait trouvé amarrée dans une chambre par les forbans. Le roi était bénaisé de voir sa fille. Il a fait un grand festin pour les officiers et les hommes du bâtiment.

Le vieux matelot était venu le soir au festin. Après, il leur a demandé à conter des histoires.

Le roi s'est déviré au matelot. Il a dit, « Vous qui passez votre vie sur la mer, vous devriez savoir des contes. »

Figure 28: Geneviève Massignon, at the time of her Acadian folklore research project.

Le vieux matelot a répondu, « Oui, si vous voulez ôter ce que ce capitaine-là a dans sa poche, je vous en conterai un. »

C'était un pistolet. Il le savait. Ils ont ôté le pistolet et il a conté son histoire. Le vieux matelot a tout conté. Il a dit, « Votre fille, c'est moi qui l'a sauvée. »

La fille a reconnu le matelot. Elle l'a pris par le cou et elle a dit, « Oui, mon père, c'est lui qui m'a sauvé la vie. »

Le petit oiseau dit, «C'est lui qui a sauvé la vie de ta fille et c'est moi qui a sauvé sa vie à lui. ».

Le roi qui a entendu ça, il était fâché après les hommes du bâtiment.

Le capitaine a été pris et le roi a fait marier sa fille avec vieux matelot.

Il y a eu des grandes noces et le vieux matelot est resté là.

Ronald Labelle

8: Voices of Acadian elders

I would like to share the words of a few of the many elders I interviewed in Chezzetcook, people who gave me a warm welcome and generously shared their memories of past life in the community. Nearly all have passed away since I began to visit them in the 1980s, and this chapter will acquaint readers with four of them: John Lapierre, Lavinia (Roma) LeBlanc, Liliane (Lapierre) Bellefontaine and Édouard Lapierre.

Lavinia LeBlanc was the only one of the four whom I interviewed in English. Like most of members of her generation, she was bilingual, but she preferred to be interviewed in English, as she had lost the habit of speaking her first language. I have translated the words of the three other informants from French.

Unfortunately, the local Acadian dialect can not be properly conveyed in a translation. Still, I hope these pages will give readers an appreciation of the richness of local culture shared by the elders of Chezzetcook.
The chapter also includes additional excerpts from Lena Ferguson's interviews with John Lapierre, Liliane Bellefontaine, Luc Bellefontaine and Mary Jane (Julien) Wolfe. Lena recorded theseduring the years when she was exploring aspects of life in the community in order to prepare a series of articles for the *Dartmouth Free Press*.

I would like to dedicate this chapter to the memory of Lena Ferguson, who spent countless hours documenting the history and traditions of the area.

John Lapierre - "Our people here used to be called Acadians"

John Lapierre was a member of the sixth generation of Lapierres who lived in West Chezzetcook. Like many others of his generation, he was well aware of his Acadian heritage. He told me his ancestor had escaped from the British at Grand-Pré and had made his way through the woods to settle at Chezzetcook.

As in most family legends, there is some truth to the story, because François Lapierre, the first of the family to have settled in Acadia during the mid-17th century, did live at Grand-Pré, while the Lapierres of a later generation actually managed to avoid being deported, although they were captured and imprisoned for a time at Fort Beauséjour before eventually settling in Chezzetcook.

John was born in 1901, the 11th in a family of 12 children. Like many members of his generation, he chose to leave his community to earn a living, but he returned to settle in Chezzetcook after only a few years in the United States.

His childhood memories are of growing up on the family farm, which produced oats and hay as well as livestock, and how he helped his father fish at Threefathom Harbour. He had fond memories of the parish church, where he served as an altar boy at the time when the interior walls had yet to be finished. He told me of how just before midnight mass on Christmas Eve, with the church filled with parishioners, the altar-boys would go around lighting candles set all along the walls.[245]

John Lapierre's first work experience was on a schooner hauling beach gravel to Halifax. This is how he recounted the story to Lena Ferguson (her questions are in italics):

> Arthur and Peter Ferguson used to haul some roofing gravel from the back of the cape. It was roofing gravel, and they had some sales for that. He used to dump it there. He would come through the cape. He had a road cut out there and he would dump it at a little place out there that's inside the cape, but that cape is gone now. It's there that Arthur used to dump that gravel. They would take it with a gundalow from there and put it in the schooner and perhaps sometimes when it was smooth, there was water enough for the schooner at the mouth of the harbour and it wasn't very far to handle it, you know.
>
> Peter's schooner was the *Shamrock*. One time, he hired me to

---

245 CEAAC, Ronald Labelle Collection, accession no. 1385 (1982).

go in town. I was only a boy. I was only about 12 or 13 years old. Arthur was home that time. (…)

Peter, the old man himself, Mr. Ferguson, he asked me if I would go. There was a Murphy working with him there, Joe Murphy (…) He wasn't fit that time, and they asked me if I would go.

"Well," I said, "I'll ask my father and mother if they would let me go," I said, "I'm willing to go".

I told father that Peter had asked me to make the trip with him.

"Ah yes," he said, "go help him".

So I went, and I worked on the schooner. That was in town. And they unloaded that—I used to be helping on the winch, you know, the gravel is all in the bottom of the schooner. He had roofing gravel in. She was loaded, and Arthur was home that time but Murphy wasn't around.

You see, they would heist her up like that on the winch there, one on each side, and they had to fill up the tub in the hole. They used to have a two-bushel tub, I think, so it was quite big. For one man, it was too much to turn, but for two men, one on each side —the other man was there, he would be on the front, and he would be pushing and turning, and then the boom would swing over on the wharf in Halifax. And Peter would stay there. That was his job, you see; he would dump that dump on the wharf and they would haul it away with horses in those days.

Old Peter was a good strong worker. He would take hjs time but he was there all the time, early in the morning.

How long would it take to get to Halifax in the schooner?

If the wind was good, easterly wind, you could sail up there in two hours. In two hours and a half, you would be there at the wharf.

Did you come back the same day?

No, it took over a half a day to unload the schooner. Old Arthur used to be cook. We would stay up front. There was lots of room there for two men; there were bunks and you could eat there.

Old Peter, now, used to stay in the back cabin. He used to sleep there. He was the captain.[246]

---

246 Eastern Shore Archives, Lena Ferguson Collection, tape 6737 (1988); tape 6808 (1980).

Chezzetcook: an Acadian stronghold

John Lapierre's most vivid memories of his early years in Chezzetcook concern his summer spent on a fishing schooner when he was 16 years old. This is how, in translation, he described to me his own personal experiences on the fishing schooner:

> I made one trip over there, to the Magdalen Islands. They had big boats that went there, some big ships. They were built in the west at Lunenburg. Ah, some big vessels. So me, I was coming from Maganchiche (Threefathom Harbour) in the spring...and old Captain Gilbert, he was a German, Gilbert Gates was his name.
>
> He said, "Do you want to come aboard the schooner this year?"
>
> "Well," I said, "I don't know yet. I'll have to ask my parents. But as far as I'm concerned, I said, I'm willing to go."
>
> "Yes? Well you find out," he said, "I want you to come, and another feller," he said, "Gregory Fillis is coming."
>
> He was a fellow from Grand-Désert. He spoke English.
>
> All right, I asked my father.
>
> "Ah, it's okay to go," he said, "if you want to. You don't have to go, but if you want to go, you're welcome to."
>
> And my mother, well, gosh, my mother wasn't too much against it either.
>
> I had a brother who was on board that big vessel also. (...) It was its fourth year in the Baie du Nord [the northern section of the Gulf of St. Lawrence]. They called that the Baie du Nord. I enjoyed it, once I got used to it, I really liked it.(...)
>
> Half the schooner belonged to Grand-Désert, and Seaforth, further down, owned half of it too. In those days, those schooners cost a lot of money. They cost thousands of dollars, but today it would be millions of dollars for a vessel like that.
>
> Ah yes, she was a nice schooner. She sailed well and she sailed fast. Ah, that was a nice boat. I guess she was almost a hundred feet long. And she was tall on the water; you know, those ships are tall.
>
> They used to lower the dories into the water, and they would haul them in every night. They lifted them in. [There were] two tackles, one in front and the other in the back. They put them all one inside the other. And they put seven on one side, and seven on the other side of the ship. There were 14 dories all together.

> There was just one man who fished in each dory. They went in the morning; they got up early, and then we had breakfast after them. At six o'clock, they were up, and they had a good breakfast. And then they put their dories afloat one after the other. There was a reef there, a shoal, and the ship didn't go that far. That's where they fished. Once they were done with the cod, they came back with it. They filled up their boat. Some of them filled their boat so deep, so close to the water's level, with cod, and some of those codfish were this long. They were big and heavy. But that cod came for a certain amount of time and stayed a while. It stayed there for maybe a week and a half.
> At one time, the fishermen went and got some bait. They had herring, and they had two nets spread alongside the ship at night. The next morning, they hauled them in. There was enough herring for all the fishing dories.[247]

The summer spent as a teenager working on a schooner with a crew of experienced fishers left John Lapierre with lasting memories. His retelling of the experience gives us an intimate view of the cod fishery in the early part of the century (my questions are in italics):

> We didn't have too much rain the time I was down there. We only had one storm. It was windy and it got pretty rough. And through the night—I remember that because I used to sleep way in the bow, the bow of the schooner—and I used to hear the water flapping on the schooner. I got used to that after a while—and the man that was watching, he had to call another man up that had been sleeping, for help. He had to give him more cable. I guess he thought he might drag the anchor. And he gave him quite a bit of cable. I remember that well.
> Once you were used to it, it went well. There was enough to eat, and I worked at splitting the cod heads. (...) That was my work all the time, splitting cod heads: splitting them on the side, and then taking the head off.
> And then there was a fellow who would split, and then take out the bone there, the middle bone, you know. And then it tumbled into a barrel of water, a barrel with some water in it, and then it was salted. It stayed in the water for maybe... as long as it

---

247 CEAAC, Ronald Labelle Collection, accession no. 1375 (1982).

took to fill the barrel. And then they would take it and there was sort of a chute that went down into the ship's hold. (...) They would salt it in the ship's hold in those days. You were gone for two and a half months, so they had better salt it!

They had to wash it first on the schooner. It had to be clean fish. And then, they would put it through a press, you know, and the water would drain out.

Then, when they were through fishing, there was still a lot of work to do. They would take it to shore, on the beach. They spread it out. Some had flakes and some just on the rocks, on the beach.

There was one week of fishing when, by Geez; the vessel had a big load on board. Everything was filled with codfish. They used to go in dories; every time they would come aboard—that was twice a day they used to go out—we'd be loaded. They would have perhaps two tons of fish there. And some of them were that long, the codfish.

That week we had to work! We worked late at night and on the Saturday night, they all turned in and gave us a hand with the fish. By Saturday night, the codfish was all cleaned, and the deck was washed. Even if you finished at 10 o'clock at night, you had to do it.

On Sunday, people didn't work. No fishing on Sunday. (...) You could go up on deck and sit there.
Did they play cards on the boat?
Not much, no. Well, you know, there were a lot of older men, Germans. They were all pretty old, and they would talk with each other...
That was the only time you went?
Only once. After that, during the fall, they went to town, they sold their fish, and there were some men who came and who wanted to buy the boat. The men from Seaforth were starting to get old, and some of them were happy to sell.

My Gosh, they sold it. I guess it was (to) people from Newfoundland.[248]

As this was during the summer of 1918, it is not surprising that the ship's crew was composed mainly of young boys and older men. The

---

248 Ibid., accession no. 1323 (1982).

Ronald Labelle

First World War was still raging, and most local men of working age were serving in the armed forces. John was a deck hand, or "mousse", and his main task was to remove the heads of the codfish, while Tom Lapierre split the fish and another "mousse" named Gregory Fillis extracted the livers to be used in preparing cod liver oil.

During the following years, John continued to work with his father and, at the age of 21, he left with two of his friends to look for work in Portland, Maine, joining several other men from Chezzetcook who were already there. He remembers that in order to get a work permit, he had to prove that he was 21, and that he knew how to read.

Arriving in Portland, he saw many familiar faces:

> There is a place that they called... Westbrook; it was west of Portland, to the west across the railroad tracks. And there were a lot of old men, the old men who worked at Thompson's Point. Some of them had jobs as machinists, the Lapierres, and some of them worked as builders—not as builders but as blacksmiths.
>
> There was a Lapierre, and there was a Roma who worked as a blacksmith. He was a good blacksmith. There were a lot of blacksmiths in that place. I think there were five or six, you know. They worked on the railroad cars there, the gondola cars, steel cars. They were big and long. And then they had box cars like you see around here. Those ones were made of wood.
> *But on the railroad, did you move from one place to the other?*
> No. That was our place, Thompson's Point it was called. It was nice, ah yes. (...)
>
> When I lived there I stayed at a boarding house with my cousin. But then he was leaving. He worked on the waterfront and he did well, but work was slack in the spring; so then he had an idea to go out west.
>
> Good, well, I said, "I'm not going out west because if my parents take sick at home, I'll have to come back."
> His parents were dead, so he went out there.[249]

At that time, John felt responsible for his parents' livelihood, he being the youngest son of the family and his father Simon over 70 years old. He therefore returned to Chezzetcook after three years in the United States and stayed with his parents during their final years. He bought a small

---

249 Ibid., accession no. 1314 (1982).

boat with which he fished for lobsters, and he took up farming again, using an ox to haul loads, as had always been done in the community. At the age of 38, he married a widow named Marie Mayette. In later years, he worked at various times on road construction crews in the Chezzetcook area, while continuing to farm. When I met John Lapierre in 1982, he had been widowed himself for several years, and lived alone in his house situated near the boundary between West Chezzetcook and Grand-Désert.

Lavinia LeBlanc - "We never gave up our French"

Lavinia LeBlanc was born Lavinia Roma in 1899. She was a member of the sixth generation of Romas in Chezzetcook, and a descendant of Jean-Baptiste Roma, who had made his way to Chezzetcook after being freed from imprisonment at Louisbourg in 1760. Her parents, Michel and Isabelle Roma, raised eleven children at the Head of Chezzetcook, in the house where Lavinia still lived when I met her in 1982.

Growing up a certain distance away from the Acadian communities of West Chezzetcook and Grand-Désert, Lavinia didn't have access to schooling in her first language, but said her family always spoke French together, despite being surrounded mainly by English-speaking people. However, as she spent most of her life in English-speaking surroundings, Lavinia gradually lost the habit of speaking French outside of her immediate family circle, and she was one of the few informants who preferred to be interviewed in English.[250]

During her childhood at the Head of Chezzetcook, Lavinia witnessed the harvesting of the marsh hay. She remembers that by the time the harvest was over, there was not a straw left standing on the entire marsh. She even helped her father haul the load of hay:

> Well there's the place. There's the marsh, right there. We used to go down and cut the hay off of the marshes and some of them would take it and haul it way down West Chezzetcook, and they had those gundalows, you know, big long black boats. They didn't have no sails on it, they'd just pole it. They pushed it with poles. They used to come up here and cut... my father used to go there and cut it and then he'd haul it. Most of the time, he used to haul it with two wheel carts. He'd have the children to push it, and

---

[250] Ibid., accession nos. 1253-1295 (1982); 1670-1680 (1983); 2573 (1986).

he'd get in the shafts and haul it and put it on the grass here and let it dry. That was done kind of late in the summer, after the other hay was cut and put away.

The gulley leading to the Head of Chezzetcook was not only used by farmers from the lower part of the inlet to reach the salt marsh. Lavinia's family used to go downstream to dig for clams and to picnic on the many islands between East and West Chezzetcook:

Do you know why they chose to live around here? Was it to be close to the marshes?
Well it was in access to almost anything, you know. If you wanted to go on a boat and get fish, if you wanted to go digging clams, there was all kinds of clams and you'd dig clams or go down and catch your own fish if you wanted to, by hand line. We used to do that. And there was islands, a bunch of islands down there. Instead of going to the beaches, we used to go to the island for our picnics – our family picnics, you know. Take a bunch, put them in a boat on a Sunday afternoon and everybody would go down... we'd all go down for a picnic and steam clams and... well, we'd bring our supper down there and eat our supper down there, whatever we had. Our father always used to go dig clams and we'd run around the flats and help him. Well, you know, then we'd come home after dark. We'd come home, sail when the tide would answer. When the tide would be coming in, then we'd leave to come up with it. And by the time we used to get up here, the tide would be high, right up. The gully would be right full.

Apart from the family picnics on Sundays, the annual parish picnic was an event that Lavinia looked forward to as a child:

We used to pick berries, when they used to have a church picnic. All the young children, they would always go and pick so many berries and sell it so we'd gather some money. We used to get about five cents a quart for blueberries or any other kind of berries we'd pick. And sell it, and gather up money for to go to the picnic. Oh boy! we were glad of that. We used to have big, big picnics. Well, we thought they were big picnics, you know. They'd have big suppers and they had a big thing made outside, like a stage. It was all covered up with branches. The fiddlers used to be inside and everybody would go inside and dance.

Lavinia not only picked berries to earn pocket money, but she also helped her father gather blueberries to sell in Dartmouth:

> Walking was nothing, you had to go. We used to go miles and miles and go picking berries a way back at Long Lake, we call now. Gee, if you would tell them to go down there now, they'd faint. We used to go there and walk there and heavens, we used to have to carry two pair of shoes with us, because one pair we'd use to go in the woods with, you know; we didn't care, the other pair we had to put on to come home with. Father used to come with us and with great big baskets of berries - blueberries. Father used to put them over his shoulders, you know; carry one basket in the front, one in the back. He'd take mostly all the load so we wouldn't have too much to carry. Then, he used to gather a whole wagonload and then he'd go in town and sell it, peddle it.
> *A wagon load of blueberries?*
> Yes, we used to have four or five boxes, big boxes, that high. And then he'd go and sell it. That was when I was only a kid. And he used to go into Dartmouth because I remember the first day I went to Dartmouth. We were scared to death. There was nothing to be scared of. The only thing, we used to smell the smoke. We never had no smoke around here, and we used to smell the coal smoke when we used to get up there. Well you'd go in with a horse and father used to put his horse in the shed, you know, a barn there. And we wasn't allowed to go too far. We were just allowed to go down parts... the end of the road to see. Then we used to listen to the horse. You know the noise the horse would make on the concrete. We never had that so that was something new to us!

Children accomplished an remarkable amount of work in Chezzetcook, and they often began to take on regular employment as soon as they entered their teens. As a teenager, Lavinia worked as a household servant in Halifax, where she was living during the terrible explosion of December 6, 1917, an event that left lasting images in her memory:

> I was working in Halifax. I was working down on South Park Street. I was looking after a bunch of kids. They were just gone to

school. They never got hurt. It was down in the South End. The school got smashed, though. Some of them might have got hurt, but the ones I was looking after didn't. But the house was all demolished. The house I was in was all busted; the windows were all busted and doors was torn off the hinges and we all had to vacate the place and go in the... where they play golf now, in the Halifax golf fields, and that's where we stayed all day. Some of them stayed all night. They were expecting another blast. It didn't come. They were saved from that. If that one had went off, I guess the whole place would have went flat. But it didn't. I went... we went downtown, my girlfriend and I went downtown. They were calling for help, you know, so we went down to... I think the post office is built there now, right below St. Mary's, there. There was a great big theatre, the old time theatre was there. And they had opened it up for a hospital. We went in there. Oh, the sight you would see there was something awful.

They had brought all the injured people in to there?

Well, as many as they could take in, you know, the hospitals were all filled up. And they took them in there, and they had... they had no trucks, they just had horse and buggies - not buggies - they had those low, low carts that the wheels was high and the cart was right almost down to the ground.[251] They used to haul them in on that. They were piled up like cord wood.

And they wouldn't have had enough doctors and nurses to look after them.

No. They had to have people to make bandages, tear up things to make bandages. So we had our share of work that night. Oh, I don't know, there was a lot of bad things happened in those years, but they all weathered. Some got killed, some didn't. Some got blind. I suppose that's life one way or the other. You get it good, and then you get it bad, and you never know how it's going to end. It can't end very much worse than that.

Apart from working in Halifax, Lavinia LeBlanc also spent some time in Boston before returning home, where she married Alban Julien in the summer of 1919. The couple then spent a few years at Grand-Désert, after which they bought a farm at Threefathom Harbour.

---

251 This was a 'sloven', a type of cart that was commonly used in the Maritimes between the mid-nineteenth and mid-twentieth centuries.

Chezzetcook: an Acadian stronghold

Her husband was a fisher, farmer and jack-of-all-trades who left home for a while to work in the shipyards at Halifax, and who also went once to Portland, Maine to earn the money he needed to pay off the mortgage on his farm. Lavinia and her first husband spent 27 years at Threefathom Harbour, where they raised five children.

During the 1920s, before the harbour itself had been joined to the mainland by a causeway, Lavinia used to observe the comings and goings of rumrunners:

> Great big boats would come in and a couple of men would go out to lead them in. They'd go out with their motorboats and then they'd lead them in, you know. They'd come so far and then they'd anchor. Then the boats would go out and get the stuff and bring it ashore. And then the cars were there to pick it up and boats and cars and trucks, wagons of all kinds.
>
> *And where did they take it from there?*
>
> To bootleggers. They'd take it to the people in Halifax, sell it, God knows where. They didn't say that, I don't know. But I know different places in Halifax had these places where they used to sell liquor.
>
> *Did the local people in Threefathom Harbour, did they make money on that?*
>
> Some of them did, you know; they used to go help, so they were getting paid. They were getting paid for hauling it up. They used to go down the shore and haul it up. Sometimes there'd be 15 or 20 vehicles (...) They had some powerful cars that used to go down there. Great big Cadillacs. Fill them right up full of liquor. I remember going in to feed my pig one morning and there was a couple of bags of bottles... whisky. They had thrown it in the pigs' yard, you know.
>
> *They had stashed them there.*
>
> I suppose with the intention of picking them up when they come back. (...) Sometimes there'd be 15 cars waiting for that boat to come in. And they used to have to park their cars different places because those 15 cars at that time in one spot would show up an awful lot. They used to hide them in the woods and byroads and any place where they could park one. And I seen them when the boats would come in and then they'd go and get the stuff and bring it in. They'd work all night on that. They'd start and they'd be working until daylight. I counted, one night, there were 15

cars. There was all kinds of liquor around.
It would all be unloaded during the night, eh?
Yeah. The cars was right there waiting for them. And where the cars couldn't go, they used to have ox teams and horse teams that would go down so that they'd bring it up to the cars. I guess everybody was getting paid. There was an awful lot of people there, you know. Well, all the people around there. There wasn't that many people living in Threefathom Harbour, but they didn't only come from Threefathom Harbour, they came from Grand-Désert. Anybody that wanted to get in.

You'd be surprised who they were. Some was big shots, you know. They weren't common people. Common people only had the scrapings. (...)

They used to come down and stay for a whole week before the stuff would land. They couldn't take no chances. There was a house on top of Graham's Head, what we were just talking about, and they used to rent the attic. There was like three flights, and up in the attic there was a place that you could look out in the ocean, and they used to stay there for weeks at a time. Nobody knew they were there. But they used to stay there.

Then they would see a boat coming from far. They'd know when the boat... then they'd notify the rest of them.
Was there some kind of signal to know that it was the rum running boat?
Oh yeah, well the boat was always black. The rumrunner was always black. You'd see it coming, you knew it was her.

My God! Those were the great old days, I suppose if you'd want to call them that. There wasn't much for the people that was living then locally. They never got rich off of it.

With so much rum running activity going on, Lavinia and her husband became familiar with the hiding places used by the bootleggers from Halifax:

We went one night to investigate a hide. They used to call them a hide. My husband was with me and he tapped the... He knew it right away, it felt right hollow. He says, "They've got a hideaway here."
He would tap what?
He'd tap the stick that he had, and it went right through the

gravel on the beach. And he scraped it, and there was the catch. I went to open the hatch, and it was right hollow, there was nothing into it.

He says, "We'll come here in about another month's time, and we'll see what they got into it."

And we did. We went down, and it was right full, right up to the cover. That was an awful temptation not to take any, you know. There was nobody around, and you found that hide.

They used to go there and they'd take their boat and go get some—steal some.

I guess some people would steal some, eh?

Oh, yeah. But it was a long way to carry it on the beach, you know. They had to get their boats and get the booze there. Those were rich people that had that catch there; rich people from Halifax.

Living close to the sea, Lavinia also witnessed shipwrecks, and her husband was hired a few times to haul cargo that had washed up on shore.

Lavinia and her husband sold their land and moved to Dartmouth in 1947, but five years later, they returned to live at the Head of Chezzetcook. Lavinia later became a widow, and was eventually remarried to Francis LeBlanc.

When I met her in 1982, she had been widowed a second time and was living alone in the house she had grown up in at the Head of Chezzetcook.

Liliane Bellefontaine - "The Acadians endured a lot so they could live in peace"

Liliane Bellefontaine was bom in 1901, the daughter of Daniel Lapierre and Catherine Bellefontaine. On her father's side, she traced her ancestry back six generations to Jacques Lapierre, the ancestor of all the Lapierres of Chezzetcook. When Liliane married Eloi Bellefontaine in 1925, she took on her husband's name, which was also her mother's maiden name.

Among all the Acadians of Chezzetcook who were born around the turn of the 20th century, Liliane Bellefontaine was one of those who had the most extensive knowledge of the early history of the community. She had an excellent command of French, her first spoken language. All the excerpts of interviews are translations from the original French, except for the first one, in which she explained to Lena Ferguson how the Bellefontaines, her maternal ancestors, changed their name from "Godin":

> They were not there (in Grand-Pré). They were away to New Brunswick. Alexander and Jean and Charlie, these three brothers, came out here from New Brunswick and they settled here. But Charlie didn't stay here. (...) Bellefontaine is a title this man got from the King of France. (...) It seems that Montreal was only a town then, that was the 16th century, a long time ago, and this man, his name was Godin. (..) A young boy, he came to Montreal, and he worked so hard for Montreal, doing so much.[252] (...)
>
> They went out there [to New Brunswick]. They were travelling a lot before the Expulsion because nobody was settled in those days. They were not settled. Young people were travelling an awful lot. They travelled to New Brunswick, these groups, the Godin. And it happened that his famly had, I think, 7 or 8 boys and he baptized them on that name. He dropped Godin.
>
> He baptized them; that's how, from generation to generation, it came to be Bellefontaine.[253]

Liliane had often listened to her parents and grandparents talk about the difficulties experienced by the early settlers, and about how the Aboriginal population had helped them:

> With the Mi'kmaq, they were all right. I have often heard that they would say, "With the Mi'kmaq, we had friends, but with the English, we had enemies." That was the saying of the old people from the early days, the first ones, I think. That's what I heard.

The eldest of five children, Liliane spent her first years in West Chezzetcook. At 11 years of age, she went to live with an Acadian family in the village of Corberrie, near Digby in Southwestern Nova Scotia. Whereas many teenage girls in Chezzetcook went to work as domestic servants in Halifax, it was unusual to leave home so young.

One advantage to sending Liliane to work in an Acadian area of the province was that she could continue her schooling in French:

---

252 Charles Bellefontaine, ancestor of the Chezzetcook branch of the family, was the son of Gabriel Godin, who had taken on the title Sieur de Bellefontaine upon receiving a large land concession along the St. John River from the Governor of Acadia in the 1690s.

253 CEAAC, Ronald Labelle Collection, accession nos. 1143 (1982); 1455-1457 (1982); 1713-1734 (1983).

Chezzetcook: an Acadian stronghold

> At 11 years of age, I went off to Digby. I stayed there four years, then I came back. I came back home and I always stayed around here, apart from working in town, you know. We had to earn our living. I had to work until I got married. (...) That was a young age, but they taught you to work in those days. They didn't teach you to smoke cigarettes! I was only 11 when I went over there, to Digby. There I could go to school, and I learned how to work. I had to do housework, and also on the farm. You know, there was a lot of work to do. You had to lend a hand everywhere.

Religion was important to Liliane's family when she was growing up, and all religious practises at that time took place in French:

> Children said their prayers in school, but they learned their prayers at home. They knew their prayers before going to school. Then, the schoolteachers taught us the catechism. We had prayer books in French. We learned our prayers in French, and the catechism was French. They were all French priests in those days, here and down around Digby. The priests' sermons were all in French. Ah yes, but now it's all English. The difference was like night and day.

Many members of Liliane's parents' generation could read French:

> In the old days, they had a French teacher who went through... or a French school master who came by. Because my grandmother, she learned French, she didn't learn English. Well, at the time when my mother went to school, they learned both. They learned the two languages then. My mother could read English and French, and I used to read her history book, from when she was in tenth grade.

Liliane's mother was active in St. Anselm's parish where she sang regularly at mass, and she sometimes led the church choir. She was also one of the founders of the local chapter of the French Canadian Catholic women's organization, *Les Dames de sainte Anne,* and Liliane followed in her footsteps later on.

Liliane had a strong attachement to her family, and although she spent eight years working in Halifax before her marriage at the age of 24, she returned home whenever she could. Her mother taught her to card, spin and knit wool, and Liliane often helped her with these tasks.

One of her jobs was to fetch the raw wool that her mother needed:

> Me and my sister, we went many times to the other side [of the inlet] with a sleigh to get wool hides. Sometimes I'd come back from town and my mother would say, "Well, I don't have much wool left. You'd better go across to see if you can find some there, at the Head of Chezzetcook."
>
> We went on the inlet with a little sleigh and we came back with a couple of wool hides. (...) Yes, and in summer, we walked down below to get some wool hides. There were always people who had sheep, you know, because in Grand-Désert they had a lot of sheep.

After her wedding, Liliane lived with her husband in one of the oldest of the Bellefontaine family residences, a house that had been built in the 1840s at the Head of Chezzetcook and later hauled over the frozen harbour by teams of oxen in order to reach its present destination in West Chezzetcook. That is where the couple raised their three children and where Eloi earned his living by operating a saw-mill.

I first interviewed Liliane Bellefontaine in 1982, and visited her on each of my later trips to Chezzetcook. The final visits took place after she had moved into a nursing home in Upper Musquodoboit.

I consider the passing of Liliane Bellefontaine in 1990 as marking the end of an era in Chezzetcook, for, with her soft Acadian accent and her gentle sense of humour, she seemed to represent more than anyone else a culture from an earlier time.

Mary Jane (Julien) Wolfe—"In the summertime, we would dance on the bridges"

Mary Jane Wolfe was born in 1921, the daughter of Walter Julien and Rose Lapierre. She is a fourth-generation descendant of Simon Julien, who came to Chezzetcook from France at the beginning of the 18th century.

Mary Jane grew up in Grand-Désert and attended school there. Interviewed by Lena Ferguson in 2001, she recounted her childhood memories of the Acadian *mi-carême* tradition:

Chezzetcook: an Acadian stronghold

> At Mid-Lent, we would just leave the school. The teacher couldn't say nothing. There was the whole bunch of us running up in the field and falling down in the mud and everything else.
>
> These tiny little cookies were made like the top of salt and pepper shakers. There were so many kids, they were made right small. She would throw a handful and we would go after her and if we got too close, she had a big fork so we didn't go any closer. (...)
>
> You had to go up in the fields, but the fields were nice and clean then. They had been all cleaned in the fall, you know, and it was nice. You went where you could see her, so the kids could see her. She would come around noontime, I would say. She would take off when we had no more cookies. She would show her bag—there were no more cookies. (...)
>
> They gave a lot of the old traditions up, like the Happy New Year. I remember going out for Happy New Year with my brother Ferdie and it was raining real hard and we had pillowcases, white pillowcases. And of course, the candy was not wrapped up. It was mostly molasses candy, taffy. And some of them, the taffy was not quite—if you make a nice taffy, you could sugar it, but some of it had no sugar, it was just pure molasses. It was raining really hard and we went to one door and the molasses candy was dripping over the bag. It was stuck together. What a mess that was. (...)
>
> I remember my mother making molasses candy and putting it on a great big board, a floured board that they used to knead their bread on. It was clean and they put all the candy on that and they took a knife and put it underneath a lump of candy and put it in your bag. Nobody got sick from it.

Mary Jane Wolfe also told the story of the short-lived lobster factory at Threefathom Harbour, where she worked as a teenager. Her memories describe not only the work environment at the lobster factory, but also provide a picture of social life in the community in the 1930s:

> I don't know how it came about, but they wanted to set up a lobster factory down at Threefathom Harbour and they had to get someone from outside who knew how to set it up to operate it. They had this Ferdinand LeBlanc who was involved in a lot of lobster factories in New Brunswick. They had them up there. I don't know who was the boss. Harry Julien was the stoker for the big

furnace to keep the boilers going and he used to blow the whistle. It was all coal, of course. They had a well up further, before the sea, to the salt water.

Where was the lobster factory located?
It was right as you entered the Threefathom Harbour fishermen's reserve before they put the causeway up. You had to go across in a little boat, a little rowboat. There was no causeway at the time.

Did you have to walk from Grand-Désert to Threefathom Harbour?
I have but we would stay down there for the week. There was like a small cookhouse, just temporary, and the bunks. The weather was nice in May and June. It was strictly for lobsters. They started the 20th of April and ended the 20th of June. You just came home on weekends.

They got this Ferdinand LeBlanc to come, and his sister. Her name was Rita LeBlanc. They came down to show us just what to do. They showed us—we were packers on the assembly line. One would put the tail parts, then one would put the arm meat, then one would put the claws on the top. And then they had to seal it. It said "United Maritime Fishermen" on the label.

What did they do? Wash them first?
Somebody used to boil them and then there was somebody to open up the shells and stuff like that, and then it was sealed.

It only operated for a couple of seasons. I don't know why. They couldn't make a go of it. A lot of the lobsters were shipped in crates to Boston. They would come and pick them up.

We would get maybe a dollar for the day. Mister Lapierre ran the cookhouse and we would go down and have at least one meal. The rest of the time, my father was in a little camp down there and he would bring food for the week and I'd go down there and have food with him.

How many were employed there?
There were 20 or 25 people. Most of the women had their relatives down there. There was a lot of camps down there and there was a lot of fishermen. That's what they did for a living. I believe that was in 1936.

Did you wear uniforms?
We had to wear white aprons made out of those sugar bags; the sugar came in cotton bags. They were bleached, and made into aprons. And we had a white thing on our heads too, like a white bag.

Chezzetcook: an Acadian stronghold

We got maybe half an hour for dinner. We would go to the camp. The camp was close by. I remember sleeping in the cookhouse and I guess we had our breakfast there in the cookhouse.

Ferdinand LeBlanc's sister showed us how to can the lobster. It had to be canned just so, and she showed us just what to do, how to pack it. I was on the claws.

They were steamed and inspected, of course. Somebody came to inspect it. The lobsters were sealed in small cans. One man used to crack the lobsters. They used to put all the claws separately and then they came to us in big basins or trays. (...)

Did they throw the bodies away?
They kept the tamale, but the rest of the stuff wasn't used. It's just the tamale that was used. (...)

I remember Florinda Lapierre, Johnny Lapierre's niece, used to work down there, and Gertrude Lapierre. I had friends there. The camps were numerous. They were just one on top of the other. Everybody was down there, you know, and it was lively. They had a huge breakwater made out of these great big wharves. The breakwater had to be built, and you could walk on that for about a half a mile. It was really nice.

Did you have get-togethers at night, when the work was finished?
At night, we would roam around on the beaches, the girls would have fun. Not the fishermen, because they were up at four o'clock in the morning. At eight o'clock, as soon as the sun went down, they were in bed, but not us.

I remember knocking on one of the doors. There was a couple of young people too—the sons went with their fathers, some of them, not all of them—and we had knocked on this cabin door one night and this fisherman came out in his underwear and chased us up the beach, throwing rocks at us. It was about ten o'clock at night. That was late.

On weekends, we would go for a walk in the evenings and a couple of the boys used to play the mouth organ. We would dance on the bridges. There was a lot of bridges then. That's how we learned to dance, five or six of us, pretty well my age. We would stick together and in the summertime, we would dance on the bridges, playing the mouth organ. (...)

One final story by Mary Jane Wolfe deals with an old Acadian tradition that recounts how daily activities used to follow natural cycles reflected by the movement of the tides and the phases of the moon:

> You would make your own butter. When they wanted to churn their butter—they made their own butter—the man who used to live across from our place, he used to go up on top of the hill and look if the tide was coming up or going down, falling or rising. Because they said if you made your butter when the tide was going out, it couldn't come to butter. That's what he said, in French of course.[254]

Norman Julien—"A lot of Acadians, after they chased them out, they drifted back here"

Norman Julien was a third generation descendant of Simon Julien. His father, Frederick, was the son of George Julien and grandson of Simon, who arrived from France between 1800 and 1805.

Norman was born in 1904 and the interview by Lena Ferguson took place in 1977. His memories touch upon the early history of the community, local brickyards, shipbuilding activities in the past and rum running in the early 20th century:

> Down around here, when the old people wanted a piece of land, they put a fence around it and they claimed it. After 20 years, it was theirs. And when they died, they signed it to their children or whoever they wanted to give it to. But you wouldn't find a record of who was the original owner because there was no original owner.
>
> You see, when the British took the Acadians, they chased them out. Well, the Indians were here first as well as the Acadians. Then Queen Victoria gave a lot of land to different people, you know, the King or the Queen would pass on this place to some of their own people, you see, and we would have to get out. Well, that's the way it was in them days. (…)
>
> There was a lot of Acadians, after they chased them out, they drifted back here. That's the old Juliens and Lapierres. (…) As far as I can understand, the Julien who came here ran away from a French war ship. (…) He ran away and he hid for a long while, and he came out after so many years. And he was originally from

---

[254] Eastern Shore Archives, Lena Ferguson Collection, tape W7-1A (2001).

Chezzetcook: an Acadian stronghold

France. This is where he settled, Grand-Désert.

The Chezzetcook people were all Acadians. Down here (Grand-Désert), there were Conrods, and Fergusons and Nieforths. It was a different breed, you see, they didn't get along with the Acadians up there. They were all French.

And these people down here wouldn't give in to them. They said, "No, we'll not call it Chezzetcook, we'll call it Grand-Désert."

They only changed the post office down here a few years ago. You would always give your address as Grand-Désert. (...)

The church is something the people should be proud of. Some of the bricks came from the brickyard but they were soft. You don't remember the brickyard, but I do.

They had an ox—not one but five big oxen. When one got tired, they put another one on to mix the clay, you know, to make the bricks with. And the ox would walk round and round, round and round.

And there were about 10 or 12 men working there. They would probably make 100 [bricks] a day or 150 a day. Them days, labour was so cheap, if they made 100 bricks a day, that was a lot of money.

I never worked there but I was up there when they were working. It was just clay, that's all, and you had to burn it. They made the brick, they put it in a mold, made the fire and then burned it.

They shipped the bricks everywhere. Old Peter Ferguson took them to Halifax. They had the *Shamrock* and I think they had another one before that, two vessels. There was the old *Shamrock* and they had another one before that. (...)

There was a boat built right down at the foot of the hill by the shore. I remember that, too. That was about 100 feet long. It was everybody's.

Protestants and Catholics around here in them days, there was no difference. They were all people. One didn't hold any discrimination against nobody.

Well, Percy Conrad's father had a share, Jimmy Julien had a share, Martin Julien had a share, Anselme Lapierre had a share and some of the Nieforths from Seaforth had a share. They all chipped in and there was no money paid. Everybody worked and when the vessel was done, they launched her. I remember they launched her in the wintertime. I think her name was the *Condor*.

Old Jim Conrod had a share.

She was launched in the winter. They had cattle and men. They pulled her right across the ice. Them days, that ice was thick. They pulled her right across to the beach on the flats until they come to the channel and they left her there then on the ice until the ice went away and the high tide come when she floated. Well then, they rigged her and took her fishing. They used to go to the Magdalen Islands.

Old George Julien, the *Black Prince*, she got lost at Shag Rock with a load of rum. It was 1911, I guess. He had it loaded with rum in a storm. He came in a storm, ran ashore, and of course he had a load of rum, he threw it overboard and he went ashore and they carried some to hide it.

But he lost the vessel; she sank. He lost the vessel but he bought another one and he was rum running until he died.[255]

Douglas Lapierre – "At New Years, we went to knock on the doors with a little mallet"

The final interview I conducted in Chezzetcook was with Douglas Lapierre. He was born in 1928. His parents were from Grand-Désert but moved to West Chezzetcook where he grew up. As was the case with most families of his generation, his parents raised their children in French, and it remained his first language all his life.

Douglas told of how he fished at Threefathom Harbour with his father during his youth and spoke about a traditional Acadian custom he has preserved. Here, in translation, are some excerpts from our discussion that took place in 2017:

> At New Year's, we went to knock on the doors with a little mallet. I have kept my mallet. It's made with a knotted branch of wood.
> *Did the other kids have mallets like that one?*
> Some had small flat mallets. I made one for my granddaughters. The last time they did the rounds on New Year's Day was in 1994.
> *When you were young, was it only the boys who went around knocking on doors?*
> It was girls and boys. We would leave in the morning early and we were gone until the evening; it was all day long. We would go

---

255 Ibid., tapes 6797-6798 (1977).

Chezzetcook: an Acadian stronghold

almost as far as Grand-Désert. When it was starting to get dark, we would go back home. We had a big bucket full of *tamarin* (molasses fudge).

They made lots of molasses *tamarin*. It was cut in pieces. You would have to knock on the doors, because if you didn't knock, they would send you away with no *tamarin*.

The doors were all made of wood in those days. (...)

I started fishing with my father in 1941, during wartime. My great-grandfather fished there, then my grandfather, my father and then me. They were all fishermen.

They had to walk from here on Sundays and they stayed in their cabins until Saturday. You carried your food on your back and you had to walk. There were no cars.

There was no road across to the island. The road was built in 1948, the causeway.

Threefathom Harbour had a different name then, eh?
Yes, Maganchiche it was called. At Maganchiche, my father's fishing cabin was built in 1925. It's still there. (...)

Lobster fishing started in April and fishing went until November. The old fishermen went to the Madeleine islands, to the *Baie du Nord*. There was a lot of cod there. Our own boats were small, about thirty feet or so.

How did you sell your fish?
A boat came every Friday and took the lobster to Boston. The codfish was all salted. In the fall, in October, they sold the fish. They took it to Halifax.

A schooner from here went to town every week, bringing fish there. They caught a lot of herring here in July. It was all sold to the West Indies, the salt herring. (...)

I started fishing at 13. The codfish that I caught, I had a small axe and I cut the end of the tail, so that was mine and the ones where the tail wasn't cut, that belonged to my father. When we sold it in the fall, the ones that had their tails cut were mine.

So you didn't go to school for very long?
I went to grade seven. I worked in Halifax on the waterfront as a stevedore in winter, and in the summer, I fished.

Fishing was a hard occupation, eh?
Ah yes. You left early in the morning; 4 o'clock or 5 o'clock and you came back in the afternoon around 3 o'clock. Then my father sent me to light the fire to make dinner. We would stop for dinner

203

for about 20 or 25 minutes. Then they came for the fish.

I would sometimes fall asleep and the fish would burn in the pot. I was 14 years old and I would fall asleep.

In the fishermen's cabins, what did you eat? Fish and potatoes?

Yes, and there was bread too. During wartime, there was plenty of food.

A German submarine had sunk an American supply ship. Everything floated up to the surface of the water and drifted to shore. It was all food for the soldiers. There was plenty of it.

We lived well for the duration of the war, for years. There were a lot of small cans—small cans of meat and different things; cookies, big tins of milk powder, icing sugar, tapioca—big containers of tapioca and raisins. There was everything you could wish for. The Germans had sunk a ship just off from Threefathom Harbour.

There were big chunks of chocolate too. Some of them had melted but others were still good.

Do you know if they saved the American sailors from the supply ship?

You didn't know much. They wouldn't say anything in those days.

You would hear the depth charges. Sometimes, the codfish would be killed by those and would float up to the surface. The submarines were close by.

When you fished there, had rum running ended?

Pretty much. After 1939, it was pretty much finished. There was still a little bit.

At Grand-Désert, they would hide the rum in the sand. They would make a space to hide small barrels of liquor, ten-gallon kegs.

What did the fishermen in Threefathom Harbour do in the evening to pass the time?

There wasn't much to do. There were young people like me who would set traps to get rats there.

Were there stories that were told to scare people or funny stories about tricks that were played?

Ah, people played tricks on each other. Down at Threefathom Harbour, at Maganchiche, they would block up the chimney pipe and then when you went to light the fire, the cabin would all fill up with smoke.

And another thing, you would go to the spring to fetch fresh water and when you would come back down with it, some men would stop you to have a chat, and while they were talking to you, one of them would take the bucket, throw away the water and replace it with salt water. Then you would go to make tea and you would find it was salt water![256]

Figure 29: Douglas Lapierre holding a homemade buoy.

---

256 Interview with Douglas Lapierre, West Chezzetcook, 29 April 2017.

Ronald Labelle

9: 20th-century decline...and renewal

An enduring French presence in the early 1900s

The French language had such a dominant presence in 18th and 19th century Chezzetcook that many local families of Irish or Scottish origin, such as the Murphys and Fergusons, became fluent in the language, and the same was true of a few Protestant families of German descent named Conrod, Fillis and Niford.

The 20th century, however, saw a reversal of the phenomenon, and Acadian families gradually adopted the English language. In outlying areas such as Porter's Lake and East Chezzetcook, the French language began its long decline in the 19th century, due to the predominance of English, although some parents made great efforts to ensure that their children would be able to speak their language.

Maud Bellefontaine, for example, who was born at Porter's Lake in 1886, remembered that, when she was growing up, local schooling took place entirely in English, as there were few French-speaking families living in the vicinity. She learned to speak French thanks, in part, to an aunt who provided her with catechism lessons. Members of her generation learned all their prayers in French.

During the first half of the 20th century, French-language decline became widespread not only in outlying areas, but everywhere around Chezzetcook. The last bastion of the French language was Grand-Désert, where it continued to be in common use for a few decades longer, but few members of the generation raised there after the Second World War learned to speak it. It had become essential to speak English both at school and in work environments, and parents no longer saw the use of passing their native language on to their children.

Francophone priests and nuns who taught at local schools headed efforts to stem the tide of language assimilation in the first half of the century. From the 1880s until 1950, French-speaking priests served Saint Anselm's parish on a constant basis, and most of them strongly encouraged their parishioners to continue using their language.

The Roman Catholic parish was at the heart of the community and the priests made sure that religious and social activities associated with it took place in French.

Artifacts preserved at the Acadian House Museum in West Chezzetcook show how Church activities continued to be conducted in French: Missals, prayer books and published collections of religious hymns used locally were all in the French language, as were baptismal and confirmation certificates.

The museum also houses a framed plaque entitled "Pour la Patrie – Volontaires de la Paroisse Saint Anselme", which lists the names of 64 soldiers from the parish who served in the Second World War.[257] Surprisingly, this formal document, dated 1945, was entirely written in French.

Another way the Church encouraged the French language was through the annual parish picnic, a tradition that has taken place for over a century. The event took on an important role in the community between 1928 and 1937, when Father Élie LeBlanc turned it into a two-day affair coinciding with Assumption Day, August 15th, the patriotic Acadian holiday. The priest took advantage of the event to preach a special sermon at mass, encouraging Acadians to maintain the French language.

Local priests also encouraged members of Saint Anselm's parish to join French Canadian Catholic organizations. A group of local women joined "Les Dames de Sainte Anne", a Québec based Francophone women's organization dedicated to religious and social causes. One certificate of membership (*diplôme d'agrégation*) is preserved at the Acadian House Museum in Chezzetcook. It informs us that Mrs. Mary Hagen of Grand-Désert was received as a member of the organization in June of 1922.[258]

"Les Dames de Sainte Anne" is a good example of an organization that built connections between local Acadians and Francophones in other provinces.

The most widespread Acadian fraternal organization was "La Société l'Assomption", founded in 1903. During the first 30 years of its existence, it established over 200 local chapters all over the Maritimes, as well as in New England.

The local chapter situated in Chezzetcook, "Succursale Étoile de

---

257 "List of Volunteers", Acadian House Museum, Artifacts Canada accession no. 2001.07.01N.

258 Ibid., "Certificate of Membership", accession no. 2012.55.01.

Marie", was one of the last to be set up. A membership ribbon preserved at the Acadian House Museum states that the local chapter was founded in November of 1946.[259]

One of the main activities of the Société L'Assomption was to offer scholarships to Acadian students, and it also provided members with mutual insurance services.

Just as 19th-century French visitors to Halifax made the trek to Chezzetcook to meet Acadians there, a delegation from France took part in a ceremony marking the community's origins in 1935. According to Aurèle Bellefontaine, the French Consul in Halifax facilitated the visit, which was part of a tour of French-speaking communities in Eastern Canada.

Thanks to the encouragement of Father Élie LeBlanc, the visit to Chezzetcook was marked by a grand ceremony, in which the delegation entered the community through an arch festooned with French flags. They were greeted with a sixty-gun salute and were led to a hall where a buffet was served, accompanied by formal speeches.[260]

Members of the delegation were so taken by the reception they received in Chezzetcook that, after their return to France, they sent Christmas gifts as a gesture of thanks. Each member of the church choir received a framed tricolour ribbon tied to a small bag of soil from Paris. The accompanying inscription read: "Terre de France – Paris 1935, Noël, Jardin de l'Archevêché – permission spéciale de Mgr. Cardinal Verdier".[261]

The fact that the Cardinal of Paris himself had granted permission to include samples of soil from the bishopric gardens shows the consideration the French delegation had for the community.

Following the departure of Father Élie LeBlanc in 1938, the next parish priest, Mgr. Isaac Comeau, continued the work of his predecessor, encouraging the maintenance of French and offering help to young people who wanted to improve their knowledge of the language.[262] While the mass was celebrated in Latin at the time, his homilies were delivered mainly in French, and he made sure that any announcements made in church were given first in that language.

Mgr. Comeau encouraged the local population to use French in daily conversation and would even refuse to answer bilingual parishioners

---

259 Ibid., "Ribbon, membership", accession no. 2010.011.001.
260 Eastern Shore Archives, Lena Ferguson Collection, tape 6753, Aurèle Bellefontaine (5 December 1977).
261 "Sample - Earth", Acadian House Museum, Artifacts Canada accession no. 2012.25.01.
262 Dwayne Doucette, "Monsignor Comeau".

when they spoke to him in English. He recognized that the future of the French language in Chezzetcook depended on young people, and he helped promising students obtain financing to pursue their education in their language, especially at Collège Sainte-Anne in Church Point.

One of his protégés was Louis Lapierre, from Grand-Désert, who later became a biology professor at the Université de Moncton and who was able to play a national role as a consultant on environmental issues, thanks to his bilingual upbringing.

Unfortunately, Louis Lapierre was an exceptional case, at a time when young people in general were abandoning the French language. He was a member of the last generation of children educated partially in French at St. Mary's school in Grand-Désert.

Despite the fact that the curriculum in the public school system was almost entirely in English, the teachers there endeavored to include as much French language instruction as possible. Several teachers were Acadian members of the Sisters of Charity who came from Acadian communities in Southwestern Nova Scotia. Soeur Claude-Clombienne (born Odette Béatrice Comeau) was one who left a mark as a tireless promoter of the French language.

When the Sisters of Charity left in 1959, the two-room school remained open for two more years, after which all the pupils began to attend school in West Chezzetcook. While bilingual nuns continued to teach at the West Chezzetcook school, it was not possible to use French informally in the classroom, as had been the case at Grand-Désert, because some of the pupils there were unable to understand the language.

During the 1960s, children from both Grand-Désert and West Chezzetcook began to be bused outside their community to pursue high school education, first at Jeddore and later in Dartmouth. This was highly detrimental to the survival of the French language, as Acadian youths preferred to hide their Francophone identity in order to avoid enduring the same kind of discrimination that was suffered by other minority groups at that time.

Rapid decline in the mid-20th century
In 1968, the *Fédération acadienne de la Nouvelle-Écosse* (La FANE) was founded to promote the development of Acadian communities in the province. Regional offices were established in all the principal Acadian areas of settlement, The Société L'Assomption wound down its activities as La FANE took up the cause of Acadian unity.

Ronald Labelle

Despite the fact that Chezzetcook had been a part of the earlier organization, La FANE disregarded the community, considering that it was no longer an Acadian district due to the decline of the French language there. In the late 1960s, a few families continued to communicate in French, but the language was used almost exclusively by elderly residents in the community.

In March 1974, Carmen Comeau, who later became Director of La FANE, wrote a newspaper article entitled "Chezzetcook a des racines françaises" (Chezzetcook has French roots). In it, she states: "...la réalité française dans West Chezzetcook est une réalité du passé" (French existence in Chezzetcook is a thing of the past).[263]

Comeau believed that the French language did not have the means to be sustainable there, as it no longer played a central role in family life. Past generations of Acadians had been strongly pressured to marry members of their own faith, a fact that encouraged them to choose a spouse from their community.

Sophie Lapierre, for example, recounted that her mother had forbidden her to frequent Protestants during her youth in the early 20th century. She recounted one case when a cousin of hers who had gone to work in Halifax married a Protestant, which caused a scandal in the community[264]

By the mid-1900s, this type of social control no longer existed, and more and more Acadians married people with no French background. In families where at least one parent was from an English-speaking background, the French language was almost never handed down to the next generation.

Although the provincial office of La FANE has been situated in nearby Halifax since 1968, the organization made no attempt to reach out to the local Acadian population. In 1982, I was even told by the Director of La FANE that the only place I would find Acadians in Chezzetcook was in the cemetery!

Because of its long history, however, Chezzetcook began to attract the interest of local historians and genealogists. Mgr. Frédéric Melanson, who was parish priest at St. Anselm's from 1968 to 1974, became extremely interested in the origins of Acadian families there. He carried out years of research on the topic, culminating in his self-published *Genealo-*

---

[263] Carmen Comeau, "Chezzetcook a des racines françaises".

[264] CEAAC, Ronald Labelle Collection, accession no. 1472 (1982).

gies of the Families of Chezzetcook, NS, in 1981.[265] These publications helped the local population become better aware of their family origins going back to the years before the Acadian Expulsion.

Mgr. Melanson was greatly concerned by the decline of the language in the community. In the course of a lecture he presented at the Atlantic Canada Institute in 1981, he stated that "until the older generation can be made to feel proud of its Acadian heritage, old French and all, little can be done."[266]

A local historical society was founded in Chezzetcook in 1974, and its most active member, Lena Ferguson, carried out more than one hundred interviews with elderly residents, dealing with all aspects of life in the past. Not being a French speaker, Lena Ferguson was unable to explore topics specific to Acadian culture, but she collected a wealth of information, much of which was published between 1976 and 1981 in a series of 70 newspaper articles in the *Dartmouth Free Press*.

One result of her efforts was the acquisition of a gundalow by the Nova Scotia Museum in 1980. The gundalow that had belonged to members of the Bellefontaine family was put on permanent exhibit in the new Maritime Museum of the Atlantic on the Halifax waterfront in 1982.

Despite a growing recognition of Chezzetcook's rich historical heritage, the distinctly Acadian identity of the community continued to erode, as was evident in a 1988 *Halifax Mail-Star* article entitled "West Chezzetcook: old Acadian ways go with a whimper".[267]

The author stated that Chezzetcook was rapidly becoming a bedroom community with few ties to its old way of life and culture. Ironically, he quoted Beverly Hugli, one of the architects of the cultural reawakening that was about to begin, saying, "The language is just about dead now."

At a time when French immersion programs were becoming a popular option in Nova Scotia, local schools could have implemented the new curriculum, therefore supplying children of Acadian descent with the opportunity to pick up French as a second language. Unfortunately, school administrators in West Chezzetcook ignored the need for a French immersion program.

Their total disregard of the importance of local Acadian culture was typical of the attitude prevalent in the region as recently as the 1980s.

---

265 Melanson, *Genealogies of the Families of Chezzetcook, NS*.
266 Melanson, "Chezzetcook – Culture", p. 8.

267 Laurent Le Pierre, "West Chezzetcook: old Acadian ways go with a whimper".

Ronald Labelle

Gaetz Brook Junior High School was the only school on the Eastern Shore where a French Immersion program was established, and this program continues to this day.

An awakening in the 1990s
When *The Acadians of Chezzetcook* was published in 1995, I hoped my book would raise awareness of the long Acadian history on the Eastern Shore, but little did I suspect the effect it would have locally. Over one hundred people attended the book launching on November 4th 1995, including Barbara LeBlanc, President of La FANE, who spoke of the important contributions of Chezzetcook to Nova Scotia's cultural heritage.

A few days later, Mr. Keith Colwell, Member of the Legislative Assembly for the Eastern Shore, presented a resolution in the Nova Scotia House of Assembly, celebrating the Acadian presence in the area. That same month, a journalist from the *Daily News* of Halifax prepared an article entitled "Acadian pride on rise again in Chezzetcook".[268]

During the following months, interest stirred up by the publication of *The Acadians of Chezzetcook* continued to increase. In early 1996, local residents founded the West Chezzetcook / Grand-Désert Community Interest Group.

Members immediately embarked on an ambitious plan to link community development to cultural heritage. Thanks to fundraising activities, they were able to purchase a house built by members of the Bellefontaine family in the 1850s. Their goal was to establish a museum devoted to the Acadian history of the area, and they wasted no time in doing so.

Almost immediately after its purchase in 1997, the newly-acquired Acadian house hosted a travelling exhibit of traditional *mi-carême* masks from Chéticamp. From then on, Chezzetcook became an active part of the Maritime Acadian diaspora, hosting not only exhibits, but also concerts by popular Acadian acts like "La Revue musicale acadienne" and "Les Tymeux de la Baie".

That same year, Chezzetcook joined in the celebration of the 150th anniversary of the epic poem *Évangéline*, hosting a weekend of activities around the theme "L'Acadie en fête".

While the poem by H. W. Longfellow resonates all over Acadia, it has special meaning locally, because the fictional heroine of the poem is named Évangéline Bellefontaine. Nowhere else in the Maritimes has

---
268 Swick, David, "Acadian pride on rise again in Chezzetcook".

"Bellefontaine" remained in use as a common family name.

During the first years following the acquisition of the future museum building, members of the community interest group concentrated their efforts on adapting the former residential home to its new purpose, while keeping its original layout dating back to the 1850s. They also gathered hundreds of artifacts, photographs and written documents from local families. The work was completed in 2001, the year of the official opening of the "Acadian House Museum".

Members of the community interest group not only strived not to renew pride in the Acadian history of Chezzetcook, but also embarked on an ambitious project to bring about a renewal of the French language. They realized that Chezzetcook would never fully rejoin the family of Acadian communities if the language was not revitalized.

In 1997, local activist Judy Doucette Bellefontaine carried out an informal survey of residents "who continue to have some speaking ability and definite understanding of the French language".[269] She compiled a working list of 104 individuals.

Because of the unverified nature of the survey, the actual number of French speakers may have varied slightly from that figure, but it is impressive to discover that at a time when the language was generally thought to have almost disappeared in Chezzetcook, there were still approximately one hundred individuals there who could communicate in French.

Chezzetcook rejoins the Acadian community

At the dawn of the 21st century, language revitalization efforts began modestly with the establishment of the "Club français", an informal group of local residents interested in creating opportunities to speak French on a regular basis.

The group has been meeting weekly for over twenty years and one of their goals has been to reach out to other minority Acadian groups in the Maritimes. This provided them with an opportunity to learn from the experiences of members of other communities.

For example, during a visit to Pomquet in Antigonish County, they heard about the difficult campaign Acadians there fought during the 1980s and 1990s in order to obtain a French language school. As the last

---

269 "Census Record", Acadian House Museum, Artifacts Canada accession no. 2020.33.1.

bastion of Acadian culture in Antigonish County, Pomquet was in danger of losing its character as a French speaking community until the establishment of *L'École acadienne de Pomquet* in 1992.

This inspired the Chezzetcook group to begin looking into the possibility of lobbying for the creation of a French language school of their own.[270]

While the desire to obtain a new school remained a long-term goal for the community interest group, their immediate concern was the approach of the 2004 *Congrès mondial acadien* or "World Acadian Congress". This is an international gathering held every five years since 1994. The third Congress marked the 400th anniversary of the founding of Acadia and was the largest yet, as it took place in Acadian areas throughout Nova Scotia.

The 2004 Congress was coordinated by La FANE, but as the provincial Acadian organization was yet to include Chezzetcook in its activities, the community was left out of the official program of events.

Not to be dissuaded by this apparent snub, the group in Chezzetcook organized four full days of Acadian celebrations from August 12th to 15th, coinciding with the Congress.

August 15th had been an Acadian holiday ever since 1881, when Our Lady of the Assumption, *Notre Dame de l'Assomption*, was chosen as patron saint of Acadia, and a mass accompanied by a parish picnic traditionally took place in Chezzetcook on or around that date, but awareness of the cultural significance of the event had declined during the last decades of the 20th century. Organizers of the 2004 Acadian Celebrations were able to restore the connection between the parish picnic and Acadian heritage.

While it was customary for local events to take place in English only in the late 1900s, by 2004 Chezzetcook had regained its pride as a bilingual Acadian community. The celebration held in August also marked the first time in decades that the Acadian character of Chezzetcook was widely recognized.

As part of "la caravanne terre et mer", a delegation of approximately one hundred Acadians from New Brunswick travelled through Nova Scotia by land and sea in August 2004, visiting not only the sites where the official Congress activities took place, but also reaching out to two Acadian communities that had been neglected until then: Larry's River in Guysborough County and Chezzetcook. The main organizer, Jean Gaudet

---

270 Beverly Hugli, personal communication, 22 April 2022.

Chezzetcook: an Acadian stronghold

of Dieppe, insisted that the caravan should make a stop in both areas.

At Larry's River, the key event marking Acadian anniversary celebrations was a re-enactment of the arrival of the first settlers from Chezzetcook, two hundred years earlier. Many of the participants, wearing period costumes, came from Chezzetcook to take part in this unique event that highlighted the historic link between the two communities.[271]

After leaving Larry's River, the delegation arrived by boat at Threefathom Harbour on August 6th and was greeted by Community Interest Group members who organized an emotional gathering symbolizing the renewal of ties between Chezzetcook and the greater Acadian diaspora.

Ties established in 2004 have been maintained and expanded over the years, as groups of New Brunswick Acadians continue to make yearly visits to the community.

One of the highlights of the August, 2004 celebration was the "Heritage Day" held on August 14th, on which family histories and genealogies were displayed in the parish hall. The members of local families who greeted visitors included bilingual individuals who wore a name tag including the words "Je parle français".

The two women representing the Robichaud family, for example, not only presented a genealogy display, but also wore traditional Acadian dress and exhibited heritage objects preserved by their parents. This is a good indication of the cultural awakening that was taking place in the community.

Family trees were also displayed on August 15th, the final day of celebrations, and the four-day event ended with the first ever "tintamarre" held in Chezzetcook.

This is a relatively new Acadian tradition that began in New Brunswick in 1979, the year marking the 375th anniversary of Acadia. The word "tintamarre" signifies a deliberate display of loud noise. In all Acadian areas of the Maritimes, a marching parade is held on the Acadian holiday, with colourfully-dressed marchers carrying Acadian flags and using various noisemakers. The joyful noise is meant to celebrate the survival of the Acadian people.

In Chezzetcook, as everywhere else in Acadia, a "tintamarre" now takes place each year on August 15th, along with various other events, such as museum displays and musical presentations.

One important result of the 2004 celebration was the way it energized

---

271 Avery, *The Forgotten Acadians*, pp. 77-78.

members of the community group, who then launched several new projects. A bilingual community history board had been installed in Grand-Désert during the previous year on land donated by the Lapierre family. In West Chezzetcook, the land surrounding the Acadian House Museum then became the focus of efforts to interpret Acadian history. A plaque depicting local history was unveiled on the site, thanks to the support of the Halifax Foundation and other donors.

In 2005, a former barn situated near the museum was renovated in order to be made available as a community meeting hall called *La Grange*, The following year, a tearoom called *La Cuisine de Brigitte* was opened on the site. The tearoom quickly became a gathering place for community members and for summer visitors, who have the opportunity to taste traditional dishes there.

From its modest beginnings in 1997, the Acadian House Museum gradually evolved into the complex now know as *L'Acadie de Chezzetcook*. The final addition to the complex was the visitors' centre. This building was relocated from its original site in Grand-Désert in 2014, and was renovated thanks to funding made available to Acadian organizations by the Department of Canadian Heritage. It now serves not only as an interpretive centre but also as a venue for art and craft exhibits.

One example of a project carried out at the new visitors' centre is a mural made up of dozens of miniature paintings depicting the traditional way of life in Chezzetcook. This project, coordinated by Francophone artist Sylvie Boisvert in 2017, involved community members of all ages, who were encouraged to choose a theme related to traditional life and work in Chezzetcook.

The Acadian House Museum itself has continued to evolve, thanks to support from the Association of Nova Scotia Museums. A database containing information about the collection was created and in 2021, and was incorporated into an online service entitled "Artifacts Canada", administered by the Canadian Heritage Information Network (CHIN). Over 1,000 artifacts and documents are included in the online database and nearly all descriptions of objects include photographs.

The museum collection is exceptionally rich and diverse, and it includes not only household objects donated by local families, but also documents pertaining to Church and school history. Many of the latter documents came to the Acadian House Museum thanks to long-term loan arrangements.

While the Acadian House Museum began as a modest, community-oriented institution, in 2014, *L'Acadie de Chezzetcook* became a full-fledged member of La FANE,. This means that local initiatives now have financial and logistical support from a province-wide Acadian organization.

The *Club français*, for example, had been providing evening French lessons for several years on an informal basis, but has now become an official member of *Équipe Alpha*, an organization that promotes literacy in Nova Scotia's Francophone communities. Senior members of the Club français also participate in projects run by *Le Regroupement des aînés de la Nouvelle*-Écosse (RANE), a province-wide seniors organization. One recent project entitled "Entre les générations" supported a much-needed dialogue between older French-speaking residents of Chezzetcook and local youth who attend the new French-language school, *École des Beaux-Marais*.

The key role of the French-language school

Efforts to foster pride in the Acadian heritage of Chezzetcook could never be entirely successful if language revitalization did not occupy a central role in the movement. The steady language decline that took place throughout the 1900s meant that, by the dawn of the new century, very few community members under 50 years of age could speak French.

For Chezzetcook to remain a bilingual community with a notable Acadian character, it was necessary to remedy this situation and the most obvious first step was to lobby for French-language education, as had been the case in Pomquet and other communities in Nova Scotia.

It was essential that requests for a French school come from parents with school-age children. Members of the Robichaud family took up the cause and contacted Darrell Samson, the head of the *Conseil scolaire acadien de la Nouvelle-Écosse* (CSAP), the provincial Francophone school board.

Circumstances happened to be favourable to their request. Samson resided nearby and was therefore familiar with Chezzetcook. He was also a university-trained specialist in second-language education and a strong advocate for the rights of French-language minority communities. Darrell Samson was able to guide the group in their efforts, which included a letter-writing campaign by local parents.

Parents were able to convince the CSAP to request government funding for the opening of a French school in Chezzetcook, but one problem still remained: How to provide schooling in French in a community where children were being raised in English by parents who had lost their native language. The solution was to proceed in stages, beginning with a French pre-primary class called *Grandir en français*, then adding an additional class each year. In that way, by its 10th year of operation, the school would be able to provide all levels of education in French from pre-primary to the 8th grade.

This approach had been used with success elsewhere, for example at Cap Saint-Georges, on the West coast of Newfoundland, where a French school began in 1975.

The first *Grandir en français* class began modestly in September 2010. It was housed in a temporary mobile classroom, but more suitable accomodations were made available the following year, when the former Lakeview School at the Head of Chezzetcook became *L'école des Beaux-Marais*, with 27 pupils enrolled at the pre-primary and primary levels.

Right from the beginning, the community strongly supported the school. Hundreds of local residents showed up for its inaugural Christmas concert. This was a very emotional event, at which many older attendees had tears in their eyes hearing their grandchildren sing in French for the first time.

Over the past twelve years, members of the Chezzetcook "Club français" have often taken part in activities at the school, explaining local Acadian traditions to the children. In 2022, for example, children received a "baskahou", a basket containing Easter eggs on a bed of straw brought by a partridge, thus reviving a unique local tradition.

The *École des Beaux-Marais* finally had a full contingent of pupils from pre-primary to 8th grade in 2019. By that time, enrolment surpassed 250 and this number has remained stable, but parents and educators have been aware for several years of the need for a new and better-equipped school.

Members of *L'Acadie de Chezzetcook* often expressed their concern about the inadequacy of the present school and they were successful in convincing the Acadian school board to include the project among its priorities.[272]

Plans for the construction of a new school were made official in the spring of 2023. Many parents hoped it would be possible to replace the existing school with a pre-primary to 12th grade facility, so that their children would no longer have to commute to Dartmouth to complete their secondary education in French. However, the present plan is to build a school that continues to provide education from the pre-primary level to grade 8.

---

272 Valentin Afano, personal communication, 25 April 2022.

Chezzetcook: an Acadian stronghold

Despite that decision, the news that a new, modern school would eventually be built was well received in the community, and should put an end to a situation where many parents choose to send their junior-high-level children either to French schools in Dartmouth or to English-language ones closer by.

Looking to the future

Participants in activities organized by *L'Acadie de Chezzetcook* see the need to maintain the ties between the generations and strive to foster a strong Acadian identity among the families of children enrolled at *École des Beaux-Marais*. They offer French classes to parents who grew up hearing the language spoken by their elders, but who never had the opportunity to learn to speak it.

Figure 30: The pupils and staff of École des Beaux-Marais, 2018.

The fact that parents are making an effort to learn French at the same time as their children are becoming fluent in the language shows how determined community members are to see Chezzetcook regain its Acadian identity.

Apart from the question of schooling, the other main area of concern is St. Anselm's Roman Catholic parish. As is the case in many parts of the country, the declining fortunes of the diocese meant that the local church had to close its doors in 2019. French-speaking priests had always played a central role in the promotion of Acadian identity in the community.

With the renewal of pride in French heritage, it would be natural for the Catholic Church to take part in the movement, both by providing French language masses and participating in the Acadian celebration of Our Lady of the Assumption on August 15th.

The large, brick church building, constructed in 1894 thanks to the collective efforts of community members, stands as a proud symbol of local Acadian identity and its closure was a terrible loss for community members who still feel a close bond to their Roman Catholic faith. Being obliged to join St. John of the Cross parish in the English-speaking community of East Chezzetcook, they have no hope of once again being able to hear the mass celebrated locally in French.

As a sign of their attachment to the now-shut-down church, a large group of local residents gathered in front of the building on Christmas morning in 2023 to sing songs of the season. They obtained permission to end their gathering by ringing the church bell, so that parishioners could once again listen to the joyful sound that was heard on Christmas morning all over Chezzetcook for over one hundred years.

One bright note regarding the closure of St. Anselm's church is the recent purchase and transfer of the former church and glebe house to *L'Acadie de Chezzetcook*. The group has now obtained funding from Heritage Canada to create the *Centre acadien de l'Anse de Chezzetcook* / Chezzetcook Inlet Acadian Centre.

Community members look forward having the opportunity to make use of their historic buildings, which have been deconsecrated by the Catholic Church. Plans are under way to house various heritage activities such as art exhibitions, musical performances, language classes and workshops.

It will also be a space devoted to reconciliation with the Aboriginal community, in recognition of the historical importance of Chezzetcook for the Mi'kmaq population in the Maritimes.

Not to be daunted by the many challenges they face, members of the community group that supports *L'Acadie de Chezzetcook* are pressing ahead with several new projects. The Acadian House Museum will soon be renovated and will become an even better site for displaying local culture.

Members have also produced a new Acadian-themed card game entitled *Le Tour Acadien*. Each of the cards illustrates an event or a person pertaining to Acadian history. The game is distributed through a partnership with Acadian organizations all over the Maritimes, and a card-playing tournament using the game is planned for the upcoming *Congrès mondial acadien* in Southwest Nova Scotia.

Chezzetcook: an Acadian stronghold

This project provides a good example of how Chezzetcook is now playing an active role in the promotion of Acadian culture in the Maritimes.

After having been long considered as a former Acadian community where French culture was no longer visible, Chezzetcook has risen phoenix-like from its long decline, and now faces a bright future as a fully-fledged member of the Acadian community in Nova Scotia. The future will bring many realizations, with a new generation of young people who are benefiting from French language education.

Thanks to the efforts of a dynamic group of volunteers at *L'Acadie de Chezzetcook*, provincial Acadian organizations have thrown their support behind the community. In the coming years, we can expect to see the completion of family histories, museum exhibits, photographic collections and cultural projects of all kinds.

My community study published in 1995 ended with a warning that unless the local population became conscious of the importance of preserving their cultural landscape, Chezzetcook would soon cease to exist as a distinctly Acadian community in Nova Scotia, and a unique element of the province's cultural fabric would be lost forever.[273] Nearly 30 years later, I can state with confidence that a reawakening has indeed taken place, and a new chapter of Acadian history in Chezzetcook has just begun.

---

273 Labelle, *The Acadians of Chezzetcook*, pp. 87-88.

Figure 31: Tricolour satchel of soil from the grounds of the Archdiocese of Paris offered to the people of Chezzetcook by the Archbishop in 1935.

Bibliography

Arsenault, Bona, *History of the Acadians*, Montreal: Fides, 1994.

Avery, Jude, *The Forgotten Acadians - a story of discovery*, Halifax: New World Publishing, 2019.

Bell, Winthrop, *The Foreign Protestants and the Settlement of Nova Scotia*, Toronto: University of Toronto Press, 1961.

Boudreau, Ephrem *Le petit Clairvaux – Cent ans de vie cistercienne à Tracadie en Nouvelle-Écosse, 1818-1919*, Moncton: Éditions d'Acadie, 1980.

Burnham, Harold B. and Dorothy K., *'Keep Me Warm One Night': Early Handweaving in Eastern Canada*, Toronto: University of Toronto Press, 1972.

Clarke, Cathy, "103 year old woman recalls Christmases of the past", *Dartmouth Free Press*, DATE?

Comeau, Carmen, "Chezzetcook a des racines françaises", *Le Petit Courrier*, 28 March 1974.

Cozzens, Frederic S., *Acadia or a Month with the Blue Noses*, New York: Derby & Jackson, 1859.

Dawson, Joan, *The Mapmaker's Eye*, Halifax: Nova Scotia Museum and Nimbus Publishing, 1988.

Delarue, Paul et Marie-Louise Tenèze, *Le conte populaire français : Catalogue raisonné des versions de France et des pays de langue française d'outre-mer*, Paris: Maisonneuve et Larose, 1964.

Dillman, Mary Alma, "How Grand Desert got its name", *Dartmouth Free Press,* 22 October 1980.

Documents inédits sur le Canada et l'Amérique, Tome 1, publiés par *Le Canada-Français,* Québec, Imprimerie L.J. Demers & Frère, 1888.

Doucette, Dwayne, "Monsignor Comeau", unpublished paper, Musquodoboit Harbour, NS: Eastern Shore District High School, 1981.

Du Boscq De Beaumont, Gaston, *Les derniers jours de l'Acadie (1748-1758)*, Geneva: Slatkine-Megariotis Reprints, 1975.

Du Hailly, Édouard, "Une station sur les côtes d'Amérique – Les Acadiens et la Nouvelle-Écosse", *Revue des Deux Mondes*, 1862, tome 42, pp.

875-900.

Dunn, Brenda, "Certains aspects de la vie des femmes dans l'ancienne Acadie", in *Un regard sur l'Acadie – Trois discours illustrés*. Halifax, N.S.: Nova Scotia Museum (Curatorial Report No. 87), 1999.

Ferguson, Lena, "History of Porter's Lake", unpublished manuscript, 1990.

_____, "History of Saint Mary's School, Grand Desert", unpublished paper, April 1980.

_____, "The Fishing Schooners", *Dartmouth Free Press*, 31 May 1978, p. 8.

_____, "The Days of the Schooner, part 2", *Dartmouth Free Press*, 15 March 1978.

_____, "Chezzetcook Clothing Factory Recalled", *Dartmouth Free Press*, 2 November 1977, p. 5.

_____, "A Time of Fasting", *Dartmouth Free Press*, 23 February 1977, 2nd section, p. 4.

_____, "Remember the Old Straw Mattress", *Dartmouth Free Press*, 8 June 1977, 2nd section, p. 1.

Griffiths, Naomi E. S., *From Migrant to Acadian – A North American border people, 1604-1755*, Montreal & Kingston: McGill-Queen's University Press, 2005, pp. 73-74.

Hardy, Lieutenant Campbell, *Sporting Adventures in the New World*, Vol. II, London: Hurst and Blackett, 1855.

Hines, Linda, *Life in Old Chezzetcook*, Musquodoboit Harbour, NS: Eastern Shore District High School.

Jean, Denis, "Le rôle des Métis dans l'histoire de la colonie de l'Acadie", *La Société historique acadienne – les Cahiers*, Vol. 48, No. 2, 2017, p. 65.

Julien, Emma B., "History of Grand Desert", unpublished essay, 1907.

Labelle, Ronald, *The Acadians of Chezzetcook*, Lawrencetown Beach, NS: Pottersfield Press, 1995.

_____, "La vie acadienne à Chezzetcook", *Société historique acadienne – les Cahiers*, vol. 22, No. 2-3, 1991, pp. 1-95.

_____, « Le déclin de la langue française à Chezzetcook », *La Société historique acadienne – les Cahiers*, vol. 23, Nos. 3-4, 1992.

Lane, P. and Associates, *Baseline Data Report and Historical Overview of the Chezzetcook Salt Marsh Prior to Highway 107 Construction*, Halifax: Nova Scotia Department of Transportation, 1986.

Le Blanc, Emery, *Les entretiens du village*, Moncton: Imprimerie acadienne, 1957.

Le Blanc, Ronnie-Gilles, "Pigiguit: l'impact du grand Dérangement sur une communauté de l'ancienne Acadie", in *Du Grand Dérangement à la Déportation – Nouvelles perspectives historiques,* Moncton: Chaire d'études acadiennes, 2005, pp. 167-246.

_____, "Les Acadiens à Halifax et dans l'île George's, 1755-1764", *Port-Acadie,* Nos. 22-23, 2012-2013, pp. 67-71.

_____, *Le voyage de Rameau de Saint-Père en Acadie, 1860,* Québec : Éditions du Septentrion, 2018.

Le Pierre, Laurent, "West Chezzetcook: old Acadian ways go with a whimper", *Halifax Mail-Star,* 21 April 1988, pp. 1-2.

Marsais, Adolphe, "Un mois de séjour chez nos Acadiens", Montreal: *L'Ordre,* 2 September 1867.

Martin, John P., *The Story of Dartmouth,* privately published, 1957.

Massignon, Geneviève, *Trésors de la chanson populaire française – Autour de 50 chansons recueillies en Acadie,* Paris: Bibliothèque Nationale de France, 1994.

Melanson, Mgr Frédéric, "Acadian Settlement at Chezzetcook", Genealogical Association of Nova Scotia, 1985 (PANS, MG 100, Vol. 68, No. 15).

_____, "Chezzetcook – Culture", in *Lectures Given at the Atlantic Canada Institute,* No. 5, 1981, p. 8.

_____, *Genealogies of the Families of Chezzetcook, NS,* Windsor Junction, NS, 1981 and Halifax, 1982, 13 volumes.

Morin, Maxime, *Le rôle politique des abbés Pierre Maillard, Jean-Louis le Loutre et François Piquet dans les relations franco-amérindiennes à la fin du Régime français (1734-1763),* M.A. Dissertation, Laval: Université Laval, 2009, pp. 100-101.

Murdoch, Beamish, *A History of Nova Scotia or Acadie,* Vol. 1, Halifax: James Barnes, 1865.

Ney, Eugène, "Voyage à la Nouvelle-Écosse", *Revue des Deux Mondes,* 1831, tome 2, pp. 390-409.

Pacifique, R. P., "Le Pays des Micmacs", *Études Historiques et Géographiques,* Société de Géographie de Québec, 1934, pp. 274-5.

Pelletier, Denise and Marie-Claire Pitre, *Les Pays-Bas,* Fredericton: Société d'histoire de la rivière Saint-Jean, 1985.

Piers, Harry, *Report on the Provincial Museum for 1934-35,* Halifax: Provincial Museum and Science Library, 1935.

Plessis, Mgr, "Voyage de 1815 en Acadie de Mgr Plessis", *Cahiers de la Société Historique Acadienne,* Vol. 11, Nos 1-2-3.

Purcell, Joseph, *Acadian Architecture and Cultural History of Chezzetcook,* unpublished report, Halifax : Nova Scotia College of Art, 1979.

Rameau de Saint-Père, Edmé, "Voyage de Rameau de Saint-Père en Acadie, 1860", *Société historique acadienne – les Cahiers,* Vol. 4, No. 8, 1973.

_____, *Une colonie féodale en Amérique: l'Acadie (1604-1710),* Paris: Plon / Montréal: Granger, 1889, Vol. II.

_____, "Un voyage en Acadie – 1860", *L'économiste français,* No. 12, 1862.

Ross, Sally, "La reconstruction d'une société" in *Un regard sur l'Acadie – Trois discours illustrés,* Halifax: Nova Scotia Museum, 1999.

_____, *Les écoles acadiennes en Nouvelle-Écosse, 1758-2000,* Moncton: Centre d'études acadiennes, 2001.

Schrepfer, Luke, *Pioneer Monks of Nova Scotia,* Tracadie, NS: St. Augustine's Monastery, 1947.

Scott, David D., "Morphological Changes in an Estuary: A Historical and Stratigraphical Comparison", in *The Coastline of Canada,* S. B. Cann, Ed., Ottawa: Geological Survey of Canada, 1980.

Shears, Robert H. J., *Examination of a Contested Landscape: Archaeological Prospection on the Eastern Shore of Nova Scotia,* M.A. Thesis, Halifax, St. Mary's University, 2013, p. 30.

Sweet, Brad, *St. Anselm's an Acadian Parish. A Short History from 1750,* unpublished paper, 1999.

_____, *Réfractaire and Mission Priests in Post-Deportation Acadian Education in Eastern Nova Scotia, 1792-1840,* M.A. dissertation, Laval, QC: Université Laval, 1999.

_____, "Chezzettcook Dyke Petitions, 1834-1877", unpublished paper, 1999.

Swick, David, "Acadian pride on rise again in Chezzetcook", Halifax: *The Daily News,* 14 November 1995.

Tattrie, Jon, *Cornwallis: The Violent Birth of Halifax,* Lawrencetown Beach: Pottersfield Press, 2013,

Vincent de Paul, *Memoir of Father Vincent de Paul,* Charlottetown: John Coombs, 1886.

Walsh, William S., *Curiosities of Popular Customs,* Philadelphia: J.B. Lippincott Co., 1898.

White, Stephen, "La généalogie des trente-neuf familles hôtesses des « Retrouvailles 94 »", in *Société historique acadienne – les Cahiers,* Vol. 25, Nos. 2-3, 1994, pp. 152-158.

Wicken, William C., *Encounters with Tall Sails and Tall Tales: Mi'kmaq Society, 1500-1760,* Ph. D. Dissertation, McGill University, 1994, p. 394.

Winslow, J. J. F., "The Bellefontaine Club", *The Atlantic Advocate,* Vol. 48,

No. 4, 1957, pp. 31-33.

Archives
Acadian House Museum
Artifacts Canada
Bibliothèque Nationale de France
Library and Archives Canada, Archives de la Nouvelle-France.
Nova Scotia Archives.

Oral history
CEAAC, Ronald Labelle Collection.
Eastern Shore Archives, Lena Ferguson Collection.

Publications
L'Évangéline, the main Acadian newspaper in the Maritimes.
The Cross, newspaper published by the Diocese of Halifax.

Other
"Community History Board – Grand Desert", West Chezzetcook /Grand Desert Community History Group.
"Fisheries Statements for the year 1882" *15th Annual Report*, Department of Marine and Fisheries: Ottawa, 1883.

Ronald Labelle

Figure 32: An Acadian flag now proudly displayed in the marsh on Chezzetcook Inlet.

Acknowledgements

I would like to acknowledge the support received from the Social Science and Humanities Research Council of Canada for my initial research project, carried out in 1982. The late professor Cyril Byrne, of Saint Mary's University, played a crucial role in the first phase of the research, as he strongly encouraged me to include Chezzetcook among the Acadian communities I was studying, as well as helping me to establish contacts in the community. The late Mgr Frédéric Melanson was also supportive, sharing the documentation he had accumulated during the years he served as parish priest in West Chezzetcook.

If not for the strong community spirit that now exists in Chezzetcook, I would not have undertaken the task of updating and completing my research in order to produce a much more complete study than my initial work, *The Acadians of Chezzetcook*, published in 1995. My thanks go out to the many dedicated volunteers who have worked tirelessly to promote Acadian culture in Chezzetcook since the 1990s. The final chapter of the book provides details about their many accomplishments.

Among all these volunteers, one who stands out is Beverley Hugli. For the past thirty years, she has been tirelessly promoting the French language in the community and it was partly thanks to her vision that efforts to obtain a French school for Chezzetcook were successful.

Finally, it is gratifying for me to see that Chezzetcook has now become a member of the *Fédération acadienne de la Nouvelle-Écosse*, after have been neglected by the Acadian leadership for many years. I thank Ms. Mélodie Jacquot-Paratte, the current Director of the *L'Acadie de Chezzetcook*, for her suggestions regarding publication plans, and thank you also to Mr. Andrew Wetmore and the team at Moose House Publications for recognizing the importance of this work.

Ronald Labelle

About the author

Ronald Labelle is a recently-retired professor of French Studies at Cape Breton University. His research has always focused on the language and culture of Acadians in the Atlantic Provinces. He began his career in 1979 as Folklore archivist at the Université de Moncton's Centre d'études acadiennes.

He has written extensively on folk traditions and oral history. In 1986, he was awarded the France-Acadie literary prize in Paris for *Au Village-du-Bois*, a book based on life stories gathered in a rural New Brunswick community.

During the past fifteen years, he has been actively involved in storytelling, most notably as Storyteller-in-residence at the Cape Breton Regional Library from 2015 to 2019. He also curated an exhibit held at the Université de Moncton's Acadian Museum in 2011, entitled "The Art of Storytelling in Acadie".

More recently, in 2023, he led a workshop on memoir writing at the Sydney branch of the Cape Breton Regional Library.